The Modern Theology of Tradition

J. P. MACKEY
Queen's University, Belfast

DARTON, LONGMAN & TODD

LONDON

Darton, Longman & Todd Ltd.,
29a Gloucester Road,
London, S.W.7
© *1962, J. P. Mackey*
First published 1962

Printed in Great Britain by Butler & Tanner Ltd., Frome and London. Nihil obstat; Joannes M. T. Barton, S.T.D., L.S.S., Censor deputatus. Imprimatur; E. Morrogh Bernard, Vic.Gen., Westmonasterii, die 3a maii, 1962. The Nihil obstat and Imprimatur are a declaration that a book or pamphlet is considered to be free from doctrinal or moral error. It is not implied that those who have granted the Nihil obstat and Imprimatur agree with the contents, opinions or statements expressed.

CONTENTS

INTRODUCTION

"GOD, who, at sundry times and in different ways, spoke in times past to the fathers by the prophets, last of all, in these days has spoken to us by his Son" (Hebrews i. 1–2). So Hebrews describes the coming of the final and definitive Word of God, the Truth that would make *us* free. But that was two thousand years ago. What forges the link between that final Revelation and us? It is in answering that question that theologians of every Christian persuasion write about Tradition. If we possess the saving truth today, it is because it was handed down, because it was 'traditioned' to us. It is fair to claim at the present time that theologians of all denominations agree in recognising Tradition in Christianity. It would be foolhardy to claim that they agree in their evaluations or descriptions of it. To most non-Catholic theologians Scripture is the only sure source of Christian truth, Tradition is always liable to corruption. In this book we intend to adopt a positive approach to the problem rather than a purely speculative one, i.e. to sift theological opinion in modern times in order to find the core of truth rather than to discuss Tradition in theory. If the Catholic teaching on Tradition takes up most of the book that is because it would be impossible to do justice both to the Catholic and to the variety of non-Catholic theories of Tradition in one book and because the present writer is better informed on the Catholic teaching. Tradition is a complex phenomenon in any theology.

The modern Catholic theology of Tradition begins with Franzelin. His work is not chosen as a starting point merely with a view to isolating a manageable period. It has been said, and it is probably true, that he gave the theology of Tradition a bent which it never had up to then: it was Franzelin who first related the concept of Tradition so closely to the infallible teaching of the Magisterium as to derive his definition of

Tradition from that relationship. But, apart from that, his treatise *De Divina Traditione et Scriptura*, written at the time of the Vatican Council and summing up the thought of that time, is the classic on Tradition from which the Catholic theology of Tradition in the period developed. Homogeneity was not always a characteristic of that development—to put the matter mildly. But the broad divisions of the Tract were laid out by Franzelin and the development took place within that structure.

Our attention is confined to theological thought on Tradition in the period: abstracting from direct consideration of official Church documents and of surveys of the pre-Vatican theology of Tradition. In reviewing the theology of the period it is the differences and the additions that must attract the main attention of this essay: the additions in order to arrive at a notion of Tradition as adequate as possible, the differences in order that the notion emerges as critically tried and sound. The subject is wide because of the number of different viewpoints on each of the different elements in the description of Tradition. Even on a broad canvas there would be little room for repetition of similarities. If the period is a manageable one, it is no more than that.

Tradition has been a live question since the Reformation, and it will be as long as its influence remains. But the definition of the two great Marian dogmas within a century of each other gave the discussion of Tradition an added boost. Whatever may be said about the dogma of the Immaculate Conception, there was no question of Catholic theologians 'finding the dogma of the Assumption in Tradition', as they had been accustomed to finding dogma in Tradition. In the absence of any agreed scriptural proof for these truths, the question of the nature of Tradition became a very important question indeed. And now, if the question of rapprochement between Catholics of East and West is in the air, Tradition will be all the more a central question, especially in view of the part played by and allotted to the Catholic Magisterium in modern times. Although Tradition is as old as the Church, in a very real sense the question of its nature is a modern problem. Different elements of

Christian truth, as Guardini remarked, have different seasons for growth.

It is substantially the suggestion of Heinrich Bacht that, even since the time that Franzelin and Scheeben began to write, all the elements required for an understanding of the nature of Tradition (such as is now possible) have been analysed by one theologian or another. It is now a question of synthesis.

There is a dispensation in the Church which the word Tradition describes. The term is taken from our common language and it refers to some spiritual possession that is passed on from generation to generation. But there are some things in the Church which are not described as Tradition there although their equivalents in any other society would be so termed. For instance, the equivalent of the Bible in any other society would be called part of the literary Tradition. With us it is separate, the Bible is Scripture and our term Tradition will not cover it. We have not taken over the term unchanged from our common language, but for any changes in meaning that we make we can show good reason.

It is the task of this essay to try to describe, by a synthesis of modern thought on the subject, what meaning theologians think this term Tradition should have in order to describe adequately an actual dispensation in the Church. For this is a doctrinal dispensation that has brought the faith to all of us; it is no accidental addition to the Church of Christ. Our religion is not one of personal illumination, or of unsupervised Bible reading, but, to use the words of Van den Eynde, 'una religione di tradizione'.

The proper place for the discussion of Tradition is not in Fundamental Theology. Indeed within the framework of the present text-book divisions of Catholic theology it is hard to say where its proper place is. It is a corollary to many tracts, and perhaps to some tracts that are not yet normally written, e.g. a tract on the laity. In any case, it is Dogmatic Theology in the full sense.

A synthesis needs a central theme; something with regard to which the different viewpoints on Tradition can be classified, something that can assimilate a thought or two from each

viewpoint until an overall unity is achieved. It has been remarked already that Tradition is a complex thing. In the
theology of the period under review one fundamental complexity is constantly described by theologians; so constantly
that it becomes axiomatic. They say that the notion of Tradition has two essential elements. They call one the objective
element and by that they mean to indicate the truth that is
handed on. The second they call the subjective or active
element and by that they indicate the process or activity of
handing it on. For Tradition in any context is some spiritual
good that is passed on to us, that advances with us and that,
through us, reaches down to future generations.

For the sake of clarity we shall use the word Tradition with
an initial capital in this essay only and always to describe
the complex thing, involving both of these elements at once.
They are often named active tradition and objective tradition,
taken separately. They can be separated only in theory. But
in so far as they can be separated, we shall take active tradition
as the central theme of the essay.

Objective tradition or the doctrine handed down, will be
taken as the deposit of Revelation. That, as we shall see again,
will confine the discussion to the fate of what will be called
divine traditions and so to the complex of act and object that
we can correspondingly term Divine Tradition. In a very real
sense other traditions in the Church—ecclesiastical traditions
merely, or 'traditiones more apostolicae'—are ultimately for
the preservation of divine traditions. If a satisfactory description of Divine Tradition could be reached by far the principal
problem would be settled and the other traditions could be
treated in a short space.

There is no benefit in conceiving of the deposit too mechanically. The very term 'traditio obiectiva' is inclined to give the
impression of a body of truth outside of all minds and handed
on as a container of material goods is handed on. But truth
has its formal existence only in the mind. It is handed on
by communication between minds: expression given and
impression received. So that one theologian will speak of
'Traditionsgeist' to bring out the point that it is the individual or collective grasp of the truth which is handed on and

in the various ways in which such a possession can be handed on. Still, provided it is not misunderstood, 'traditio obiectiva' is the accepted term for this aspect of Tradition.

It is the discussion of Tradition from its active aspect that gives most scope for noticing the differences between theologians in the period and the development. It is from this point of view that a unified notion can be achieved in the period while allowances are made, too, for those elements of thought in the period that cannot be brought into such a unified notion. The concept of objective tradition has remained comparatively stable.

In discussing active tradition, the agents in or, to use a better phrase, the bearers of Tradition will be usually before the mind. These will be divided into groups—according to the classical division—on the basis of their qualifications and activities. As one person may be active on different levels, so the same physical person may belong to different groups. Keeping in mind, then, the fact that the groups are not mutually exclusive, we discuss Tradition where Catholic theologians claim to find it. We begin with that group whose activity undoubtedly belongs to Tradition, the Magisterium.

Chapter One

TRADITION AND THE MAGISTERIUM

"In the nineteenth and twentieth centuries many theologians say it quite clearly: Tradition is Church preaching. . . . Indeed, some say: Tradition is the Church Magisterium."
DENEFFE, *Der Traditionsbegriff*, p. 96

MODERN Catholic writing contains many surveys of the theological thought on Tradition in the period under review, some judgments, too, on the general trends of thought on Tradition in the period. A strong group of these surveys and judgments maintain that the theological thought of the period is characterised by a conception of Tradition in terms of magisterium, i.e. in terms of the official teaching of the Catholic Church. Of course, the members of the group forming these particular judgments are themselves of the opinion that Tradition is properly defined as the continuous and official teaching of the Catholic hierarchy. That is no reflection on their judgments; for, in spite of the fact that they often disagree amongst themselves in details, their judgments are in general accurate enough and of their main thesis there can be little doubt: the principal line of thought in the period under review amounts to this identification of Tradition with magisterium. We may maintain that their inventories of theological opinion were not complete—most of them are 'dated' even by now—and that they were not fair to individual theologians, but we cannot deny that they do describe the main stream of thought on Tradition.

Before examining some of the surveys that trace this Tradition-magisterium line of thought, it is necessary to clarify the meaning of the word 'magisterium'. In this book the term 'the Magisterium'—with the definite article and initial capital—will always refer to that moral body which claims in the Catholic Church to succeed the Apostles as authoritative teachers: in other words, the Catholic hierarchy as a teaching body. The term 'magisterium'—without initial capital—will always refer to the teaching of this body, i.e. to the teaching activity and its object, the truth taught. This may seem an arbitrary distinction, but some distinction like this must be clearly formed and firmly kept in mind if the confusion latent in the use of the term magisterium is to be avoided.[1] Here, then, are some surveys that trace the modern tendency to define Tradition as magisterium.

According to Walter J. Burghardt our period is divided at the beginning. He describes the main stream of thought to which we have just referred but he does not think it began with Franzelin or that Franzelin's theology of Tradition belonged to it. The Tradition-magisterium line of thought, he thinks, began later in the period. "Although Franzelin summed up the Catholic theology of tradition as it existed at the time of the Vatican Council, and his work was the framework in which that theology would evolve in the decades to come",[2] he still belongs to a period in which "there are no remarkable insights in regard of the fundamental concept".[3] Although "he set in strong relief the role of the living magisterium",[4] although the period in which he is included is one which lays an "increasing insistence on a tradition that includes a living rule of faith",[5] in which there is "a striking emphasis on tradition as itself a living, dynamic thing",[6] nevertheless the period which brought what was for Burghardt

---

[1] It is obvious that a possibility of confusion is latent in the use of this term since the term, as used in Latin and English, can refer to the moral body or to its activity or to the truth taught. The same can be said for the French 'magistère'. And it is often not clear in what sense authors intend these terms in individual instances. In quotation, of course, we simply transcribe the term as found.

[2] W. J. Burghardt, 'The Catholic Concept of Tradition in the Light of Modern Theological Thought'. *Proceedings of the Sixth Annual Convention of the Catholic Theological Society of America*, 1951. Reprint, p. 17.   [3] idem., op. cit., p. 3.

[4] idem., op. cit., p. 17.   [5] idem., op. cit., p. 3.   [6] ibid.

the significant development in the Catholic notion of Tradition began after Franzelin.[7] That period seems to have begun with the post-Franzelin text-books, although only with Bainvel and Billot did the significant development—that of identifying Tradition with magisterium—find its first fully consistent expression. "The contemporary, twentieth-century theology of tradition (*a*) regards tradition not so much as a source, as rather the rule of faith; (*b*) it stresses the active aspect, the preaching of the Church, as the formal aspect; consequently (*c*) it insists upon identifying tradition properly so called and magisterium." [8]

This survey of Burghardt's is very closely dependent on the account of the development of the notion of Tradition since Trent as that is described in Michel's *Dictionnaire* article on Tradition[9]—the dependence is acknowledged.[10] It is not surprising then to find that Michel had much the same ideas of Franzelin and of the period which followed him. Whereas he reserves his remark: "theology . . . hardly contributes any new elements to the study of Tradition",[11] for the eighteenth century, he still relegates Franzelin to a period before that which for him, as for Burghardt, brought the significant development in the doctrine of Tradition. Again the glory of the final precision falls to Bainvel and Billot and particularly to the latter.[12]

The assessment of Franzelin's thought as found in these two surveys has been challenged. Judgments of a general character have been passed on Franzelin and his followers which would regard him also as identifying Tradition with magisterium and which would consequently deny any division in our period. Deneffe, for instance, in describing the characteristic notion of Tradition in the last century or so as that which identifies Tradition and magisterium, quotes Franzelin in particular as being in favour of that concept.[13]

---

[7] idem., op. cit., p. 18.　　　　[8] idem., op. cit., p. 3.
[9] A. Michel, art. 'Tradition', in *D.T.C.*, tome 15, part 1, Paris, 1946.
[10] W. Burghardt, art. cit., p. 3.
[11] A. Michel, art. cit., col. 1327.
[12] idem., art. cit., col. 1341 ff.
[13] A. Deneffe, *Der Traditionsbegriff*, Münster i. W., 1931, pp. 109–10.

Zapelena, in an attempt to justify Deneffe's own definition of Tradition as the official teaching of the Catholic Church, picks a selection from the period and in doing so also bears out Deneffe's judgment on Franzelin.[14]

There is one more surveyor who would divide Franzelin from the main stream of thought on Tradition in our period, but for a very different reason from Michel's or Burghardt's. C. Davis writes: "There has been in recent Catholic Theology, chiefly under the influence of Billot, a tendency to identify tradition with the magisterium. This is regrettable, because the older approach, represented for example by Franzelin, which gave a wider meaning to tradition is far sounder."[15] And he goes on to describe a wide concept of Tradition which neither Michel nor Burghardt would find in Franzelin. If C. Davis is mentioned here, so long before the line of thought on Tradition to which he belongs and for which he claims Franzelin's patronage comes under review, it is only to point the more sharply the necessity of evaluating Franzelin's contribution with special care in order to decide if the Tradition-magisterium line of thought can honestly claim his very considerable authority.

Now what precisely is meant by saying that Tradition is identical with the teaching of the Catholic Magisterium? And what is meant by the statement that Tradition should now be described as a rule of faith rather than as a source of Revelation? The answers to these questions must be given by examining the theologians who held and elaborated and sought to justify this concept of Tradition. First of these in the period is the controversial Franzelin. His work on Tradition is constantly quoted by Catholic writers since it is regarded

[14] T. Zapelena, art. 'Problema Theologicum', in *Greg.*, 25 (1944), p. 68: "Long before Deneffe Cardinal Franzelin proposed and described very well the same concept of Tradition. He was followed by Bainvel, Van Noort, Dorsch, Dieckmann, Lercher and others. Deneffe however provided a more detailed examination of this whole matter and threw much more light on it." Cf. also G. Proulx, *Tradition et Protestantisme*, Paris, 1924, pp. 90–3 for a similar appreciation of Franzelin's position.

[15] C. Davis, art. 'The Church and Unity—Notes on Recent Work', in *Cl.R.*, 43 (Aug. 1958), p. 484.

as a classic amongst his own writings and a classic, too, in the Catholic theology of Tradition.

1. FRANZELIN'S THOUGHT ON TRADITION

Franzelin, who was born in the Tyrol in 1816, was Prefect of Studies at the German College in Rome from 1853. He was a Jesuit and taught at the Gregorian University. He aided in the preliminaries for the Vatican Council and was Papal Theologian to that Council when it was convened in 1869. He was made Cardinal in 1876 and died ten years later. He was one of those German theologians who were again beginning to see the value of a return to the patristic sources for theology and his works are rich with the insights of the Fathers.

The background of thought against which Franzelin sets his concept of Tradition, as that is revealed in his work *De Divina Traditione et Scriptura*[16] is as follows. The Lord chose a body of men to whom he entrusted his Revelation. He sent them to preach this truth and he threatened punishment on those who would not listen to them. He conferred on them and on their successors for ever the charism of the Spirit and he promised them his own abiding presence. Armed with this guarantee and entrusted with this mission, the Apostles and their appointed successors have taught all generations the revealed truth which came from Christ. This perennial body is—in view of the helps promised it—infallible when it proclaims revealed truth and demands—in virtue of its divine mission—the obedient assent of men to its teaching.

There is no point in discussing the various views on Franzelin's doctrine of Tradition, the various claims made to his authority by men who hold widely differing views on Tradition, before an attempt has been made to present a positive analysis of his thought on Tradition as it appears particularly in the first section of the *De Divina Traditione*

[16] J. B. Franzelin, *Tractatus De Divina Traditione et Scriptura*, ed. 4, Rome, 1896.

et Scriptura. This positive analysis will also provide a fundamental concept of Tradition which will serve as a basis of discussion in the rest of this chapter and in the rest of this book.

In his first thesis Franzelin presents his first general analysis of the concept of Tradition. He describes it as doctrines and institutions (and precepts[17]) pertaining to religion which are handed on to the Church by our predecessors for preservation.[18] There is in this description an objective and an active element.[19] The objective element consists of doctrines, institutions, precepts, in short, of the traditions. The concept of Tradition in so far as it refers to this objective element is called objective tradition. The active element is the act or series of acts or of 'means' by which the doctrines, whether theoretical or practical, are handed on and the concept of Tradition in so far as it refers to this active element is called active tradition. But just as neither active tradition nor objective tradition can be conceived without reference to the other, so the full and proper concept of Tradition refers exclusively to neither. The full and proper concept of Tradition is a complex concept combining both elements. Yet in the complex concept one element is more proper to Tradition than the other (in an analogous way a species has one element in common with other species under the same genus and an element that distinguishes or specifies it). The more proper or formal element is the active element, the 'way' in which the truth is handed on, the series of acts or of media involved in handing it on. It is not the doctrines so much as the way in which doctrines are preserved which is peculiar to Tradition and so which represents the formal element in the complex concept. That is quite clear from a comparison of Scripture and Tradition.[20] For Scripture also contains doctrines, theoretical and practical, pertaining to religion. Its objective element coincides at least in part with the objective element in Tradition. So that the essential distinction be-

[17] cf. op. cit., p. 13.   [18] op. cit., p. 11.
[19] cf. J. L. Murphy, *The Notion of Tradition in John Driedo*, Milwaukee, 1959, pp. 44, 45.
[20] Franzelin, op. cit., p. 17.

tween Scripture and Tradition is sought, not in the division of doctrines but in a distinction of the ways in which these doctrines are preserved and propagated.[21]

The discussion is then narrowed down by some divisions.[22] These are divisions of traditions or of objective tradition and they are formed on the basis of the different origins of different traditions. Divine traditions are those revealed by God himself, whether revealed through Christ or directly to the Apostles by the Holy Spirit. Traditions which originated from the Apostles acting as pastors of the Church rather than as promulgators of revealed truth are simply apostolic traditions, while those that had their origin in the post-apostolic Church are ecclesiastical traditions.

It is important to note the implications of these divisions for the rest of this book. From now on our attention—like Franzelin's—will be confined to the fate of divine traditions. If we say that Tradition is magisterium, we are speaking of the handing on, the teaching of divine traditions: we are speaking of Divine Tradition and we mean to say that Tradition is defined as the teaching of *revealed* truth *as such* by the Catholic hierarchy. We are not concerned with any teaching which the Church might impose authoritatively but to which it does not demand the assent of faith as to a revealed truth. Similarly if we write of the Fathers' part in Tradition we are not concerned with their private opinions but only with their teaching of what they regard as revealed truth. Our attention is confined to the handing on of revealed truth, of divine traditions as such.

We gather from Franzelin's Prolegomenon that it is in connection with the objective principles (i.e. the sources) of Christian knowledge that he will deal with Tradition.[23] In order to show the necessity of perennial principles of Christian knowledge it is only necessary to assume, as Franzelin does,[24] that the Christian Revelation—and this is materially equivalent with what we have called divine tradition above[25]— was destined in its integrity for all men of all ages. This

---

[21] This paragraph is a paraphrase of Franzelin's thesis 1, pp. 11, 12.

[22] Franzelin, op. cit., pp. 12 ff.

[23] op. cit., p. 9.   [24] op. cit., p. 4.   [25] ibid.

assumption is stated more clearly in thesis VI[26] where Franzelin takes the essential properties of the Christian Revelation to be universality, or the exigency for universality, and unity. He argues that God in his wisdom and providence would have provided for these essential properties by positing a cause that would ensure their presence.[27] The cause which is to ensure that the divine Revelation reach all men in its integrity will itself be what he calls the principle of Christian knowledge. He argues further in thesis VI that, without immediate revelation to individuals, there can only be one such adequate principle: the legitimate Magisterium, although he does not thereby rule out the possibility of a contributory one.[28] It is in the context of searching for these principles that he deals with Tradition.

Franzelin appeals to the Council of Trent to confirm that Revelation is contained in the Scriptures and in divine traditions and that the organ conserving these traditions is the perpetual apostolic succession in the Catholic Church.[29] It appears from this context—as it does from the argument in thesis VI—that to Franzelin's mind the adequate principle or source of Christian knowledge is the apostolic succession, the teaching authority, the Magisterium. Scripture is also regarded as a principle of Christian knowledge in this context but a secondary one since it needs interpretation by the primary principle.[30] Hence, Tradition is linked very closely with the Magisterium.[31]

In the body of the argument in this first section of the work —theses I–XI—it is again the teaching hierarchy that holds most of his attention. The argument is in two chapters. The first is entitled: "Concerning the concept of Divine Tradition and its formal element as that is seen from the very nature of the institution of the Christian Religion as described in the

---

[26] Franzelin, op. cit., pp. 40 ff.
[27] op. cit., p. 41. [28] op. cit., p. 42.
[29] op. cit., p. 9. Note, however, that in the paragraph quoted by Franzelin, Trent speaks only of conservation by a continual succession in the Catholic Church and does not refer specifically to the apostolic succession.
[30] op. cit., p. 9. [31] ibid.

apostolic writings";[32] the second: "Concerning the formal element of Divine Tradition as that is revealed in the constitution of the Church from the apostolic age onwards".[33] Yet the whole weight of the argument goes to prove that the divinely appointed organ for the preservation and propagation of the Christian Revelation—and the only adequate one —is the apostolic succession, the Catholic hierarchy as a teaching body divinely equipped and commissioned for that task.

In all this argument Franzelin is dealing with the formal element in the concept of Divine Tradition and in doing so he is all the time describing the nature of and defending the divine institution of the Catholic Magisterium. One might argue from these facts that Tradition must be identified in a very complete way with the Magisterium itself. Together with its teaching activity and the object thereof, the teaching hierarchy must be identified with the complex concept of Tradition. Such a definition of Tradition appears later in the period[34] but its advocates do not appeal to Franzelin.[35] An appeal of this nature would too obviously be an unwarranted interpretation of Franzelin's thought. He has already described active tradition as an "action or, better, a whole series and complex of actions and means",[36] has identified that with the 'form' of Tradition[37] and hence it is clear that in the body of the argument he is describing this activity which constitutes active tradition when he writes of the organ with which it is inseparable in the concrete. In a strict definition of Tradition the elements are: an activity and its object. Reference to the organ to which the activity belongs is unavoidable but the organ or body itself is not an element in the strict definition. Tradition is not *the Magisterium*.

So we find in thesis XI. In his statement of the thesis Franzelin proposes his final definition of Tradition: it is "the

[32] op. cit., p. 11.   [33] op. cit., p. 60.
[34] cf. section 3, part iv of this chapter.
[35] Filograssi does appeal to Franzelin when he proposes his own definition of Tradition: I. Filograssi, art. 'Traditio Divino-Apostolica et Assumptio B.V.M.', in *Greg.*, 30 (1949), p. 448; but not later on when he proposes his extreme identification of Tradition with the Magisterium.
[36] Franzelin, op. cit., p. 12.   [37] ibid.

whole doctrine of the Faith"—presumably what he has referred to as the objective tradition, the material element in
the concept and in the thing—"in so far as"—this presumably
introduces the formal element in the definition, under this
aspect the doctrine is tradition—"it is preserved, with the
assistance of the Holy Spirit, in continuous succession by the
unanimous teaching of those who are guardians of the deposit
and divinely instituted teachers, and appears in the profession
and life of the whole Church".[38] In the body of this thesis,
which takes the form of a reminder of the points he has made
already concerning the Magisterium and its handing on of
Revelation, there is another form of this definition: "Divine
Tradition is the divine doctrine and discipline preserved and
propagated from the Apostles onward, when it is considered
together with the means and the organ of propagation which
was instituted by Christ and is distinct from the Scriptures."[39]
Here are the two elements of a strict definition of Tradition:
the teaching activity and the truth taught, with a necessary
reference to the body which teaches but which is not part of
the strict definition.

The definition, he claims, is confirmed by the terms for
Tradition in the usage of the Fathers of the Church, and here
is how he interprets these terms. One group of patristic terms
for Tradition—terms like "common understanding of the
Faith",[40] refer primarily to the grasp or understanding of
doctrine by the *teaching Church*. A second group of patristic
terms: "ecclesiastical preaching", "rule of faith", etc.[41] refer
more to the objective doctrine. These two groups of terms,
Franzelin explains, do not describe two completely distinct
things, but rather two elements or phases of the one complex
thing.[42] The groups refer respectively to the "Church profession" and the "faith handed down",[43] to an active element
and the object of the activity.

[38] op. cit., p. 90: "doctrina fidei universa quatenus sub assistentia
Spiritus Sancti in consensu custodum depositi et doctorum divinitus
institutorum continua successione conservatur, atque in professione et
vita totius Ecclesiae sese exserit".

[39] op. cit., p. 92.   [40] op. cit., p. 95.

[41] ibid.   [42] ibid.   [43] ibid.

It is clear now that Franzelin's definitive concept of Tradition combines that of the activity of the infallible Magisterium with that of the deposit of Revelation which it transmits; "that guarding of the deposit, that perennial Church preaching which is under the guidance of the Holy Spirit, is Tradition in the best theological meaning of the word".[44] Again, referring back to thesis XI, Franzelin gives further expression to his view that the teaching of the Magisterium is the formal element in Tradition when he writes that the concept of Tradition is essentially verified in the infallible preservation of the true meaning of revealed doctrine.[45]

In this last context just referred to, the expression used to describe active tradition—"the perennial and infallible preservation of the true sense, the true understanding of the deposit of faith"—draws together two hitherto interchanging expressions for active tradition. In one set of expressions: "Church profession", "propagation",[46] the activity described seems to be an external one of preaching and teaching; whereas in expressions such as "general understanding of the faith",[47] active tradition seems to be something internal in the realm of knowledge. It appears now that this active tradition is itself a complex thing comprising a right understanding and an expression of that understanding; that it can be described by either set of terms provided we realise that the understanding of the faith is one that is expressed and that the profession is not of dead formulae but of intelligible and understood truth.

In view of all this it is very difficult to understand why Michel writes: "The great merit of Franzelin was to have placed in relief the role of the living magisterium of the Church",[48] and yet refuses to place him in the same category as Billot who, "in placing the emphasis on the 'living' magisterium . . . shows his intention of demonstrating the identity of that magisterium with active tradition",[49] or why Burghardt, too, refuses to place Franzelin amongst those who

[44] op. cit., p. 241.   [45] op. cit., p. 272.
[46] op. cit., pp. 95, 92.   [47] op. cit., p. 95.
[48] Michel, art. cit., col. 1339.   [49] art. cit., col. 1341.

identify Tradition with magisterium. It is quite true that Franzelin does not say in so many words that Tradition is identical with magisterium, but without using that precise expression it is hard to see how he could have more definitely proposed the same idea.[50] Hence, although Deneffe regards the definition of Tradition in Franzelin's statement of thesis XI[51] as a definition of objective tradition only, he adds that the active tradition can be shown to be, according to Franzelin, the teaching activity of the Church Magisterium.[52] And so with Zapelena[53] and Filograssi,[54] too, we include Franzelin in the school of thought that defines Tradition as magisterium. That is not to say that Billot, for example, said nothing more than Franzelin did on the subject. It is simply to maintain that they have the fundamental concept in common.

There is still another line of interpretation of Franzelin's thought on Tradition intimated by C. Davis,[55] and found more specifically in an article by Ternus. This is a line of interpretation which would have us believe that the concept of Tradition was wider, to Franzelin's way of thinking, than we have supposed. Franzelin, it claims, included in his concept of Tradition far more activity than that of the Magisterium. And so Ternus claims the authority of Franzelin for a concept of Tradition that includes the activity of priests and laity, of theologians and teachers.[56] If we consider briefly the evidence offered for this contention it will help to elucidate one more phrase in Franzelin's main definition.

Ternus appeals[57] to a phrase used by Franzelin in his main

---

[50] Baumgartner also attempts to show that Franzelin does not identify Tradition and magisterium, but with inconclusive arguments. Cf. Ch. Baumgartner, art. 'Tradition et Magistère', in *R.S.R.*, 41 (1953), p. 181.

[51] Franzelin, op. cit., p. 90.

[52] Deneffe, op. cit., p. 98.   [53] art. cit., p. 68.

[54] I. Filograssi, art. 'Tradizione divino-apostolica e Magistero della Chiesa', in *Greg.*, 33 (1952), p. 163. Apropos of Franzelin's concept of Tradition he remarks: "Identica é l'idea di tradizione eposta dal Billot."

[55] cf. p. 4 above.

[56] J. Ternus, art. 'Beiträge zum Problem der Tradition', in *D.T.* (Fr.), 16 (1938), pp. 39–40.   [57] art. cit., p. 48.

definition of Tradition: "(it) appears in the profession and life of the whole Church".[58] Since this is one of the phrases which specify the doctrine in question as traditional, does it not envisage an organ of active tradition that extends beyond the Magisterium? With Filograssi we would prefer to explain that phrase as referring to the activity, both ordinary and solemn, of the universal teaching body in the Church.[59] That would be more in keeping with what we have seen to be the sequence of thought under thesis XI, where the term 'Church profession' is equivalent to the activity of the Magisterium and to active tradition.[60]

The choice of the narrower notion as that most accurately representing Franzelin's thought is borne out by another important aspect of his teaching. For Franzelin Tradition must

[58] Franzelin, op. cit., p. 90.

[59] Filograssi, art., 'Traditio Divino-Apostolica', p. 448. "Per incisum illud 'in professione et vita totius Ecclesiae sese exserit' intelligitur muneri Ecclesiae docendi respondere elementum visibile totius constitutionis et actuum Ecclesiae tam in vita (si ita loqui fas est) quotidiana, quam in solemnibus gestis." Cf. also, for confirmation on this point: J. V. Bainvel, De Magisterio vivo et Traditione, Paris, 1905, pp. 39–40.

[60] Franzelin, op. cit., p. 95. Perhaps the main proof of Ternus' claim proceeds from a further statement of Franzelin's about this 'conscientia fidei', which is a term for Tradition: "Neque vero nomine 'conscientia fidei' intelligitur solius discentis sed immo totius Ecclesiae sensus et consensus" (Franzelin, op. cit., footnote 4, p. 94). If this can be written about the phrase 'conscientia fidei' and that phrase is used as a synonym for Tradition, then Tradition must extend beyond the activity of the Magisterium. Yet the phrase appears in the footnote from which Ternus quotes it, as it appears again later, amongst those by which is described that understanding of revealed truth which the teaching Church possesses infallibly (Franzelin, op. cit., p. 95). The full statement quoted just above from Franzelin's footnote is, in its context, one refutation of the error of those who would use such an equivalent for Tradition as 'conscientia communis fidei' as evidence that the teaching Church can only profess what the faithful believe (Franzelin, op. cit., p. 94). To give the phrase 'conscientia fidei' the wider sense that Franzelin gives it in the footnote was one way of preventing the erroneous doctrine just mentioned from applying it to the faithful only, but it was not consistent with Franzelin's usage in the body of the thesis. And no one will base an interpretation of Franzelin's concept of Tradition on an inconsistency, however pardonable.

have its own authority. But whence comes this authority? He writes that not only the preservation and integrity but also the "force and authority"[61] of Tradition (i.e. of objective tradition) depend upon the active element in tradition, and so upon the organ to which the active tradition belongs. The authority of Tradition cannot be discussed, he maintains, unless the organ of Tradition is pointed out since the authority of Tradition derives from the authority of this organ, or rather, is identified with the authority of its organ.[62] The authority which belongs to traditions is the authority of the organ which hands them on.[63]

Now it is clear that the authority Franzelin seeks for Tradition is the authority of a divinely instituted and infallible teaching body. It is to establish the existence and identity of such a body that the burden of the argument in the first section of the work has been devoted. The Catholic Magisterium is this body, not only because it is divinely instituted and commissioned to teach but because it has the charism of the Spirit and the continued help of Christ, both of which are given it in view of its teaching mission. It is the authentic Magisterium of the Church which lends the tradition the authority it possesses.

Franzelin's concept of authority demands some comment. When we speak of the authority of a proposition we can mean one of two things; a proposition has authority when it is imposed by a superior, and that seems to be what is primarily intended when we speak of the authority of a proposition. But we also say that a truth has authority when it is spoken

---

[61] op. cit., p. 12.   [62] op. cit., p. 20.

[63] Franzelin claims that Trent, too, vindicates the authority of Tradition from its connection with a particular organ. He assumes that the Council receives traditions 'pari pietatis affectu ac reverentia' because they are conserved in the Catholic Church—because of the organ of preservation. But on a simple verbal analysis the Council seems to receive these traditions 'pari pietatis affectu' more because of their origin in Christ and the Holy Spirit than because they were preserved in the Catholic Church. There is no mention of the Magisterium or of its authority in the tridentine context. Cf. Franzelin, op. cit., p. 12. Cf. H. Holstein, art. 'Tradition d'après le Concile de Trente', in R.S.R., 47 (1959), pp. 387-9.

by one who is in a position to know it. So we speak of the 'authorities' on a subject. It appears that a truth taught by the Catholic Magisterium has both these types of authority: it is taught by a superior—so that it demands the assents of subjects—and that superior is infallible in this matter. When Franzelin writes of the authority of Tradition he intends both meanings of the word, for he describes the divine institution of the Magisterium whereby the hierarchy is placed in authority over the faithful and he also thinks authority to belong to Church teaching "because of the help of the Holy Spirit leading her to the knowledge of all truth".[64] In the strict sense, authority is that quality of a truth which it has in virtue of being imposed by a superior. The second sense of the word is really a secondary sense.

One might very well object that the concept of authority in the strict sense is inapplicable to the process of accepting truth. One could quote freely from Berdyaev.[65] The mind accepts a truth either on its own direct evidence or on the indirect evidence supplied by someone in a position to provide it ('authority' in the secondary sense). What has the authority of a superior to do with truth? If the revealed truth were of a purely theoretical nature with no direct bearing on the purpose of human life then its propagation could be left to a suitably equipped body and to the chance enquiry of interested people. In fact, however, it is an integral part of God's practical plan for human salvation. So God did not only equip a body of men to proclaim it; he ordered them to teach all nations and threatened punishment on those who would not hear them. Needless to say (or is it needless?) such authority does not destroy human freedom in any way.

Apart from the fact that he held discussion of the active element in Tradition to be logically prior, it was to settle this question of authority for Tradition that Franzelin set out to discuss first active tradition, first the means and consequently the organ of Tradition.[66] And he found the latter to be the

---

[64] Franzelin, op. cit., p. 90.
[65] N. Berdyaev, *Freedom and the Spirit*, London, 1935, e.g. p. 331.
[66] Franzelin, op. cit., p. 20.

infallible Magisterium of the Catholic Church. Franzelin was the first exponent of this Tradition-magisterium concept and he is mainly responsible for its popularity. After Franzelin it become common enough in text-book theology. Billot in particular accepted it and developed it.

For Franzelin, as for most Catholic theologians since the Protestant Revolt, the treatment of Tradition goes hand in hand with anti-Protestant polemics. The Prologue to his treatise reveals his preoccupations with contemporary Protestantism and all through the work the 'Sola Scriptura' principle is under attack directly or indirectly as often as possible. He could try to prove that truths of Revelation are handed down that are not contained in Scripture. In fact he does try to prove this later in the treatise. But he knows that something is logically prior, namely, the proof that an organ exists which is infallible in handing on these truths. If the 'Sola Scriptura' position is to be adequately met it is this latter point which must be established.[67] So he does not dwell first on the objective content of Tradition, but on its active element. If he is to provide an answer to the exponents of 'Sola Scriptura' he must point to the basis for the authority of all Tradition, both traditions which are also contained in Scripture and traditions which may not be. It is the search for this authority of Tradition that urges Franzelin to devote so much of his treatise to the organ of active tradition, to the Magisterium.[68]

It is undoubtedly also true that a growing emphasis on the official Church Magisterium by the Magisterium itself—and particularly an emphasis on the Papacy—had an influence on the theory of Tradition at this time. In 1854 the Pope defined the dogma of the Immaculate Conception and at the Vatican Council, which was in session when Franzelin published his work on Tradition, the infallibility of the Pope was solemnly defined.[69]

[67] Franzelin, op. cit., pp. 6–8, esp. footnote p. 8, pp. 45 ff.
[68] op. cit., p. 20.
[69] It is interesting to note that when Courtade lists the formulae which the Magisterium borrowed from Franzelin, none of them are taken from

It is as the product of a man with these preoccupations and working in this climate of ecclesiastical thought, that Franzelin's concept of Tradition must be viewed.

He is concerned with the Christian Revelation and its transmission. The Revelation when, considered as something to be handed down, it is called divine tradition is described as doctrines, precepts and institutions. Institutions? He means teaching about institutions, for 'institutiones' can be in Scripture, too.[70] Revelation, divine tradition, is essentially a corpus of doctrine. Here is no shadow of a theory we meet later which regards Revelation as being made through activity and presence as well as through formal teaching.

And the authority of which he speaks? It belongs to objective tradition because of the organ which hands it on. It belongs to the truth in virtue of the divinely appointed mission of the organ which teaches it and in virtue of the infallibility of that organ in teaching it.

So he arrives at his concept of Tradition and at his answer to the Protestantism that he knew. The Lord conferred on those on whom he appointed to proclaim his message to mankind, on the Apostles and on their legitimately appointed successors for ever, the charism of the Spirit and he promised them that he would always be with them. They had this guarantee that in handing on his Revelation to all generations —whether this was done by more solemn definitions or by the daily teaching and activity of their scattered members ('in professione et vita totius Ecclesiae')—there would be no error, no failure. The activity of this body together with the doctrine thus preserved and handed on formed the elements of Franzelin's concept of Tradition. It seems a very serviceable concept and it has this advantage at least over most others: there is a great clarity about it.

---

his 'principal work', on Tradition—G. Courtade, art. 'J. B. Franzelin: Les Formules que le Magistère de l'Église Lui a Empruntées', in R.S.R., 40 (1952), pp. 317 ff.

[70] cf. Franzelin, op. cit., p. 19.

2. POST-FRANZELIN CONTRIBUTIONS

Of the theologians who follow Franzelin in this stream of thought some simply repeat his position, some add further developments. Amongst the former Hurter can be counted.[71] In most of the matter in his treatise on Tradition he reproduces Franzelin's thought in more summary form. He does not really add anything new when he writes that Tradition is written, oral or practical, according to the nature of the activity used to hand on the truth.[72] This sub-division is implicit in Franzelin's treatment, too, for Franzelin never specifically confines active tradition to oral preaching. On the contrary, he acknowledges that the Magisterium makes use of written documents to hand on the faith,[73] he knows that some truths are handed on "more in practical usage and custom",[74] and all this can be seen already indicated in that phrase of his definition where he writes that the doctrine is propagated by the preaching and life of the Church.[75] The Church preaches in her very practices.

Hurter repeats all the main characteristics of Franzelin's treatment of Tradition. To his mind also the formal element in the concept of Tradition is found by concentrating on the activity involved in Tradition.[76] That activity is the infallible teaching of the Catholic Magisterium. And so his definition of Tradition merely echoes Franzelin, with the addition of some accidental details.[77] He states even more strongly than Franzelin that the authority of traditions derives from the organ of transmission, the Magisterium.[78] Altogether Hurter's

[71] H. Hurter, *Theologiae Dogmaticae Compendium*, vol. 1, Oeniponte, 1896, pp. 157, 158.   [72] op. cit., p. 121.

[73] Franzelin, op. cit., pp. 152 f.   [74] op. cit., p. 262.

[75] op. cit., p. 90: "in professione et vita totius Ecclesiae sese exserit".

[76] Hurter, op. cit., p. 123.

[77] Hurter, op. cit., p. 138—Franzelin, op. cit., p. 90. Precisely the same concept of Tradition is introduced by Ranft into the *Lexikon für Theologie und Kirche,* except that he defines separately active tradition and objective tradition: J. Ranft, art. 'Tradition', in *L.T.K.*, tome X, ed. 2, Freiburg i. B., 1938, col. 243.

[78] Hurter, op. cit., p. 139.

is a typical example of a text-book which took over Franzelin's theology of Tradition.

Another text-book, by Dorsch, proposing the same ideas on Tradition, complains that this question of Tradition could be completed very summarily were it not for the exigencies of anti-Protestant polemics.[79] He will not, he says, re-introduce proofs of the existence and nature of the Magisterium in this context—as Franzelin does—in order to elaborate his doctrine of Tradition. Yet he must show the perennial Magisterium to be the fundamental, essential, perpetual and necessary source of Christian doctrine;[80] which amounts to a re-introduction of much of the material found in Franzelin's work. That goes again to point the influence of the Protestant position in directing the Catholic treatment of Tradition. But now we find Dorsch writing of another concept of Tradition which is termed a stricter concept.[81] This suggests that we discuss the remainder of those who hold concepts of Tradition equivalent to Franzelin's in connection with any new ideas which they also introduce. It will save the repetition of first listing them all here. We can meanwhile proceed to describe the development of this Tradition-magisterium identity which is found in Franzelin, the first explicit exponent of it in modern times.

3. DEVELOPMENT OF THIS DEFINITION

i. The Rule of Faith

It is a commonplace of the modern theology of Tradition to link the concept of Tradition with that of the rule of faith. Some theologians call Tradition a remote rule of faith, some insist that it is a proximate rule of faith, some describe it as remote under one aspect, proximate under another. Whatever their position may be, all presume by this linking of concepts to throw some light on their thought about Tradition or to segregate their ideas from others. It might be supposed that those who are in essential agreement on the concept of Tradition as the teaching of the Magisterium, those theologians

[79] A. Dorsch, *Institutiones Theologiae Fundamentalis*, vol. 2, ed. 2, Oeniponte, 1928, p. 679.   [80] op. cit., p. 689.   [81] op. cit., p. 681.

within the stream of thought now under review, would also agree in their ideas of the rule of faith. But that is not so. In this there is an indication of a development of the Tradition-magisterium concept itself.

The oldest and most fundamental notion of the rule of faith regarded it as an objective body of truth, the deposit of Revelation, the Gospel, the apostolic doctrine. It was a rule of faith because it measured the material extent of the object of faith and it carried with it the authority of God, its Author, thereby demanding the formal assent of faith. The question of the concrete application of this rule of faith was a distinct question. It could be applied, for instance, by Church teaching which might carry and add its own specific authority. But the rule of faith was prior to all that. So we find the rule of faith described, and distinguished from an application of it by Church authority, in St Augustine.[82]

So we find it, too, in Franzelin—although he mentions the matter only incidentally—except now the terms 'remote' and 'proximate' are added, the former to describe the rule of faith, the objective Revelation, apart from its application to us, the second to describe the applied rule of faith.[83] In one other context Franzelin writes of the rule of faith and betrays the same approach to the concept.[84] There again the Word of God is 'the rule for believing'; it is applied—now by means of explanation—by the teaching of the Church. It is regarded as being contained prior to this application in documents and records (it is found in Scripture, too, but that is outside our present interest). And Franzelin comments: "This is exactly what is normally said . . . Tradition (objective, contained in records and documents) is a remote rule of faith; the Church (the 'living' magisterium or preaching of the Church) is the

---

[82] Augustine, *De Baptismo contra Donatist.*, lib. V, c. XXVII, n. 38— P.L. XLIII, 196; "regulam fidei diligentissime inquisitam firmissime tenent, et si quid ab eo deviant, cito auctoritate catholica corriguntur". Franzelin admits too that the Patristic term 'regula fidei' refers to an objective body of doctrine—cf. op. cit., p. 95.

[83] Franzelin, op. cit., p. 263.

[84] op. cit., p. 155.

proximate rule of faith." [85] Substantially the same idea of the rule of faith appears in Ranft's *Lexikon* article.[86]

Objective tradition, then, is a rule of faith, remote for lack of application or explanation. If it is a rule of faith it has an authority of its own, the authority of God who revealed it. The very notion of a rule of faith implies authority. Why then should Franzelin write that the authority of Tradition cannot be discussed unless a divinely instituted organ of transmission be pointed out, for the authority of Tradition is identified with the authority of that organ?[87] We may well agree with the former point made in that same context: that it is of primary necessity to discuss the active element of Tradition since that is the formal element. But if in seeking this activity he specifically intends to seek an authority that is lent to Tradition by a divinely instituted organ, has he not limited his search artificially? Why limit the search for the activity that will be called tradition to seeking an authoritative organ and on the plea that otherwise there can be no question of authority for traditions, when it is admitted later on that objective tradition is a rule of faith and when, as such, it must have an authority of its own?[88]

Franzelin sees this objective tradition, this remote rule of faith, extant in documents and records.[89] Suppose in some cases it was placed there by agents other than the Magisterium and that it was not placed there or recorded simply as teaching of the Magisterium. It would still be objective Revelation.[90] We would have to question the qualifications of the agents who put it there, to ask about some kind of authority in them, but a priori at least, we cannot begin by demanding that the qualifications take the form of a teaching authority and a charismatic infallibility such as the Magisterium possesses. Now Franzelin does not rule out the possibility of such agents placing revealed truth in records.[91] And once that

[85] ibid.   [86] art. cit., col. 247.   [87] Franzelin, op. cit., p. 20.
[88] cf. Ternus, art. cit. Beiträge, pp. 48–50.
[89] op. cit., p. 155.   [90] op. cit., p. 263.
[91] Except in so far as a footnote on p. 8 mentions only past teaching of the Magisterium as an objective—and so a remote?—rule of faith.

B

possibility is entertained the thin edge of the wedge is already inserted between objective tradition and its absolute identity with the teaching of the Magisterium.

Neither can the question of remote or proximate, a question of application, represent a complete dichotomy. As Zapelena remarks, for those who are competent to judge documentary evidence Tradition in documents can also be a proximate rule of faith.[92]

It is a tribute to the consistency of Billot that he discarded the older concept of the rule of faith and defined that term in a sense that completely accorded with the Tradition-magisterium line of thought. Billot, like Franzelin, was a Jesuit and a Cardinal—from 1911—and he lectured in the Gregorian University in Rome. His book on Tradition is, as the title reveals, directed against 'the new heresy' of Modernism. That movement is most often connected with the names of Loisy[93] and Tyrrell. Billot attacked it in 1904; it received official condemnation in September 1907 when the Encyclical *Pascendi* was published. In the following year Archbishop Mercier made the Encyclical the subject of his Lenten Pastoral and in the pastoral he describes the modernist position of Tyrrell as follows:

> Revelation, he thinks, is not a deposit of doctrine committed to the charge of the teaching Church, and of which the faithful are to receive authoritative interpretation from time to time. It is the life of the collectivity of religious souls, or rather, of all men of good will who aspire to realise an ideal higher than the earthly aims of egoists. The Christian saints form the elite of this invisible society, this communion of saints. While the life of religion pursues its invariable course in the depths of the Christian conscience, 'theological' beliefs are elaborated by the intellect and find expression in formulae adapted to the needs of the day, but which lose in conformity to the living realities of Faith what they gain in precision. The authority of the Roman Catholic Church—the bishops and the Pope—interprets the interior life of the faithful, recapitulates the results of the general conscience, and proclaims them in dogmatic formulae. But the

[92] art. cit., p. 60.
[93] cf. A. Loisy, *Autour d'un Petit Livre*, Paris, 1903.

interior life of religion remains itself the supreme directive rule of beliefs and dogmas. In addition, the intellectual effort being subject to a thousand fluctuations, the code of beliefs is variable; and the dogmas of the Church, on their side, change their sense, if not necessarily their expression, with the ages to which they are addressed; still the Catholic Church remains one and faithful to its beginnings, because, since the time of Christ, one and the same spirit of religion and holiness animates the successive generations of the Christian community, and all agree at bottom in the same sentiment of filial piety towards our Father who is in Heaven and of love for humanity and the universal brotherhood.[94]

Tyrrell has much to say to the Cardinal in his reply but he does not attack the accuracy of that description of his position. It is put, as he says, more or less in his own words. It is inadequate—as a brief description must be—but not inaccurate.[95]

Modernism, according to Congar[96] derived from a conjunction of two factors: (1) a claim that there existed a certain discord between doctrine currently taught by the Church and the teaching found by historical and critical study of documents from the past, (2) a trend of thought in the philosophy of religion which inclined to separate religious faith from the intellectual formulations to which it gave rise in history. By the time Billot came to write, development of dogma had already become a major theme for Catholic theology —one need only recall the work of Newman. And it was

[94] This quotation is actually taken from a text of the pastoral letter which is published in Tyrrell's reply to it: George Tyrrell, *Medievalism —a reply to Cardinal Mercier*, London, 1908, pp. 9–10.

[95] One of his points against the Cardinal does strike home. He quotes from the pastoral: "The episcopate in union with the Pope is the organ of transmission of the revealed teachings of Jesus Christ. Be it said, in passing, that the organ of transmission is what, in one word, is called Tradition" (cf. op. cit., p. 6) and observes, "I should have thought that Tradition was the process of transmission or else the thing transmitted, and not the organ of transmission. But for this confusion you have excellent precedent in the words of Pius IX, La tradizione son' io" (op. cit., p. 55).

[96] Y. M.-J. Congar, *La Tradition et Les Traditions*, Paris, 1960, p. 264 f.

undoubtedly the traces left by such development in the historical records which provided the Modernists with the ammunition they needed to bombard the alleged immutability of Christian truth. So Loisy remarks: "What disquiets the faithful as far as Tradition is concerned is the impossibility of reconciling historical development of Christian doctrine with the claim made by theologians that it is immutable." [97] Billot did not try to reconcile the fact of development with the claim to immutability by examining a type of development that would not substitute for or add objectively to the original truth. Instead he based his case on the authority and infallibility of the Magisterium. Whatever it defined must be the traditional truth of the Christian Revelation—explain its development how you will. So, as Michel remarks, "Modernism provided Billot with the occasion to give more theological precision to the Catholic concept of Tradition as a remote or proximate rule of faith." [98]

Billot does not admit that objective tradition is a rule of faith.[99] And when he has fully described what the rule of faith does mean we can see clearly that it can only be the teaching of the Magisterium, and that not as an objective body of doctrine but as an activity expressing with authority the doctrine to be believed. It is a complexity of act and object[100] and it must be infallible.[101] Tradition, since it is described as the preaching of the Magisterium,[102] is the rule of faith then, as that has just been defined.[103] Billot still makes a distinction between remote and proximate rules of faith. He explains it as follows: The same Tradition, the same complex thing that is the preaching of the Church (1) is a remote rule of faith when considered "in that intervening chain of past centuries to which it belongs and right through which it forms a 'continuum' with the preaching of those who first promulgated the revealed word";[104] for under that aspect of 'pastness' the preaching of a truth can be known only through scientific

---

[97] Loisy, op. cit., p. 215.   [98] Michel, art. cit., col. 1342.
[99] L. Billot, *De Immutabilitate Traditionis contra Modernam Haeresim Evolutionismi*, ed. 3, Rome, 1922, footnote p. 20.
[100] op. cit., p. 20.   [101] ibid.
[102] op. cit., p. 25.   [103] op. cit., p. 19.   [104] op. cit., p. 29.

examination of records. It is (2) a proximate rule of faith
"when it is no longer considered in coherent and continuous
succession from the first origin of Revelation, but absolutely as exercised at this present and particular point of
time".[105]

Under both these aspects the requirements he demands for
the rule of faith are fulfilled: there is always the infallible
preaching of the Magisterium. The rule of faith is remote
when this infallible preaching is seen belonging to the past,
coming down the ages from the first promulgators of Revelation, for then it has to be ascertained by investigation of
whatever records that activity has left. It is proximate when
the Magisterium speaks here and now. At no stage is objective
tradition, whether extant in records or not, a rule of faith.
And so Tradition, the teaching of the infallible Magisterium,
and the rule of faith are completely identical. If there is
question of authority, of a rule directing faith, "we ought not
to look to that which is believed, but rather to that which
guides our belief by proposing the truth to be believed".[106]
In Billot's thought, the word of Revelation was spoken once
by God and has been repeated infallibly and authoritatively
since by the Magisterium.[107] Within this framework he defines Tradition and specifies accordingly what must be meant
by the rule of faith. It is an advance in consistency. The
authority implied in the rule is now seen to come always from
the activity of the Magisterium. It is now no longer attached
to the objective doctrine, just as the term 'rule of faith' is
no longer attached to the doctrine apart from the Church's
teaching of it.

So Deneffe complained that the primary concept of Tradition—for him also, as we shall see, Tradition in its full sense
was the authoritative teaching of the Magisterium—was
obscured in previous centuries.[108] He attributes the obscurity
partly to the proposition: tradition is the remote rule of faith,
the preaching of the Church is the proximate rule of faith.[109]
He excludes Franzelin from complicity in the obscurity by

---

[105] ibid.   [106] op. cit., footnote p. 20.   [107] op. cit., p. 10.
[108] Deneffe, op. cit., p. 116.   [109] op. cit., p. 117.

pointing out that Franzelin, although he did make the proposition his own, expounded the proper notion of Tradition
very clearly elsewhere.[110] Yet it is an account of the rule of
faith such as Franzelin gives that Deneffe is criticising for
causing obscurity. When we remember the standpoint on
Tradition from which Deneffe writes, this criticism is only
to be expected. It looks to Billot's clarification—although
Deneffe does not mention Billot in this context. But it does
not seem so good to have to change the older, accepted meaning of an old term such as 'rule of faith' in order to bring
consistency to what is claimed to be the old and proper notion
of Tradition.[111]

Consistency and inconsistency. There is another aspect of
this section of Billot's thought and perhaps inconsistency is
too strong a word for it. Better to say that there is a nicety
about Billot's thought which we would expect from Billot but
which hardly belongs here. There was an earlier and slightly
different version of the work[112] we have been examining. In
it there is this certain finesse in part of his discussion of
Tradition not altogether lost in the later version. He shows
a certain reluctance in deciding the present, actual teaching of the Magisterium—precisely as such—to be completely
equivalent to Tradition. The reluctance is shown in this
way. Having described Tradition as the remote rule of faith
"in the intervening chain of past centuries", he adds: "In
this first sense, therefore, Church preaching essentially veri-
fies the formal concept of Tradition, i.e. the transmission
of the revealed truth as from hand to hand down from the
Apostles. That is, I say, Tradition in essence." [113] Whereas,
when he comes to describe the proximate rule of faith,
Church preaching "simply as such", he seems to think that
he needs to explain why he calls it Tradition. "Under this
aspect it is still indeed Tradition in so far as it hands on
what it received either explicitly or implicitly from our fore-

[110] op. cit., p. 118.
[111] cf. R. Draguet, 'Review of Deneffe's Der Traditionsbegriff', in
E.T.L., 9 (1932), p. 94.
[112] L. Billot, De Sacra Traditione contra Novam Haeresim Evolutionismi, Rome, 1904.   [113] op. cit., p. 8.

bears, but now it is Tradition under the precise aspect of authoritative teaching." [114]

It is as much as to say that there are two 'formalities' or formal elements involved in Church preaching: one, the transmission element, makes it Tradition; the other, the magisterial element, makes it authoritative—although that is suggested more than expressed. We shall see it expressed by Scheeben. In the later version of Billot's work the sharpness is taken out of the distinction when he merely writes of the remote rule of faith: "it is Tradition in the precise sense of transmission . . . or Tradition precisely as such" and there is no use of the phrase 'ipsissima traditio', Tradition in essence; although he still thinks the same explanation is required when he regards the proximate rule of faith, Church preaching "exercised at this present and particular point of time" as Tradition. [115]

As the word itself sounds in our ears, Tradition suggests something received out of the past and handed on into the future. It belongs to the historical aspect of man's existence. As Semmelroth puts it, "Since mankind has historical existence, Tradition automatically exists." [116]

The teaching of the Magisterium has two characteristics that are proper to it. It is authoritative in the strict sense. It commands assent. That is because the Apostles and their successors have a mission from God to teach; they share in God's authority. The teaching of the Magisterium also authenticates truth, places the official stamp of authenticity and integrity upon it; because the Magisterium has the charism of infallibility—a charism that belongs to it in view of its mission, in view of its function. Indeed its mission would hardly be conceivable without such a charism.

To take an activity such as that of the Magisterium, to regard only its present value, the authority it gives, its official authenticating effect on truth, without any reference to past or future, is not to speak of Tradition as the word normally suggests itself to our minds. The word will have a technical

[114] op. cit., p. 9.   [115] *De Imm. Trad.* (1922), p. 29.
[116] O. Semmelroth, art. 'Überlieferung als Lebensfunktion der Kirche,' in *S.Z.*, 48 (1951), p. 2.

meaning in theology, of course, but to be of any value it must still carry the essential traits of its normal meaning with it.[117] So the possibility is suggested of distinguishing within the activity of the Magisterium itself its authoritative and authenticating effect on truth and its 'handing-on-what-it-received' effect. Provided the emphasis is not immediately on an effect which is proper to magisterium and to it alone—and in a scientific enquiry it is hard to see why the emphasis should be immediately there—the bearers of Tradition need not be automatically limited to the Magisterium, and may not be limited to the Magisterium at all. Such a line of thought is suggested by Billot, but only suggested, when he writes that Church preaching in the intervening chain of past centuries is Tradition in essence and that Church preaching simply as such is also Tradition since it hands on what it received from predecessors, but not Tradition under the precise aspect of authoritative teaching.

ii. The Contribution of A. Deneffe

Deneffe is the most thorough of those who identify Tradition with the teaching of the Magisterium. Nowhere in his work is there a foothold for another concept. Despite what Michel writes of him, that he takes his concept of Tradition from Billot and without acknowledgment,[118] Deneffe has his own additions to make towards clarity. In contradistinction to Franzelin and Billot, the exigencies of polemics against non-Catholics make no claim upon his thought. Spurred on by a controversy with Dieckmann, his aim is to search Christian thought since the beginning in order to discover what has always been the principal concept of Tradition.[119] In spite of his protest that he has not sought to 'prove' with chosen

[117] cf. Ternus, art. cit. 'Beiträge', p. 53. On the other hand, Josef Pieper's article on the common concept of Tradition suffers because he seems to have the peculiarities of religious Tradition too much in mind: Josef Pieper, art. 'Le Concept de Tradition', in La Table Ronde, n. 150 (June, 1960), pp. 74 ff.

[118] Michel, art. cit., col. 1346. True enough, Deneffe only appeals once to Billot, to confirm a very minor point—cf. Deneffe, op. cit., p. 146.

[119] Deneffe, op. cit., p. 1.

evidence a concept of Tradition already held,[120] Draguet
thinks that he was too prone to see in the evidence from
the past a concept of Tradition which had become popular
more recently and which Deneffe himself as a theologian had
adopted:[121] Müller and Baumgartner[122] openly accuse him of
bending the import of the evidence to bear out a concept of
Tradition that he had made his own; while Michel and Van
den Eynde are satisfied to criticise him for often misunderstanding the evidence which he did bring forward from the
past.[123] Certainly he did not represent some of the post-
Vatican theology as accurately as he might. Still the work of
this German theologian, written in 1931, remained until very
recently the only full-scale attempt in this period to present
the 'positive theology' of Tradition and, even if it has not got
the basis in Christian history that he would like to claim for
it, we can judge Deneffe's positive account of Tradition on
its own merits. For many of his critics accept his main concept
of Tradition even when they reject so much of the evidence
on which he claimed to base it.

Already in his introduction Deneffe is prepared to tell us
what he has found to be the main concept of Tradition.
Tradition is the infallible teaching of the Church which
began with the Apostles, and at that stage is called constitutive
Tradition; which is continued ever since by their successors
and is then termed continuative Tradition. It is the proximate
rule of faith.[124] His only addition in this sphere of definition
is to insist specifically that the teaching of the Church which
is authoritative but not infallible—such as is found in various
decrees and encyclicals—does not as such belong to Tradition

---

[120] op. cit., p. 106.   [121] Draguet, loc. cit., p. 94.
[122] O. Müller, art. 'Zum Begriff der Tradition in der Theologie der
letzten hundert Jahre', in M.T.Z., 4 (1953), p. 166. Ch. Baumgartner,
art. cit., p. 167.
[123] Michel, art. cit., col. 1346. D. Van den Eynde, 'Review of Deneffe's
Der Traditionsbegriff', in R.D'H.E., 27 (1931), pp. 853 ff.
[124] Deneffe, op. cit., pp. 1–2: "Tradition im Hauptbegriff ist die
lebendige, unfehlbar kirchliche Glaubensverkündigung, die mit den
Aposteln begann (traditio constitutiva) und von ihren Nachfolgern mit
derselben Autorität fortgesetzt wird (traditio continuativa). Diese Tradition ist nächste Glaubensregel."

in its primary sense: "in that case the word (Tradition) would be used in a subsidiary sense".[125] Yet this addition has its implications. If in order to be Tradition, teaching must be not only authoritative but also infallible, it may not be possible to indicate the full content of Tradition in practice, and it must often be difficult to say whether a particular truth that is widely taught is Tradition or not. A solemn definition in matters of faith or morals by the Pope or a General Council is held to be infallible and is clearly Tradition as Deneffe defines it. But the morally unanimous teaching of all the legitimately appointed bishops of the world in union with the Pope is also infallible and so it is Tradition. Then may each papal encyclical, each pastoral letter from a bishop be called Tradition? Each is authoritative but each by itself is not infallible (an encyclical or part of it may be). Whether or not the truth expressed in such a letter or encyclical (where that latter is not clearly infallible in any part) is unanimously taught or not is a question of fact. If it is, then this teaching in this letter is part of Tradition, is Tradition in a partial or subsidiary sense. To take a slightly different angle on the subject: in all probability the teaching on the Assumption of Our Lady was explicitly Tradition in Deneffe's sense of the word before the definition of 1950. But for how long before 1950? It would be impossible to say. So the position of Deneffe implies this: if infallible Church preaching is Tradition and we are asked to identify Tradition in practice—to say whether this or that is unanimous Church preaching—we can only do so with complete certainty by referring to definitions of

[125] op. cit., p. 131. In view of this it becomes difficult to understand this criticism of Deneffe by Zapelena: "In notione primaria traditionis desideratur consideratio traditionis authenticae quidem sed non infallibilis" (art. cit., 71). The point made here by Deneffe was later explained in his own way by Filograssi. The full and proper concept of Tradition, he writes, is verified in a definition or consensus of the Magisterium; the concept is verified "quasi in fieri et via ad perfectam cognitionem" in the progress of an implicit truth in so far as the Magisterium intervenes, but not infallibly, in this progress (e.g. by approving a Mass or Office)—cf. art. cit., 'Tradizione divino-apostolica', p. 163; also art. cit., 'Tradition Divino-Apostolica', p. 472.

the Pope or to decrees of the General Councils. So much might be gathered from Franzelin and Billot, but only Deneffe is explicit enough to suggest these implications.

Together with this primary concept of Tradition, Deneffe claims to have found a secondary or derived concept which he describes as follows: 'Tradition' also describes the records of Church teaching that accumulate with the passage of time and from which the teaching of the Church of past ages can be known. This 'Tradition', this corpus of 'monumenta'— writings of Fathers and Theologians, inscriptions, the beliefs of the faithful etc.[126]—can be called a remote rule of faith in so far as it leads to a knowledge of Church teaching, the proximate rule of faith.[127]

In this double definition we have Deneffe's reformed teaching on the rule of faith, for he says that it was his idea of Tradition as a remote rule of faith which obscured his own understanding of the concept of Tradition before his controversy with Dieckmann and subsequent enlightenment.[128] His thought is slightly different from Billot's. He uses the term 'rule of faith'—or, rather, allows it to be used—for the records themselves rather than for the preaching of the Church to which they bear witness. This, however, involves him in a difficulty, noted by Zapelena.[129] Consider the written definitions of the Magisterium. Are they a proximate rule of faith considered as a form of actual teaching? Or are they documentary 'Tradition' and a remote rule of faith? The same difficulty does not arise for Billot because it was an element of pastness rather than the form, documentary or otherwise, that made a rule of faith remote to his way of thinking.

Yet again Deneffe makes his own explicit contribution. He makes it quite clear that there is nothing in the records of Tradition that is not formally and materially teaching of the Magisterium, irrespective of the agents who placed it in these records. He cannot at all conceive of objective Revelation other than as itself the object of official teaching.[130] If the

---

[126] Deneffe, op. cit., p. 113.
[128] Deneffe, op. cit., p. 1.
[130] op. cit., p. 111.

[129] art. cit., pp. 71, 72.
[127] op. cit., p. 2.

Magisterium is not itself responsible for the records of its preaching, then those who are responsible are so confined to simple transcription of what the Magisterium of their time teaches that the Magisterium of a later age, in drawing doctrine from the records they produce can be said ultimately to be drawing the doctrine from itself.[131] And at this stage the theory that would identify Tradition with magisterium, is fully consistent at least.

The logical conclusion to this series of thought was stated, however, by another theologian, the contemporary French writer, Journet. Two things, he writes, are required in order that a truth be believed on divine faith: it must be included in the deposit of Revelation and its inclusion there must be proclaimed.[132] And it is clear from that section where the proclamation is said to belong to a 'lieu déclarant'[133] right down to where this 'lieu déclarant' is declared to be the Magisterium[134] that, for Journet, in order that a truth be believed on divine faith it must be proclaimed by the Magisterium. As far as truths handed down in Tradition are concerned there is no believing on divine faith only. All truths which reach us through Tradition are believed on divine and catholic faith because the agent in Tradition is always the infallible Magisterium; and without its action at every stage no truth, whether explicit or implicit, reaches us. That is a statement of fact based on the identity of Tradition with the teaching of the Magisterium.

iii. Constitutive Tradition and Development of Doctrine

There is one other aspect of doctrine for which we may allow Journet to act as spokesman in the stream of thought we are now examining. It is the question of development of dogma in its relation to Tradition. It is obvious to every Catholic theologian that there is much more explicit in

---

[131] Deneffe, op. cit., pp. 163, 164.

[132] cf. C. Journet, *Esquisse du Developpement du Dogme Marial*, Paris, 1954, p. 15: "Deux éléments requis pour qu'une vérité puisse être crue de foi divine: l'un ontologique, ou inclusion dans le dépôt; l'autre gnoseologique, ou proclamation de cette inclusion."

[133] op. cit., p. 16.   [134] op. cit., p. 46.

Church teaching today than was explicit in the teaching of the first Christian centuries. The transmission of the revealed word, then, cannot have been a monotonous repetition of numbered formulae. There was obviously development. Emil Brunner will grant us that such development is inevitable (and justified) in the preaching of the faith: "it would be a very short-sighted and, even from the standpoint of the New Testament, an unjustifiable Biblicism which would disallow the notion of development out of the embryonic to the finally mature".[135] It is not possible here to examine the problem directly connected with development of doctrine, i.e. must the Dogma of Our Lady's Assumption, for instance, be a syllogistic conclusion from two revealed premises in order that we may know it to be revealed, or could it be connected with the deposit of revelation in some other way? This problem has produced a literature of its own.[136] But even if a treatise on Tradition cannot direct its attention to the more theoretical problem, it must take account of the factual and evident process of development in framing its description of Tradition.

According to Journet development of dogma belongs to the activity of Tradition itself. As he puts it: "The deposit of faith is not transmitted except through development." [137] And he deals with it accordingly in discussing Tradition as it was in apostolic times and as it is in the post-apostolic Church.

Deneffe, too, has distinguished apostolic Tradition which he terms 'constitutive Tradition' from Church or post-apostolic Tradition, which he refers to as 'continuative Tradition'.[138] But this merely indicates that the Apostles first handed over the deposit of Revelation in its entirety to the Church, in that

[135] Emil Brunner, *The Misunderstanding of the Church*, London, 1952, p. 39.
[136] For an introduction to this problem, cf. E. Dhanis, art., 'Revelation explicite et implicite', in *Greg.*, 34 (1953), pp. 187 ff.
[137] Journet, op. cit., p. 47.
[138] Deneffe, op. cit., p. 163. The terms 'apostolic Tradition' and 'Church Tradition' refer to the handing on of divine traditions by the Apostles and the post-apostolic Church respectively. These terms must be kept distinct from two others: 'apostolic traditions simpliciter' and 'ecclesiastical traditions' which refer to truths handed on that are other than revealed truths or divine traditions.

sense constituted a deposit, while the Magisterium of later ages passes this deposit on. Deneffe is concerned with the similarities of these two activities, apostolic and post-apostolic, especially with their similar authority, for he is anxious to prevent a restriction of the term 'Tradition' to the activity and doctrine of the apostolic age.[139] With Journet, on the other hand, it is the differences of apostolic and post-apostolic Tradition that are emphasised. He even distinguishes two principal theological senses of the word in order to clarify these differences. In the first sense Tradition refers to "the transmission of the totality of the revealed deposit, made by Christ and the Apostles to the primitive Church—and by extension to the whole of the revealed deposit thus transmitted".[140] Of this apostolic Tradition he writes as follows: the Apostles did not receive mere formulae to hand on, they had from Christ and the Holy Spirit a prophetic illumination which showed them the deepest meaning of the truths with which they were entrusted. This illumination was, in fact, a revelation.[141]

Of course, the term 'illumination' is a generic term. It can cover many kinds of influences on mind—some of them equivalent to revelation, some of them not. Suppose some words were spoken by Christ to the Apostles of which they retained the verbal memory, but the intelligible content of which quite escaped them (that the intelligible content of Christ's words was sometimes hidden from the Apostles is clear from the Scriptures, e.g. Luke xviii. 34). If the meaning of these words later came to them by 'illumination', in that case illumination would be equivalent to an infusion of knowledge, equivalent to revelation. Similarly if a new aspect or a new implication of a truth already understood were infused by illumination, then again it would be equivalent to revelation. But if illumination is simply taken to describe an activity other than the infusion of knowledge, if it refers to the

[139] op. cit., p. 12.
[140] C. Journet, *The Church of the Word Incarnate*, vol. 1, London, 1955, p. 523 footnote. This definition of Tradition is given in reference to his description of Tradition in his *Esquisse du Developpement du Dogme Marial*.   [141] op. cit., *Esquisse*, pp. 21, 22.

ordinary dispensation of graces and gifts of the Holy Spirit by which the mind itself is enabled to see deeper into the truth it already understood, then it is not equivalent to revelation at all. The illumination of which Journet writes is, as he says, equivalent to revelation. As a result of it the apostolic knowledge of the deposit of Revelation surpassed in depth any knowledge later achieved in the Church; the latter always tends towards the former as a polygon to the perfection of a circle.[142]

Yet it is not this appreciation of the truths that the Apostles handed on to the primitive Church, since that depended upon a light which was not transmissible. Rather they had to conceptualise and formulate their vision and so transmit it to the Church.[143] The immediate post-apostolic Church had to begin with the understanding it attained of these meaning-saturated sentences of the Apostles.[144] There was now no renewal or continuation of revelation and yet the task of the Magisterium would be to strive towards the perfection of the Apostles' understanding of the truth they spoke. In this continual effort at understanding and explanation the handing on of the truth is achieved.[145] We have now arrived at the other principal sense of the term Tradition where it means the "transmission from generation to generation, by divinely assisted Magisterium, of the whole of the primitive revealed deposit".[146] This activity preserves and explains the deposit of faith. As an explanatory activity he writes of it: "The passage from implicit to explicit is made with rigorous logic alright, but in the darkness of faith, and it is not possible without the (infallible[147]) help of the Holy Spirit." [148]

The development of dogma which had become a major theme for Catholic theology some time before the period presently under review, and the historical results of which came under heavy fire from the Modernists, was tackled by Catholic theologians in our period in two different ways. As

---

[142] op. cit., pp. 28, 29.   [143] op. cit., pp. 26, 27.
[144] op. cit., p. 29.   [145] op. cit., p. 47.
[146] op. cit., *The Church of the Word Incarnate*, p. 523 footnote.
[147] op. cit., *Esquisse*, p. 55.   [148] op. cit., p. 53.

Congar has pointed out the three great definitions of 1854, 1870 and 1950—which were themselves prime instances of development of dogma—were justified by their authors principally by an appeal to the faith of the Church, of pastors and of faithful.[149] So one tendency amongst theologians was to insist on the infallibility of the Pastors or bishops as a teaching body and on the infallibility of the Pope; to justify the development by showing the divine guarantees possessed by those who defined it. A second tendency was to describe the faith of the Church as a subjective and divine gift with its own powers of penetration and with an objective content; to justify development by describing it in this supernatural setting. The contemporary exponents of this second tendency are men like Dillenschneider, Koster and Bacht —we shall examine their contributions later—who are concerned particularly with mariological instances of development.

A theologian's approach to Tradition must be closely connected with whichever of those tendencies he follows, i.e. with his approach to the problem that development of dogma poses for one who holds that Revelation comes down to us unaltered.[150] Generally theologians of the second tendency since they appeal to the faith of the Church, the 'sensus fidei', do not restrict their definition of Tradition to magisterium. Hence it is curious to find Journet at once appealing to this "loving instinct of faith",[151] a factor in development and in Tradition, and yet defining Tradition as magisterium. On the other hand, theologians of the first tendency (Billot, for example) have very little to say about the actual process of development. They are mainly concerned with the infallible definition in which it results. Deneffe is content to point out that development is possible in the Christian dispensation and to give the simplest illustration of how it comes about. He writes: "In the teaching 'Mary is free from all sin', the

[149] Congar, op. cit., *La Tradition*, p. 255.
[150] It is significant that Hocedez treats of the theology of Tradition only in conjunction with his section on the development of dogma: E. Hocedez, *Histoire de la Theologie au XIXe Siecle*, vol. III, Paris, 1947, pp. 170 ff.   [151] op. cit., *Esquisse*, p. 55.

proposition 'Mary is preserved from original sin' is implicitly contained and handed on." [152]

Franzelin, like Journet, emphasises the necessary connection between active tradition and development of dogma. His thesis is that it is essential for Tradition to preserve the proper understanding of the doctrines of the faith: the doctrines of the faith are not so straightforward and simple as to preclude all controversy and misunderstanding. Hence it is impossible to preserve the deposit pure and integral over the ages "unless those who preserve the faith are also infallible teachers of its meaning".[153] It is obvious from this that active tradition and development of dogma are one and the same process. But Franzelin again does little more than indicate the possibility of development of dogma from the fact that there can be truths implicit in truths handed over by the Apostles and carried forward in Tradition, truths in Tradition may be obscure and controverted for a time, or a truth may be implied for years in a practice or custom in the church before it becomes the subject of specific preaching.[154] His only hint as to how he thinks the development comes about in fact—and it is consistent with his description of active tradition—is when he insists that it is the work of authentic doctors or members of the Magisterium.[155] He knows that other agents have their part in preparatory stages of development that precede formal definition but, just as these were allowed no part in active tradition, so they have no part in the activity properly called development of dogma. That must take place under the direct influence of the Holy Spirit and Franzelin does not regard the activity of these other agents in that way. So these other agents are merely instruments in the hands of the Magisterium.[156] Development of dogma, like Tradition, is the monopoly of the Magisterium. And Franzelin makes no attempt to describe in any detail the part he allows the general body of the faithful in the stages of doctrine preparatory to definition.

It is a sign of the relevance of discussing a theologian's

[152] Deneffe, op. cit., p. 136.   [153] Franzelin, op. cit., pp. 272, 273.
[154] op. cit., p. 260; op. cit., p. 262.
[155] op. cit., p. 273.   [156] op. cit., pp. 277, 278.

attitude to development of dogma to any discussion of his notion of Tradition that here, too, Franzelin's reason for confining active tradition to the Magisterium is revealed: he sees active tradition as he sees development of dogma only where he can also point to a charism of infallibility. The charism of infallibility itself comes in contact with agents other than the Magisterium only indirectly. It is obviously this charism, then, that Franzelin has in mind when he writes that other bodies prepare only indirectly for the development or definition[157] and equivalently rules them out of development and active tradition on that account.

With these additions from the theology of Journet, the essential contribution of this stream of thought to the theology of Tradition is complete. It only remains to examine what must honestly be described as a freak description of Tradition by some theologians of this same tendency—the tendency to define Tradition in terms of magisterium—and to comment on a term which, like 'the rule of faith' is also used to describe Tradition, i.e. 'a source of Revelation'.

iv. The Extreme: Tradition identified with the Magisterium

The type of description of the Catholic concept of Tradition with which we are now dealing is exemplified first by Pesch: "we understand by Tradition that organ by which revealed truths are handed on, and the organ in question is the Church Magisterium".[158] That description is slipped into a footnote and is completely outside the sequence of thought in the section in which it occurs. It could be dismissed as accidental were it not for the fact that it reappears later in the period in a more deliberate way. Dieckmann, who helped Deneffe change his views on Tradition, has it too. He is so absolutely logical about his identification of Tradition with magisterium—with the Magisterium, rather—that his little tract on Tradition appears as a scholion to "De existentia magisterii Ecclesiae".[159]

---

[157] op. cit., p. 278.

[158] C. Pesch, *Praelectiones Dogmaticae,* I, ed. 4, Freiburg i. Br., 1909, p. 382, note 564.

[159] H. Dieckmann, *De Ecclesia,* II, Freiburg i. Br., 1927, p. 27.

And he describes Tradition as follows: "Church Tradition is
. . . that physical or moral person, in so far as he preaches
with the authority of Christ, on whom Christ has conferred
the teaching office." [160]
It would be pleasant if he could be taken to mean no more
here than Franzelin meant when he declared that if he considers Tradition in the concrete he must consider the organ
which conserves and transmits;[161] if he only meant to indicate
the organ without including it in his strict definition: or if he
could be excused, as Deneffe excuses him, on the grounds of
metaphorical usage. Deneffe justifies such a metaphor since,
he says, the hierarchy is a vessel holding tradition and handing
it on—"so, pointing to a jug that holds wine, a man can say:
that is wine".[162] But it seems from its position in Dieckmann's
treatise—it comes immediately after he has laid down the
qualities which true, dogmatic Tradition must possess[163]—that
this is a strict definition of Tradition in which metaphorical
usages cannot be presupposed. Yet to define Tradition as the
Magisterium not only adds nothing to our knowledge over
and above what we have found already, it goes against every
normal and theological usage of the word otherwise known
to us.

Perhaps the best commentary on this new aspect of the
stream of thought now under review is the retreat from this
position by its most recent exponent. When Burghardt was
expounding his identification of Tradition with magisterium
he remarked, with an air of condonation: "in fact, Filograssi
has tried to show recently that the magisterium in its totality
is identical with tradition in its totality",[164] and he refers to
an article written by Filograssi in 1949. There is nothing
unusual about Filograssi's definition of Tradition in this
article,[165] but when he discusses the relation of Tradition to
the Magisterium, he claims that, provided 'Magisterium' is
taken to cover the organ or body of teachers, the teaching

---

[160] op. cit., p. 29.   [161] Franzelin, op. cit., p. 9.
[162] Deneffe, op. cit., p. 103. Cf. Dorsch, op. cit., p. 680.
[163] Dieckmann, op. cit., p. 29.
[164] Burghardt, op. cit., p. 25.
[165] Filograssi, art. cit. 'Traditio Divino-Apostolica', p. 445.

activity and its object, it is equivalent to Tradition; for the concept of Tradition also has these three elements.[166] He clearly means that Tradition involves all three elements, that the Magisterium itself is part of the concept of Tradition together with its teaching activity and object.

But a year after Burghardt had quoted him Filograssi retreated substantially from this position[167] when he opened a section on relations of Tradition to the Magisterium—a section corresponding very closely to the one just quoted—with the words: "However close is the relationship between the Magisterium and Tradition, strictly speaking, as Church documents hint, the one is distinct from the other and they are not identified."[168] It is not a complete retreat, however. It is only a retreat behind Dieckmann. For, having described the Magisterium as living and traditional and having enumerated its functions, he points out that there are theologians who do not hesitate to identify it with Tradition.[169] He then proceeds to outline the exact position he held in 1949 and to quote Dieckmann (in a footnote).[170] He claims that this same position, but now under different patronage, is perfectly orthodox and has the advantage of fully portraying the role of the Church Magisterium in Tradition.[171]

By 1957, with the publication of Filograssi's sixth edition of De Eucharistia, the retreat is complete. Now the identification of Tradition with the Magisterium is mentioned with detachment. Dieckmann's definition is no longer paraphrased in Filograssi's own words. It is in the body of the text; Dieckmann is to speak for himself. And the view is no longer declared: "absolutely orthodox, held by most reliable theologians".[172] The retreat deserves praise, not only because of the

---

[166] art. cit., pp. 450, 451. If, however, Magisterium is taken 'distributive' to indicate one or other of the elements enumerated above without extending to all three, it is no longer identical with Tradition (pp. 452, 453). This shows that Tradition for Filograssi involves all three elements in its definition.

[167] art. cit. 'Tradizione divino-apostolica', 1952.

[168] art. cit., p. 144.   [169] art. cit., p. 145.

[170] art. cit., pp. 145 ff.   [171] art. cit., p. 147.

[172] I. Filograssi, De Sanctissima Eucharistia, ed. 6, Rome, 1957, pp. 18 ff.

neatness of its execution but because the position retreated
from was so untenable. It is one thing to say that the activity
which is active tradition cannot be discussed without reference
to its organ or principle; it is something completely different
to say that Tradition is identical with this organ or—with
organ, acts and object—to say that the organ is part of the
strict concept of Tradition. No reason can be given for such
complete identity. No reason is given. It can only lead to
confusion.

4. DECLINE OF THE DEFINITION: THE SOURCE
OF REVELATION

Already before any of the texts quoted above in favour of
the identity of Tradition with the Magisterium had been
published, Pohle had criticised just such an identification and
for an interesting reason. It is such a definition of Tradition,
he claims, that Protestants attribute to us in the course of
anti-Catholic polemics. And on the basis of it they accuse the
Catholic Magisterium, and specifically the Pope, of arbitrary
caprice in dealing with the Word of God. To them Tradition
in the Catholic sense is the arbitrary imposition of doctrine
which follows upon the Pope looking into his own heart,
'scrinium cordis pontificii'.[173]
Essentially the same objection is still repeated today.
According to Dejaifve, modern Protestants like Ebeling and
Schweitzer contend that Catholic theology has placed the
Magisterium in such a supreme position that its power over
the Word of God is completely arbitrary. There is not any
point in saying that the Magisterium defines only what is in
Tradition if in the same breath a Catholic theologian will
say: and Tradition is what the Magisterium teaches. That,
they object, is a mere quibble.[174] The answer to this objection
which Pohle and Dejaifve both think at once most effective
and truest to the proper concept of Tradition is the denial

---

[173] J. Pohle, art. 'Tradition', in *Kl.*, Freiburg, 1899, vol. II, col. 1939.
[174] G. Dejaifve, art. 'Bible, Tradition, Magistère dans la Theologie
Catholique', in *N.R.T.*, 78 (1956), cf. esp. p. 138.

of that statement 'and Tradition is what the Magisterium teaches', i.e. a rejection of the Tradition-magisterium concept in all its forms. It is curious to see the very Tradition-magisterium concept which men like Franzelin and Dorsch built secure against the Protestants so turned against them.

Of course, strictly speaking, the Tradition-magisterium concept need not be rejected in order to answer the objection. Even if Tradition be identical with authoritative teaching of the Magisterium that still does not mean that the Pope defines what he likes, that the Magisterium teaches anything other than what was originally revealed. Indeed if the Magisterium is infallible it cannot teach anything other than what was originally revealed. But Pohle thinks a more realistic notion of Tradition would meet the objection more effectively. There are many aspects of this more realistic notion of Tradition, of this more effective reply. Here we must concentrate on one of them. Tradition is regarded as a source of doctrine to which the Magisterium is bound. The same point is sometimes made when theologians write of the authority of apostolic teaching which constituted this source and to which all subsequent teaching is subject. But we shall leave that aspect to a fuller discussion of apostolic Tradition. Here we watch Pohle and Baumgartner establish that the Pope does not look into his own heart; he looks into a source of revelation, which is quite distinct from his heart.

To answer the charge, Pohle feels that he must regard Tradition as somehow distinct from the Magisterium and its teaching. Mostly he is insisting that Tradition is a treasury, 'Traditionsschatz', to the contents of which the Magisterium in its teaching activity is absolutely bound.[175]

Here two ideas are involved. One, the idea of an objective body of truth with its own authority, even over the Magisterium, reminds us of a term already discussed, the term 'rule of faith'. The other idea concerns the same objective body of truth but now regarded as a treasury, a source from which the Magisterium draws the truths which it teaches with its own infallible authority. 'Traditionsschatz' is Pohle's word for

[175] J. Pohle, art. 'Tradition', in *K.l.*, Freiburg, 1899, vol. II, col. 1939.

it. The English equivalent is obviously that 'source of revelation' which theologians do call Tradition. Now we must ask
if the theologians who identify Tradition with magisterium
speak of Tradition as a 'fons revelationis', a source of revelation from which the Magisterium draws its doctrine. We find
a certain difference of opinion.

The tract in which Tradition is discussed in the manuals
of theology is normally entitled 'De Fontibus Revelationis'.
And in many of those who identify active tradition with the
teaching activity of the Magisterium we find the following
statement or its equivalent: "The Church does not receive
doctrine in new revelations, but, by the help of the Holy
Spirit, she draws it from the different sources of revelation.
. . . We deal with both of these sources, beginning with
Tradition." [176] A similar introduction to the tract can be
found in Hervé's work, for example.[177]

Dorsch, on the contrary, entitled his treatise on Tradition:
'De ecclesia fonte revelationis sive de traditione', and adds
below this "it is obvious that the teaching Church, i.e. the
authentic Magisterium, fulfills the definition of a source of
revelation".[178] From that it is clear that Dorsch does not think
Tradition to be a source of revelation from which the Magisterium draws the doctrine it teaches. Rather the Magisterium
is a source of revelation by reason of its own teaching. A
somewhat similar understanding of the term is found in the
thought of Burghardt. Tradition may be called a source of
revelation or source of the faith to his mind simply because
magisterium, with which it is identified, may. He does say
that Revelation is—or was, rather—a source of faith in the
primary sense: "Properly speaking, as Michel has pointed out,
there is only one source of faith, and that is revelation. But
revelation has been transmitted to men in two ways: by inspired writings and by the living preaching of the Church,

[176] A. Tanquerey, *Synopsis Theologiae Dogmaticae*, I, ed. 16, Paris,
1919, p. 617. He describes active tradition as the teaching of the Magisterium—p. 619.
[177] J. M. Hervé, *Manuale Theologiae Dogmaticae*, I, Paris, 1952, p. 536.
He describes active tradition as the teaching of the Magisterium—
p. 546.
[178] Dorsch, op. cit., p. 679.

i.e. by Scripture and tradition. Under this aspect of the mode of transmission, we may speak less properly of two sources of faith."[179] Again there is no question of Tradition being called a source of faith for the Magisterium.

There is an inconsistency in the position adopted by Hervé. To regard Tradition as a source of doctrine for the Magisterium seems incompatible with the Tradition-magisterium concept. For the writers referred to seem to envisage Tradition as a source of doctrine existing contemporaneously with the Magisterium and, since the Magisterium draws its doctrine from it, at least not identical with the teaching of the Magisterium, therefore somehow distinct. Then is it not illogical to regard Tradition as at once a source for the teaching of the Magisterium while yet identified with the teaching of the Magisterium itself? Dorsch and Burghardt are, therefore, more logical when they no longer regard Tradition as a source for the teaching of the Magisterium, contemporary with the Magisterium, but as a source of revelation precisely in its identity with magisterium.

Unfortunately for those who believe Tradition to be identical with the infallible teaching of the Magisterium, however, the notion of the 'fons revelationis' which is Tradition and which is spoken of in a manner that would suggest that Tradition is something not identical with the infallible teaching of the Magisterium, is not so easily dismissed. For the whole matter will be raised again by Baumgartner when he maintains that the official documents of the Church have consistently used the word 'Tradition' to refer to a source of the faith from which the Magisterium must draw its doctrine and have consequently suggested, to him at least, that Tradition is not identical with the infallible teaching of the Magisterium.[180] When the encyclical 'Humani Generis', for instance, speaks as follows about Tradition, the source of revelation: "theologians must always return to the sources of divine revelation: it is their task to point out exactly how the truths taught by the Magisterium are 'contained either

---

[179] Burghardt, op. cit., p. 25. Cf. also T. Simar, *Lehrbuch der Dogmatik*, I, Freiburg i. Br., 1879, p. 19.
[180] cf. Y. M-J. Congar, op. cit., *La Tradition*, pp. 257, 258.

implicitly or explicitly' in Sacred Scripture or in divine 'Tradition' ",[181] Baumgartner asks: "In what sense does this encyclical use the word 'Tradition'? And since it is one of theology's first laws to use a key-word like 'Tradition' with the meaning given it by the Magisterium, here is undoubtedly a guiding light for the theology of Tradition." [182] It was probably in view of the 'modus loquendi' of official Church documents—particularly 'Humani Generis'—that Filograssi retreated from his extreme Tradition-Magisterium position.[183] It is substantially the suggestion of Baumgartner that one should retreat from the Tradition-magisterium position altogether.

Before we examine Baumgartner's contribution let us consider the proposals of another theologian who studied the 'modus loquendi' of Church documents and defined Tradition as a source of faith for the Magisterium; the theologian in question is Proulx.[184] Proulx emphasises greatly the concept of Tradition as a source of faith distinct from the teaching of the Magisterium. He insists, in fact, that Tradition be defined as an objective deposit of truth, the verbal deposit handed over to the Church by the Apostles.[185] In other words Tradition could only have been a complex thing in apostolic times.[186] After that Tradition is defined as an objective body of truth.

Suppose for a moment that such a definition of Tradition were accepted as the full and proper definition.[187] Would it

[181] A.A.S., vol. 42 (1950), p. 568. The quotation marks within the quotation indicate that the phrases are taken from Pius IX, 'Inter Gravissimas'.

[182] Baumgartner, art. cit., p. 163.

[183] cf. Filograssi's references to these documents in art. cit. 'Tradizione divino-apostolica', p. 135 and in op. cit. De Eucharistia, 'prologue'.

[184] cf. Proulx, op. cit., pp. 97 ff. for his treatment of Church documents.

[185] op. cit., p. 154.   [186] op. cit., p. 188.

[187] Proulx claims the authority of Van Noort and De San for this definition of Tradition—op. cit., p. 89. But De San insists that active and objective are inseparable elements in the notion of Tradition—L. De San, De Divina Traditione et Scriptura, Bruges, 1903, p. 9. And Van Noort speaks of a complex concept even when he regards Tradition as a source of faith—G. Van Noort, De Fontibus Revelationis, Amsterdam,

be a source of revelation for the teaching of the Magisterium such as that is normally understood? It seems not. Because the source of revelation is normally understood as something existing contemporaneously with the Magisterium, not as something from which the first post-apostolic Magisterium drew its teaching and with which no subsequent Magisterium can be in direct contact. Van Noort supports this point with particular clarity. He asks where the present Magisterium gets the doctrine it teaches. He quotes the Vatican council to the effect that the Magisterium draws its doctrine from two sources: one is Tradition.[188] The point is implied clearly, too, in the quotation from 'Humani Generis' given above. The Encyclical does not ask theologians to compare present teaching with past teaching of the Magisterium in order to arrive at a judgement concerning consistency; it asks theologians to ascertain how the teaching of the Magisterium is contained in two sources of revelation and so obviously regards these sources, Scripture and Tradition, as at once equally contemporary with and yet not identical with the teaching of the Magisterium. Hence, Tradition even as a source must exist now. That means that traditions must now be borne along by somebody and that implies active tradition. Since the Tradition-source is not identical with the teaching of the Magisterium which is drawn from it, neither can this active tradition be identical with the teaching of the Magisterium.

Therefore neither the definition given by Proulx nor the Tradition-magisterium definition will satisfy the implications of referring to Tradition as a source of revelation for the Magisterium. For, as it has just now been proved, the Tradition-source is a complex thing (Van Noort is again explicit on the point)[189] and yet the activity involved in this complex

---

1954, p. 3. Proulx is better supported later on by D. Van den Eynde, art. 'Tradizione e Magistero', in *Problemi e Orientamenti di Teologia Dommatica*, Milan, 1957, p. 245.

[188] Van Noort, op. cit., pp. 1–3. Note, however, that Van Noort also describes active tradition simply as magisterium—p. 106.

[189] op. cit., p. 3.

thing cannot be identified with the teaching of the Magisterium.

Baumgartner concludes from his examination of Church documents that the word Tradition is used in them to convey primarily the objective element of Tradition, objective tradition, as a source of doctrine on the same plane as Scripture.[190] He thinks that over-emphasis on the active tradition exercised by the Magisterium—for all must admit that the Magisterium does exercise active tradition—has obscured the concept of Tradition as a source of revelation.[191] But he, too, is faced with the task of describing a complex concept, the active element of which is not identical with the teaching of the Magisterium although it does coincide with that teaching in part and in some respects. If Church documents understand Tradition primarily in its objective sense, even on their own 'modus loquendi' it cannot be left at that.

Baumgartner's explanation is as follows. In one section of his article[192] he maintains that the active tradition of the Magisterium is governed by the active tradition of the Apostles which it attains in 'the word written and handed on', the sources of the faith.[193] What does he mean by this? He lays great emphasis on that Tradition of the Apostles which was constitutive: it constituted the deposit of revelation a complete whole. This deposit is at once a norm for the preaching of the Church—another way of saying it is the rule of faith, having authority of God who revealed it—and, precisely as it is handed down, i.e. precisely as (Scripture or) Tradition, it is a source of faith. Now how does Baumgartner explain the fact that the oral deposit becomes a source of faith for all succeeding generations? In other words, how does he describe Tradition, the source of faith?

He writes that the faith of the Church was the result of apostolic preaching.[194] But this faith did not remain internal. It was expressed in many ways, developed and so handed on.[195] Ask now where is the source, the Tradition that provides for

[190] Baumgartner, art. cit., p. 170.
[191] art. cit., p. 163.
[192] art. cit., pp. 171–6.
[193] art. cit., esp. p. 174.
[194] art. cit., p. 173.
[195] ibid.

present preaching and the answer is: it is the deposit of revelation as it is held and carried forward by the universal Church,
"this deposit of faith is 'lived' and so transmitted in a certain
way by the entire Church".[196] Hence, Baumgartner's remark:
"However essential the active tradition of the Magisterium
in the full concept of 'Tradition', it should not be emphasised
to the point of minimising . . . the dignity and authority of
the source which is the norm for ecclesiastical preaching."[197]
The activity of the Magisterium is an active tradition, not
active tradition simply, not all of it. We have already noted
the possibility of distinguishing two aspects within the teaching of the Magisterium itself: one by which it is tradition (and
on a par with the tradition of other bodies in the Church—
if such is found to exist), the other by which it is formally
magisterium, authoritative and authenticating. If some such
distinction were made Tradition could perhaps be thought
sufficiently distinct from teaching of the Magisterium to be
regarded as a contemporary source for it.

Baumgartner's attempt to construct a theology of Tradition
is by no means detailed. His aim was mainly negative—to
show that the Tradition-magisterium school of thought does
not accord well with the usage of the word 'Tradition' in
official Church documents. It cannot completely dismiss the
Tradition-magisterium concept. The Church has not defined
Tradition and the exponents of the Tradition-magisterium
definition could perhaps—although with a certain amount of
strain—interpret official statements to suit their own mode of
thought. Then, much more detail would be demanded of
Baumgartner's account of Tradition before it could be considered as a serious rival. Still, there can be little doubt about
the fact that this Tradition-source idea belongs more logically
to another concept of Tradition than that adopted by the
line of theologians we have examined. To that extent it
suggests another approach. It prompts the mind to a wider
search.

[196] art. cit., p. 174.   [197] art. cit., p. 163.

5. SUMMARY

Early in this chapter we said that the Catholic concept of Tradition comes in answer to the questions: how does Revelation, which was completed at the death of the last Apostle, reach all generations and what guarantees us that it reaches all generations in its integrity? If an attempt were made to give a consistent answer to these questions in accordance with the theory of Tradition we have just been examining it would read something like this:

Christ sent his Apostles and their successors into the whole world to preach his Gospel with authority. He promised them his help and the charism of the Spirit so that their mission would not fail. The Apostles enjoyed a revelation from the Spirit, or at least an illumination equivalent to revelation by which they saw the truth unfold before them. Their successors were not so favoured, but their infallibility as a body is the same as that of the body of Apostles and that of their head is a personal infallibility similar to that which individual Apostles had. Their teaching has the same authority as that of the Apostles. Their activity, like the Apostles', is active tradition; the Revelation is objective tradition when it is 'in transit'. Tradition is the infallible preaching of the Church.

The activity of this hierarchical body which can be called tradition is not confined to speech. The Magisterium also promulgates Christ's doctrine in documents. And even in actions which have to do, for example, with conserving the structure of the Church or with dispensing the divine mysteries, in actions like these which the Magisterium performs or commands, there is truth involved. By what is done or commanded to be done men can sometimes see what Christ taught the Apostles. Active tradition involves all these things.

Active tradition is not merely conservative. It does not confine itself to keeping intact a group of formulae. If it did, the content could gradually seep out of them. Because it hands on truth, active tradition involves an effort at understanding. Because the truth contains divine mysteries this effort presages development. There is more implicit in the deposit of Revelation than was explicitly grasped by the Apostles who received it from Christ or than was grasped by their successors who received it from the Apostles. How this implicit is contained in the explicit, by what process it is brought out, are other questions. One thing is certain, the handing on of the deposit of Revelation involves development of dogma. This explanation or explication of doctrine is active tradition, the infallible work of the Magisterium.

The question may be asked: is Tradition a rule of faith? Provided one understands by rule of faith the authoritative proposition of truth to be believed, then Tradition is a rule of faith. If a distinction is to be made between remote and proximate rules of faith it can only be explained by calling the actual, present teaching of truth a proximate rule of faith and the teaching of the past remote. The latter is remote because it can only be reached by documentary evidence. It would give rise to confusion if one were to say that objective tradition is a remote rule of faith while the teaching by the Magisterium is a proximate rule of faith. In the monuments of Tradition one reaches the teaching of the Magisterium, formally as such.

Similarly, if there must be question of Tradition as a source of revelation, it can certainly be called that. The infallible teaching of the Magisterium is a source from which men of every age draw the divine truth.

Regarded in its most consistent form, that is how the Tradition-magisterium theory would read. We have seen exponents of it write about Tradition as a rule of faith or as a source of revelation in a way that does not logically belong to their theory of Tradition. We have noted a case where the infallible teaching of the Magisterium was 'ipsissima traditio' under one aspect—a case where a distinction was hinted that can be used by exponents of another view. But these 'lapses' were always rectified by more consistent exponents of the Tradition-magisterium theory. So much for synthesis.

It must be clear from the most general analysis of the stream of thought just reviewed that the leaders are Franzelin and Billot. Leaving Scheeben out of consideration, no other theory of Tradition in the period can appeal to theologians of such weight. Whatever impetus the Tradition-magisterium theory has in the period must be due largely to those two. One factor, however, cannot be left out of consideration. It is this: Billot wrote a controversial work, against Modernism or Evolutionism, and the exigencies of anti-Protestant polemics played a large part in Franzelin's approach. It is all too easy to say that it is in times of attack from heresy that Catholic doctrine is developed, and to forget that the heat of controversy seldom sees the full truth carefully and systematically exposed. It was of primary importance to Billot in showing the immutability of the Christian truth over the centuries to point to infallibility where it could most readily be found—in the teaching of men with a divine mission. And Franzelin, in his concern with anti-Protestant polemics, shows a characteristic that is evident in those same polemics down to our time. When the skirmishes over the 'traditiones mere orales' had gone on for some time after Trent, it was seen that the primary point to be established against the Protestants was the existence of a divinely commissioned body of teachers, since it was this body which they mainly accused of corrupting the Word of God. When Franzelin has established the existence, authority and infallibility of such a body and committed Tradition to its care, his case is complete. This exclusive preoccupation with the Magisterium is undoubtedly to be expected in those works which 'ex professo' deal, not with Tradition in general, but with refutation of a Protestant theme.[198] It seems that Franzelin's preoccupation is to be traced to a similar source.

Perhaps a mind less influenced by the demands of polemics or less influenced by Franzelin and Billot, would discover a fuller truth. We have seen hints of other notions of Tradition even in theologians who propose the identity of Tradition

---

[198] cf. G. Mitchell, art. 'Scripture and Tradition; a recent book', in *I.T.Q.*, 23 (1956): H. Bacht, art. 'Tradition und Sakrament', in *Schol.*, 30 (1955): H. Pinard de la Boullaye, art. 'L'Écriture est-elle La Règle Unique de la Foi?' in *N.R.T.*, 63 (1936). An exception to this preoccupation, although it is a polemical article, is H. Tavard's 'Scripture, Tradition and History', in *D.R.*, 72 (1954).

with magisterium. In so far as other notions differ from the Tradition-magisterium theory, they will differ in their views on active tradition. They will not identify active tradition with the authoritative teaching activity of the Magisterium. They will envisage other agents active in Tradition beside the members of the Magisterium. But they must safeguard the divine doctrine, too. It cannot be left to just anyone for preservation. The doctrine must always be guaranteed. Let us begin the wider search by examining the claims of the Fathers and Theologians of the Church. In our text-books the argument from Tradition is normally given as an argument from Fathers and Theologians—mainly from the former. If anyone has a claim to a part in active tradition, they have.

Chapter Two

FATHERS AND THEOLOGIANS

*"In the midst of the Church he taught and the
Lord filled him with the spirit of wisdom and
understanding."*

Introit. *Mass for Doctors*

It is just a little easier to decide the place of Fathers in
Tradition than to decide the place of theologians. So it is
better to begin with them. And only one aspect of their teaching concerns us, their teaching on matters of faith. There are
many practical questions touching Patrology that must be
passed over here. For instance, by what formulae, by what
'modus loquendi' do we know that a Father of the Church
is teaching something to be held on divine faith and not
merely offering a private opinion, a private interpretation of
the truth? Again, if Patristic teaching has full value only when
there is unanimity on a point of doctrine, and if moral
unanimity suffices, then when is moral unanimity attained?
These more practical questions are beyond our present scope
and it is the more theoretical question that interests us,
namely: when the Fathers do teach a truth to be of divine
faith, is this Patristic teaching Tradition in its own right or
not?

Whatever disagreement we may find concerning the role
of the Fathers vis-à-vis Tradition, there is general agreement
amongst theologians of our period concerning the 'notes' or
characteristics which gain for these men the title 'Father of
the Church'. These characteristics are enumerated as four.
The first is orthodoxy in significant doctrine. The second is
sanctity. Different theologians explain differently why this
must be a characteristic of Fathers of the Church according

to their conception of the role of Fathers in the Church and in Tradition. The third characteristic is official recognition or approbation by the Church. This recognition may be very specific and explicit in some cases but it suffices that it be implicit—tacit approval of the allocation of the title by theologians for example.

The fourth characteristic is given as 'antiquity': those who may be called Fathers of the Church must belong to the first centuries of the Church's history. From this characteristic a Patristic age is named which, although there is some variation, is normally taken to extend to the death of John Damascene (A.D. 754) in the Eastern Church and to the death of Isodore (A.D. 636) in the West. Normally the Fathers are discussed in a section entitled 'Monumenta Traditionis' or 'Criteria Traditionis' where writings are mainly in question: at times 'Writer' is added as a fifth note in describing them, as by Salaverri.[1] So that it is as writers that the Fathers are generally considered in connection with Tradition. It is mainly their writing activity that determines, therefore, whether—precisely as Fathers of the Church—they are agents in Tradition or not.

1. RECORDERS OF CHURCH TEACHING

It is of primary interest to ask how those who define Tradition as the infallible teaching of the Magisterium regard the activity of the Fathers of the Church. For them active tradition is the monopoly of the Magisterium. How is the activity of the Fathers explained?

For many of them the Fathers are recorders of the teaching of the Magisterium, witnesses in writing to what was once officially taught. So they appear to Deneffe, for instance. His main concern is to ascertain that the records that reach us from the past do in fact contain witness to Church teaching.[2]

[1] P. Nicolau and P. Salaverri, *Sacrae Theologiae Summa*, vol. 1, Madrid, p. 757. He extends the Patristic age in the West to Bede the Venerable and A.D. 753 while Franzelin extends it to St. Bernard and A.D. 1153. Cf. Franzelin, op. cit., p. 167.

[2] Deneffe, op. cit., p. 139.

Accordingly, the unanimity of the Fathers will be definitive proof that something was part of Church teaching.[3] He claims that the Magisterium itself so regards the teaching of the Fathers[4] and Michel will be found in almost verbal agreement with this position.[5] Burghardt, too, surveying the matter from the point of view of the 'Argument from Tradition' as that appears in Catholic text-books, writes:

> Partially at least for polemical purposes we have divided our theological 'proofs' into categories: magisterium, Scripture, Fathers, theologians . . . these are not adequately distinct categories. Actually, the sole legitimate theological method is the argument from tradition, from the preaching of the Church. The argument from the magisterium is an argument directly from the Church's preaching, directly therefore from tradition. The argument from the Fathers and theologians is the same argument, but indirectly, virtually. The Church does not derive her doctrine from the Fathers and theologians; the Fathers and theologians derive their doctrine from the preaching of the Church, from tradition.[6]

And again the role of the Fathers has been defined as that of recording the preaching of the Church, without any further complications. The uncomplicated nature of the Fathers' essential task is brought out especially by Ranft when he writes of their witnessing as an echo of contemporaneous Church teaching.[7] For this reason the writings of the Fathers are called "a Source of Tradition";[8] they contain the teaching of the Magisterium as such. It is interesting to notice that this view of the activity of the Fathers of the Church is not confined to theologians who identify Tradition with the teaching of the Magisterium. It will be found, for instance, in Liege,[9] who holds a wider notion of Tradition and whose view of the

[3] op. cit., p. 145.　　　　[4] ibid.
[5] art. cit., col. 1348. "L'autorité des Pères n'est qu'un argument pour trouver par dela l'enseignement patristique ou theologique, l'enseignement formel du magistère."　　　　[6] Deneffe, op. cit., p. 26.
[7] art. cit., col. 247.　　　　[8] art. cit., col. 246.
[9] A-M. Liege, art. 'Parole de Dieu et Tradition', in *Initiation Theologique*, vol. I, Paris, 1952, p. 34. Speaking of the ordinary and universal magisterium: "Les Pères de l'Église tiennent leur importance doctrinale de ce qu'ils en sont les temoins primitifs par écrit."

Fathers is borne out by his collaborator in the same volume who contributed the article on the Fathers of the Church.[10]

If this were the full contribution of the Fathers of the Church one would wonder why they were in fact so few and why they had to be so outstanding. They are considered solely as writers. They recorded what was in fact the teaching of the Magisterium of their time. It seems as if the task attributed to them is one that could have been performed by lesser men. They are reduced to the plane of historical witnesses. That is not to say that the argument from the Fathers, even on this view of them, is a purely historical argument rather than a theological argument. As Burghardt has been quoted to say above, the argument from the Fathers is indirectly an argument from Tradition and is therefore theological. But the task of the Fathers themselves is almost a mechanical one. What becomes then of the characteristics that are demanded before the title 'Father of the Church' is admitted to apply? What can the qualification named 'sanctity' supply to their work any more than the ordinary veracity and dedication required from every historical witness?[11] It might supply evidence of these qualities to a higher degree but that would still allow no essential difference between the Fathers and, say, a collector of conciliar texts like Denzinger. Orthodoxy could also be reduced to a test of veracity, and Church approbation to a confirmation of that veracity. So that this view of the Fathers' role is at once unsatisfactory in itself and perfectly consistent with the Tradition-magisterium theory. For we normally think of the Fathers as more than even outstanding recorders of infallibly preached truth: and yet, on the Tradition-magisterium theory, we can see that they have no part—especially as described here—in active tradition. Their characteristics are not considered to be sufficient qualification for such activity. The qualification needed for that is the

---

[10] Th. Chamelot, art. 'Les Pères et les Docteurs de l'Église', in *Iniation Theologique*, vol. I, p. 154.

[11] So Pohle includes sanctity amongst characteristics which "bieten schon ebenso viele natürliche Bürgschaften für die Reinheit der Lehre und die Glaubenswürdigkeit des Zeugnisses der Betreffenden"—art. cit., col. 1959.

charism of infallibility in the agents. The characteristics which the Fathers possessed only qualified them to record.

2. APPROVAL BY THE CHURCH

In Pohle's *Dogmatik* the account of the Fathers by a theologian who identifies Tradition with magisterium[12] is given a different twist. He writes that the teaching of the Fathers does bind us to believe, if only mediately.[13] Their teaching is dogmatic Tradition. But his explanation accompanying this claim shows him consistent with his notion of Tradition. With him all the emphasis is on one note—on the Church's approbation, mainly as it approves a Father's orthodoxy.[14] That approbation is at once the definitive qualification by which the Fathers are given the title and the element that allows the teaching of the Fathers to be called dogmatic Tradition. This Church approbation, he claims, so lends Church authority to the teachings of the Fathers that these teachings are thereby drawn under the influence of active tradition.[15] Hence if the teachings of the Fathers are to be mediately binding to faith we must first ascertain that their teaching has this (at least tacit) authorisation of the Church.[16] The teaching, precisely as affected by this act of approval, becomes Tradition.

From this it is clear how he thinks of the Fathers. They lived well, they wrote well and died. Afterwards the Church, by approving themselves, approved their teachings so that these became, by such approval, Tradition and binding on believers. Consistent again with a Tradition-magisterium theory but hardly realistic. The Church in rare cases has lent her authority to specific teachings of the Fathers—the case of Cyril's Anathemas is often mentioned—but in fact the Church normally lends her approval to the men themselves, to the

[12] J. Pohle and M. Gierens, *Lehrbuch der Dogmatik*, vol. I, ed. 9, Paderborn, 1936, p. 53.
[13] op. cit., p. 67. "Neben der unmittelbar verpflichtenden Lehre der Kirche gibt es eine mittelbar verpflichtende dogmatische Tradition. Sie ist enthalten in den Schriften der Väter."
[14] ibid.   [15] op. cit., p. 70.   [16] op. cit., p. 46.

conferring of the title 'Father of the Church' on certain men whom she thereby certifies to have the qualities demanded for such a title.[17] Her approval is thus lent indirectly to the teachings of the Fathers in general, but not so as to make their teachings authoritative in the same way as her own are.

Whereas the theologians quoted above will only allow for the Fathers recording what the Magisterium teaches, this textbook should be prepared to envisage them as thinkers in their own right. It certainly does not rule out such a possibility; but their work will have no value for faith or Tradition until it is later approved by the Church. And again it is hard to see any essential difference between Fathers and anyone else who happened to write down orthodox doctrine; it is hard to see why such outstanding qualities as we demand in Fathers of the Church are *necessary*—they are obviously useful—in these men and, particularly, how the demand for sanctity is sustained. The Church could approve the teaching of any conscientious writer who wrote orthodox doctrine. Yet we would not say that such approval would constitute him a Father of the Church.

3. MEMBERS OF THE MAGISTERIUM

So far we have seen theologians who identify Tradition with magisterium guard their consistency by not allowing the Fathers any activity which, as exercised by them, could be called tradition. Indeed, on their view, the Fathers in order to take an active part in Tradition would have to be infallible teachers. It is startling at first to find a theologian who identi-

---

[17] The Church does not decide irrespective of personal characteristics who are Fathers of the Church. She decides on the basis of three characteristics—orthodoxy, antiquity and sanctity. These three might be referred to as constitutive marks whereas the approbation of the Church is a declaratory mark. It is the business of the official guardians of revealed truth to say who are the men who have the qualifications that will recommend their work in connection with this truth. As Heinrich says of these three notes: "Die drei übrigen Requisite geben die Gründe an, aus welchen die Kirche den Vätern solche Anerkennung zu Theil werden lässt und solche Autorität beilegt." J. B. Heinrich, *Dogmatische Theologie*, vol. II, Mainz, 1873, p. 100.

fies Tradition with magisterium, regarding them in that precise way: as infallible teachers. But it is, after all, another way of being consistent. The theologian in question is Franzelin.

The Fathers of the Church were, for Franzelin too, men apart. They were distinguished by the four marks already enumerated.[18] It is on the basis of these marks, or rather on the basis of the personal qualifications which they indicate, that Franzelin measures the authority of a single Father or of a few Fathers who teach a doctrine without the unanimity of their fellows.[19] It is when he writes of the unanimous teaching of the Fathers that we see him write of them as he could only write—and does in fact write—of the infallible Church Magisterium. For now he points to a fault in a distinction which, he says, is sometimes made between Fathers as 'witnesses of Tradition' and Fathers as 'teachers': where in their former capacity their testimony is definitive but in the latter it may at times be rejected.[20] His objection is that the Fathers can act as 'authentic teachers' or as 'private teachers'.[21] It is the function of a teacher or 'doctor' to explain the meaning of an obscure doctrine, to make explicit what remains implicit, to define strictly what is still ambiguous.[22] Then, still speaking of the Fathers: "These same men who are guardians of the deposit, are also divinely appointed teachers and although the two aspects of their task admit of distinction they do not admit of any separation, as we prove elsewhere." [23]

It can only be because he is writing of the Fathers of the Church as the divinely instituted guardians of the deposit, as the Magisterium, that he can now add: "Under one and the same condition the Fathers infallibly guard the tradition and explain with the assistance of the Holy Spirit, the revealed truth, declaring its authentic meaning; this condition we have often stated to be unanimity amongst themselves and with the centre of unity." [24] Again writing about the Fathers as 'authentic teachers' he writes of their unanimity as the 'catholic understanding' formed under the infallible assistance and

[18] Franzelin, op. cit., pp. 165, 166.   [19] op. cit., pp. 165 ff.
[20] op. cit., p. 162.   [21] op. cit., p. 162.
[22] op. cit., pp. 162, 163.   [23] op. cit., p. 162.   [24] ibid.

direction of the Holy Spirit, with a clear reference to thesis XI, n. II, where such a term was used for Tradition, there the monopoly of the Magisterium.[25] Lastly, if the unanimous teaching of one age cannot be found to be at variance with the unanimous teaching of the Fathers of any other age, this is precisely because "the charism of truth which was promised by Christ is always joined to (their) firm agreement in the profession and further explanation of the truths of faith".[26]

Consequently, instead of distinguishing two tasks of the Fathers, the one in which they are really witnesses of Tradition, the other in which they are teachers who offer an explanation, Franzelin distinguished two cases of Patristic teaching: in the first they teach unanimously, in the second they do not.[27] If the term 'private doctors' is to be used it must refer to the Fathers taken individually and outside unanimity, for outside unanimity they have not got the charism of infallibility attributed to them in the last quotation above. Taken individually, 'singillatim spectati', the value of the Fathers' doctrine depends upon the personal qualifications which their characteristics indicate;[28] in unanimity, their teaching enjoys infallibility—a charismatic, not a derived infallibility.

There can be no doubt both from the distinctions drawn and from the derivation of their authority that Franzelin writes of the Fathers as of the Magisterium. Nobody will deny that a writer may quite legitimately use the term 'Father' in this sense. It was so used in the earlier centuries of the Church[29] and we still speak of the Fathers of the Council of Trent, for instance. But in this context Franzelin describes exactly what he means by the title and to whom it applies. His description is in accordance with theological usage in modern times. He further makes a distinction between Fathers 'in unanimous agreement' and Fathers 'taken individually', and since what he says about them taken individually is quite in keeping with his description of them and indeed derives from

---

[25] op. cit., p. 163.   [26] op. cit., p. 167.
[27] op. cit., p. 163.   [28] op. cit., pp. 165 ff.
[29] cf. H. Perennes, art. 'Tradition et Magistère, in *D.A.F.C.*, tome 4, Paris, 1928, col. 1792.

that description, we are entitled to expect in the interests of consistency that what he says of the Fathers in unanimous consent should also be in keeping with that same description. Quite clearly it is not. In effect another factor is added to the description of Fathers—a charism of infallibility.

In order to defend what Franzelin has written about the Fathers 'in consensu' it would be necessary not only that all the Fathers have been bishops but that all the bishops during the Patristic age should have been Fathers of the Church as Fathers are generally described. Only then would that body of men known as the Fathers of the Church be equivalent to that perennial moral body known as the Church Magisterium. But Franzelin himself recognises that not all the Fathers of the Church were bishops.[30] He does not demand membership of the episcopacy as one of the marks that constitute a Father. And it is quite clear that not all the bishops who were contemporaries, i.e. who formed the Magisterium even at any one time during the Patristic age, were Fathers of the Church, possessing the four characteristics. On these grounds, too, De San refuses the Fathers 'in consensu' just that type of infallibility that Franzelin grants them.[31]

Franzelin is not just saying that the teaching of the Fathers is infallible because it coincides with the teaching of the Magisterium. He is saying that the Fathers themselves are infallible, when they preserve and explain the faith unanimously; precisely because they have the charism of infallibility from the Holy Spirit and the help promised by Christ. The Fathers of the Church are, therefore, active in Tradition because in Franzelin's writing they are the Magisterium. There is no other satisfactory explanation for the things he has written about them.

As far as the general theory of Tradition is concerned, there is nothing that smacks of arbitrary exclusion here; any more than there is, if their own account of the Fathers is accepted, with those other exponents of the Tradition-magisterium theory who regard the Fathers as recorders of Church teaching or who allow their teaching into the stream of Tradition only after the Church has somehow taken official responsibility for

[30] op. cit., pp. 166, 167.   [31] De San, op. cit., p. 153.

it. But there is as little realism. In all cases the Tradition-magisterium theory remains credible and the Fathers of the Church remain as inexplicable as before. There is undoubtedly an element of truth in all the above explanations of the Fathers of the Church and the role they have to play, but it is only appreciable when the full truth is known. And it seems as if the price of realism in dealing with the Fathers must be an arbitrary exclusion by those who insist on identifying Tradition with the teaching of the infallible Magisterium and rejection of that identification by all others. In other words, it does seem even at this stage that if one wishes to make active tradition the monopoly of the Church hierarchy one cannot provide a realistic account of the activity that distinguished the Fathers of the Church. If the Fathers are described realistically and are yet excluded from active tradition because this is thought to be the monopoly of the Magisterium, that exclusion must seem arbitrary. It must be based on some predisposition—perhaps a predisposition to seek Tradition only where charismatic infallibility can be found? It does seem even now that realism in discussing the Fathers could involve a broader concept of Tradition.

Perennes seems hesitant to exclude the Fathers from a part in active tradition, although he undoubtedly favours the Tradition-magisterium theory. But he does not describe in any detail what this active role is or explain how it is a part of active tradition. Active tradition or 'traditions' are the different ways or organs or acts by which transmission of truth is effected.[32] Amongst those he lists: magisterium, liturgies, the writings of the Fathers, inscriptions etc. Magisterium is the principal mode of transmission and the others are subordinate to it.[33] But from this on he is concerned only with magisterium, until he finally defines active tradition in terms of magisterium only[34] and we gain no more information about the other ways or acts of transmission mentioned earlier. Of the Fathers we are simply told later that they are authentic witnesses of divine Tradition when they are morally unanimous in teaching.[35] Even from what we have already seen,

[32] Perennes, art. cit., col. 1785.   [33] ibid.
[34] art. cit., col. 1790.   [35] art. cit., col. 1792.

that could mean a number of things. The question remains: are the Fathers as such active in Tradition and if so on what understanding of the nature and qualifications of their activity?

4. INSTRUMENTS OF THE TEACHING CHURCH

Dieckmann has appeared above as one of those who identified Tradition with the Magisterium itself, the teaching body. When he comes to write of the Fathers, he describes them according to the usual four characteristics.[36] But he says that they teach in the Church: "qui in consensu Ecclesiae docuerunt".[37] The note of orthodoxy is demanded precisely because of this magisterial function of theirs.[38] This orthodoxy, of course, cannot be ascertained fully ('constare') apart from the testimony of the Magisterium, whether explicit or implicit. The Church itself recognises the Fathers as teachers "in consensu Ecclesiae".[39] Does this mean that there was in the Church a group of teachers not altogether coinciding with the Church Magisterium and that not merely because some of its members were not members of the Magisterium but because all its members, precisely as Fathers of the Church, had a teaching function to perform which was distinct from, though subordinate to, the teaching authority of the Magisterium? According to Dieckmann, the authority of the Fathers depends upon their connection with the Magisterium. A single Father may, in exceptional circumstances, be the organ through which the Magisterium speaks.[40] The Fathers in unanimous consent are, 'a fortiori', the 'voice of the Magisterium'[41] and consequently their doctrine, which is in fact that of the Magisterium, possesses the same infallibility as Church magisterium.[42] Now that still does not explain

---

[36] op. cit., p. 183.   [37] op. cit., p. 32.
[38] op. cit., p. 183. "Doctrina orthodoxa est praerequisita; nam ob ipsam solam potest quis in Ecclesia auctoritate magisteriali guadere, tale, qualem attribuimus Patribus Ecclesiae."
[39] ibid.   [40] Dieckmann, op. cit., p. 32.
[41] op. cit., p. 187.   [42] ibid.

whether the Fathers were mere lifeless instruments of the Magisterium, repeating what the Magisterium taught so that their doctrine was simply that of the Magisterium and was *therefore* infallible, or whether the Fathers, while instruments of the Magisterium in a sense, had their own contribution to make and an infallibility in their teaching which could not then be altogether explained simply by the exact coincidence of their teaching with that of the Magisterium. Unless Dieckmann wished to seem arbitrary in confining Tradition to the activity of the Magisterium, he would have to choose the first explanation. There is an indication that he would in fact choose it because when he writes of the documents of antiquity —including the writings of the Fathers—he considers that they simply testify to the teaching of the Magisterium itself.[43] And yet, when he explains why such holiness of life is demanded of the Fathers, part of his explanation suggests that such sanctity brings with it a profundity in appreciation of sacred doctrine ultimately attributed to the work of the Holy Ghost in them.[44] And that in turn suggests that the Fathers are more than instruments simply to repeat what the Magisterium has to say; that, consequently, if their teaching is infallible, the fact is not fully explained by saying it is but a repetition of the teaching of the hierarchy; that, ultimately, they have qualifications proper to them that might give them an active part in Tradition.

Clearly, with Dieckmann we have been introduced to yet another way of conceiving the role of the Fathers in the fate of Christian doctrine. The Fathers are no longer just reliable recorders of Magisterium teaching, nor writers of orthodox doctrine who happen to have been favoured by subsequent Magisterium approval. They now possess some active association with the contemporaneous hierarchy. They constitute an active organ or instrument in the possession of the Magisterium. This particular outlook on the Fathers of the Church has found acceptance with others also. It never goes as far as Franzelin does when he wrote of the Fathers as the Magisterium, nor as far as Parente when he inexplicably subsumes "the teaching of Fathers and Theologians" under the general

[43] op. cit., p. 33.   [44] op. cit., p. 184.

title "Magisterium ordinarium complectitur".[45] And, as with
Dieckmann, it is seldom fully clear what is meant.

According to Lercher active tradition must not be confined
to authoritative teaching such as the Magisterium provides.[46]
He thinks that wherever the direct action of the Holy Spirit
is found there also will be active tradition. Hence the whole
Church is involved in active tradition, although the Magisterium undoubtedly is the principal organ of it.[47] Since he
is prepared to consider direct influence of the Holy Spirit on
the ordinary faithful, we might expect that he would envisage
it 'a fortiori' in the case of the Fathers and discuss their part
in active tradition. Instead, we find them relegated to a section
where the question to be answered is "How do we know what
was taught and believed in past centuries?"[48] They are again
witnesses to a preaching of the Magisterium and a belief of
the whole Church, both of which, but not the Fathers' witnessing of them, are Tradition.

Again the clarity of the pattern does not survive a more
detailed discussion of the Fathers' activity. They act as 'witnesses of the Catholic faith', when they relay doctrine which
was publicly professed in the Church at the time. They act
as 'authentic teachers' when they explain or develop the sense
of dogma.[49] Just as in the case of those Fathers who were
bishops the function of preserving and that of explaining
doctrine could not be separated, so too with all the Fathers
recording and development went hand in hand.[50] When it
comes to showing that the Fathers provided a certain criterion
of divine Tradition,[51] he has no trouble in showing that their
activity, precisely as witnesses of the Catholic faith, provided
a reliable evidence of doctrine once professed. But what of

[45] P. Parente, *Theologia Fundamentalis*, ed. 3, Marietti, 1950, p. 227.
S. Bullough has a similar description of 'magisterium ordinarium' in his
art. 'Scripture and Tradition', in *E.C.Q.*, 7 (1947), pp. 32, 33.
[46] L. Lercher, *Institutiones Theologiae Dogmaticae*, ed. 4 (Schlagenhaufen), Barcelona, 1945, p. 311.
[47] op. cit., p. 309.   [48] op. cit., p. 319.   [49] op. cit., p. 322.
[50] ibid. Although there is a reference to Franzelin (op. cit., pp. 162,
163) in this context and an echo of his treatment of the Fathers, Lercher
never writes of the Fathers as of the infallible Magisterium.
[51] op. cit., p. 321.

their activity as authentic teachers? In order to explain why the unanimous teaching of the Fathers in their exercise of this function is beyond doubt a criterion of Tradition, he is forced to say that they participate in the infallibility of the Magisterium; they are somehow—"quodammodo"—an intermediary organ between the Pope and the other bishops and faithful.[52]

If he means that the Fathers are instruments of the Papacy in teaching the rest of the episcopate and of the Church, that they repeat the Pope's doctrinal developments, that they participate in his infallibility in this way, then his position is historically unrealistic and he no longer has much reason for calling the Fathers 'doctores': he *has* reason for not allowing them an active part in Tradition. Yet again, as with Dieckmann, we find a passage in which Lercher suggests that the Fathers do not simply repeat Church teaching, that their activity is not to be explained and evaluated solely in terms of their relationship with the Magisterium, that they may yet have a claim to a part in active tradition—although they are not allowed it here. He writes that the Fathers enjoyed a special aid of divine Providence in conserving and explaining divine tradition and he quotes Leontius to say that God placed doctors in the Church according to the providence of the Holy Spirit "in opus ministerii ad aedificationem corporis Christi",[53] to function in the ministry towards the building up of the Body of Christ.

With Zapelena we meet a theologian who uses this same idea of an instrument of the Magisterium, to explain now how the Fathers—especially as doctors—do have an active part in Tradition. His concept of Tradition is wider than the Tradition-magisterium concept and the activity of the Fathers has part in it. But if we now meet a wider concept of Tradition, it is because Zapelena's ideas have changed. In 1944 Zapelena was quite content with Deneffe's definition of Tradition; none of the criticisms he made then of Deneffe's work really affected the essential concept of Tradition found in it.[54] He even proved it then to be a 'traditional' concept by quoting

[52] Lercher, op. cit., p. 323.   [53] op. cit., p. 326.   [54] art. cit., p. 71.

Franzelin, Dieckmann and others in favour of it.[55] Ten years later when he begins to discuss Tradition it seems at first that he has not changed his position: for he says that he has already dealt with 'subjective tradition' when he proved the existence of the Magisterium.[56] Later on in the work, however, he adds to his former criticisms of Deneffe and the change of ideas is apparent. He writes that the complete identity of Tradition with magisterium cannot be admitted, and one of the reasons for this is: "because persons who take part in active tradition can be found outside the hierarchy: think of Jerome, Damascene, Justin . . . who handed down so much and so well and yet were not amongst those endowed with the office of authentic and infallible teaching".[57] Once such agents and such activity are admitted to be 'extra magisterium' and yet to have part in Tradition the question of their qualifications will come up. How does Zapelena answer it?

The extra-hierarchical agents mentioned above are Fathers. We might add that all Fathers, when they act precisely as such, act in an extra-hierarchical capacity; their activity is no longer part of infallible magisterium because precisely as the work of a Father of the Church it is part of a different unanimity than that of the apostolic succession.

Zapelena describes the Fathers of the Church in the normal fashion[58] and agrees that they are not the subject of charismatic or active infallibility.[59] Their doctrinal activity is twofold: they are witnesses to the belief of the Church of their time but they are doctors too who develop doctrine.[60] What guaranteed their activity against error and corruption? What qualifications had the Fathers for their task in Tradition? It is not enough to say, as Zapelena does, that the Fathers could not err because their unanimous teaching—whether as witnesses or as doctors—reaches the believing Church and it could not be led into error; the teaching Church professes to follow their doctrine and it could not err.[61] These considerations explain very clearly why the unanimous teaching

[55] art. cit., pp. 67, 68.
[56] T. Zapelena, *De Ecclesia Christi,* vol. II. Rome, 1954, p. 267.
[57] op. cit., p. 279.   [58] op. cit., pp. 285–8.   [59] op. cit., p. 289.
[60] op. cit., pp. 288, 289.   [61] op. cit., p. 291.

of the Fathers must have been correct. They do not at all explain *how* it could not have been incorrect. So again the connection of the Fathers with the Magisterium is brought forward and therein lies the only attempt to solve our problem. The value of the Fathers' teaching, Zapelena writes, is found in their connection with the Magisterium.[62] What is this connection? "Patristic teaching is simply one particular way ('modum quondam particularem') in which the authority of the authentic and infallible teaching of the Church reaches us." [63] Here again is the idea of instrumentality but there is no more attempt to explain the 'modum quandam particularem' here than there was to explain the 'quodammodo' above. The question is simply left at that.

De San does make an attempt to say what is meant by referring to the Fathers as an organ of the Magisterium in teaching. He, too, is inclined to favour a wider concept of Tradition that would include the doctrinal activity of the Fathers.[64] The primary agent in Tradition is still the Magisterium and Tradition is still defined primarily in reference to its teaching.[65] The other agencies serve the Magisterium in its task.[66]

The Fathers, according to De San, too, have a twofold function: they are "witnesses of the Church's faith for their age" and they act also as "public and catholic teachers of the Church".[67] The latter function has to do with development of doctrine.[68] Again the trouble crops up when an explanation must be given for the claim that the Fathers in so far as they exercise this latter function are irrefutable. For, in reference to this same developing activity, De San goes so far as to claim that Councils of the Church appealed to the Fathers not only as witnesses but "even as masters and judges".[69]

The explanation takes the form with which we have become familiar: the Fathers were in some way "instruments of the teaching Church".[70] De San does not mean that they were only organs of the Magisterium in their developing function but it is mainly in connection with that function that he urges

[62] op. cit., p. 279.   [63] op. cit., p. 290.   [64] De San, op. cit., p. 8.
[65] op. cit., p. 168.   [66] op. cit., pp. 8, 9.   [67] op. cit., pp. 139, 140.
[68] op. cit., p. 174.   [63] op. cit., p. 290.   [70] op. cit., p. 140.

the point. Already because of their sanctity the Fathers had a certain aptitude for explaining and defending the doctrines of the faith,[71] but it was the help of the Holy Spirit that was mediated to them through the Magisterium—whose organ they were in teaching contemporary faithful and the future Magisterium—which was decisive in guaranteeing their teaching.[72]

When we try to discover what he means by calling the Fathers instruments of the hierarchy we are given two clues. First, he claims that the Fathers were so much under the supervision of the Magisterium that their teaching in the last resort was the teaching of the Magisterium.[73] Secondly, the very silence of the Magisterium was equivalent to approval of the teaching of the Fathers:[74] the Magisterium could not allow them to teach something which was contrary to the faith because their teaching affected the faithful so much.[75] It seems then that to be an organ of the Magisterium means to be under the supervision of the Magisterium and to have at least the approval of its silence. Without this approval and supervision the Fathers would be only historical witnesses to divine Tradition.[76] At this stage we have an activity which belongs to Tradition, which is not magisterium but which still derives all its value from the approving supervision of the Magisterium.

It must be clear, however, that the notion of the Fathers as instruments or organs of the Magisterium cannot explain any part allowed them in active tradition—certainly if it is required to do that by itself. For we have seen Dieckmann and Lercher call the Fathers instruments or organs of the Magisterium and it was not on that account that these two can have their exclusion of the Fathers from active tradition criticised. Does it make any difference that De San seems to explain the instrumentality of the Fathers by pointing to the supervision and approval of the Church of their time? Will the notion of instrumentality so explained be sufficient to justify attributing an active part in tradition to the Fathers?

When we examine this approval and supervision by the Magisterium of which De San writes, we notice that it could

[71] op. cit., p. 132. [72] op. cit., p. 174. [73] op. cit., pp. 153, 154.
[74] op. cit., p. 174. [75] op. cit., p. 153. [76] op. cit., pp. 168, 169.

be made to mean too much for his purpose but that, in fact, it means too little. That it could be made to mean too much we see from Dorsch's use of it. He, too, declares that the unanimous teaching of the Fathers—and exercising their function as doctors—cannot be in error because they had the approval of the Church of their time which itself could not err.[77] But for Dorsch this same idea means much more than it does for De San. With Dorsch it robs the Fathers of any active part in Tradition—for Dorsch remains consistent in his Tradition-magisterium theory. By the approval given, the doctrine taught by the Fathers becomes in effect the doctrine of the Magisterium. The Fathers' writings can be said simply to reflect the teaching of the Magisterium.[78] The teaching has nothing from *them* by which *they* could be given an active part in Tradition.

But, looking at the matter objectively, we can see that Church supervision and approval means too little for De San's purpose—and that Dorsch's position is completely untenable. The Church has always supervised theological thought and especially theological writing, but her approval is necessarily slow, especially in the ferment of ideas involved in development; and certainly her silence can never be taken for approval. Too many heretical or misleading ideas have been condemned after a silence. Hence, with that aspect of the Fathers' teaching which involved development of doctrine to be accounted for, it is hard to see how its value can be made to depend upon official supervision and an approval that is mostly only silence.

In all the contributions mentioned in this section what creates difficulty is this: the Fathers are admitted to have seen deeper into Church doctrine, to have developed doctrine, to have been 'doctores'. First, on the position of Dieckmann and Lercher: it would seem that they would have to regard this function of the Fathers as one of simply repeating what the Magisterium had developed in doctrine—which would at once be an unrealistic view of the Fathers and make nonsense of the title 'doctor'. Second, on the position of Zapelena and De

[77] Dorsch, op. cit., p. 739.   [78] op. cit., p. 732.

San: it seems that it is not possible to explain, solely by reference to this instrumental relationship with the Magisterium,
the guarantee which that developing activity of the Fathers
must have if it is admitted to be part of Tradition.

Hence, some theologians merely record this activity of the
Fathers in development and leave it unexplained. When
Billot discusses the development of dogma it is the Fathers
who are primarily in question. When he describes the three
phases in development—simple faith, discussion and controversy, precise explanation—it is their work and their expressions of doctrine that come under review all the time.
Yet if we ask why such importance is given to this activity
of theirs, what guarantee we have that it does not lead astray
the Church which pays so much attention to it, we get no
answer apart from this: "In point of fact all those Fathers
whose authority has always been and is still accepted could
not have departed from that (official Church) understanding
(of the faith)." [79]

That completes the case for those who seek to explain the
Fathers of the Church, the nature of their functions and the
value of their work, by connecting them as instruments or
organs with the Church Magisterium.

5. SO FAR: CONNECTED WITH THE MAGISTERIUM

The theologians discussed so far in this chapter have one
thing in common: they seek to explain the value of the
Fathers' teaching solely in terms of the relationship of the
Fathers to the Magisterium. No other factor—although others
may be mentioned—has an integral part in the explanation.
We may summarise and analyse this approach before con-
sidering another.

If only because of Franzelin's treatment of them, it is
necessary to point out that the Fathers were not at any time
the Magisterium of the Church. Because of four characteristics which they had in common and which marked them off
from everyone else, they formed a body 'sui generis' in the
Church. The members of this body may have been to a large

[79] Billot, op. cit., *De Imm. Trad.* (1922), p. 69.

extent members of the Magisterium of the Patristic age. With those who were even the activity by which they discharged their twofold office, that of Father of the Church and that of bishop, may have been to some extent the same activity. But even then the criteria used in judging its value will be different: according as it is regarded as performed by a bishop or performed by a Father of the Church. In either case its full value will depend on the fact that it is part of a wider consensus. But the wider consensus of which it is part, and consequently its precise value, will differ according as the one who performed it is regarded as a bishop or as a Father of the Church. The unanimous teaching of the Fathers is never simply the unanimous teaching of the Magisterium. It may reflect the teaching of the Magisterium in its own way, but that is not the same thing. Its value may be similar to that of the unanimous teaching of bishops but it is never the same. The Magisterium is infallible by the promise of Christ and the charism of the Spirit. The Fathers received no such promise and they were not granted the same charism. Even if the Fathers of the Church had all been bishops their function and the worth of their work as a body 'sui generis' would still have to be described differently from those of the Magisterium.

In the view of the first group of theologians mentioned in this chapter, the task of the Fathers was to witness in writing to the teaching of the Magisterium of their time. There is no mention of that function performed by the Fathers when they acted as 'doctors', developing doctrine and teaching the developed doctrine as part of the faith. Their value is that of men who recorded. Of course, the Fathers did incorporate in their writings the teaching of the Church of their time and to that extent they provided a record. And there is this much to be said, too, for the position of this first group: it brings out the point that the essential activity of the Fathers was writing. But writing and recording are two different things. Writing is one of the arts of expression. It goes with thinking. And when the Fathers wrote, their thought went deeper than that of their contemporaries. Writing was essential to the work of Fathers, but there is a better explanation for that. It is necessary for the continuity of thought and influence within the Patristic body itself, for they lived in different places and at very different times. It is their unanimity that is valuable and only writers can show unanimity in those circumstances. It is through their writings that the Fathers appear to posterity as a "Council of teachers".[80]

There is something to be said for the position outlined in Pohle's *Dogmatik*, too. It is true that Church approbation must enter into discussion of the Fathers. The Magisterium is the divinely instituted guardian of truth and especially equipped for its task. Once it is presumed that the Fathers of the Church influence the Church by their teaching, it will automatically fall to the Magisterium to approve or disapprove. The approval of the Magisterium will naturally be decided to a large extent by orthodoxy of doctrine. It is one thing to say that the Church approves some men who are thereby fully acknowledged to be outstanding men of sanctity and learning, approved teachers in the Church—(though not approved precisely as official teachers sharing a divinely instituted office). It is an altogether different thing to say that the Magisterium thus makes its own the doctrine of the Fathers. Church approval of the Fathers does reach the doctrine in a general way through the persons. It does not—except in a few cases of explicit approval meant as such—attach to the doctrine directly, and certainly not in such a way as to lend the doctrine the Church's authority so that it becomes Tradition on the Tradition-magisterium definition. A teaching of the Fathers may be taken over and taught by the Magisterium. Perhaps that is the goal of all their teaching. But it had its own worth prior to that, precisely as teaching of the Fathers of the Church, and the question as to whether it belongs to Tradition or not will be decided on that prior worth. Once it becomes Magisterium doctrine it is obviously Tradition— in any theory of Tradition—but at that stage it is no longer simply a teaching of the Fathers.

The theory found in Pohle's *Dogmatik* might well be classified as an attempt to explain the value of the Fathers' doctrinal

[80] M. J. Scheeben, *Handbuch der Katholischen Dogmatik*, B. I. ed. 2 (Grabmann), Freiburg i. B., 1948, p. 167.

work by its consequent connection with the Magisterium. The remainder of the theologians discussed after that attempt to explain the worth of the Fathers' teaching solely on the grounds of its connection with the concomitant or contemporary Magisterium. They are all agreed that the Fathers of the Church as a body be described as 'an organ of the teaching Church' or 'a voice of the Magisterium', or by some phrase equivalent to 'instrumentum Magisterii'. Most of them do not attempt to explain this instrumental relationship any further: to say how it worked out in actual historical fact. The only attempt at such an explanation points to supervision and approval by the Magisterium. We have already noted the doubtfulness of that explanation, when it regards approval as a concomitant factor. It is some indication of the inadequacy of this appeal to a relationship of instrumentality that it can be used by theologians of almost diametrically opposite views on the claims of the Fathers to an active part in Tradition.

Most of the trouble for those who seek to explain the role of the Fathers and the value of their activity solely by their relationship with the Magisterium arises out of the fact that the Fathers had their own insights into revealed truth. When Franzelin wrote that the work of witnessing to truth and that of explaining and developing it could be distinguished but not separated he pointed a very important factor in any realistic discussion of the Fathers, even if his view of the Fathers themselves was not altogether realistic. Undoubtedly the Fathers received their doctrine from the Magisterium, they were subject to its teaching as everyone else was. But it meant more to them. There was not one section of their works in which they simply repeated doctrine and one section in which they tried to expound its deeper meaning. They wrote down their insight into the truth they had received and that insight was their own. If the truth is handed on by being explained and developed, then surely those who were outstanding in the development of doctrine cannot be excluded from some part in the activity of handing it on. And yet, if they are allowed such a part, it must be admitted that the guarantee which their activity must have as part of Tradition, has not yet been satisfactorily explained.

6. ANOTHER APPROACH: GIFTED MEN

Another approach to the treatment of the Fathers of the Church is inclined to depend on their own gifts to explain their function and to explain the value of their contributions towards the preservation and development of doctrine. For the theologians dealt with here will allow the Fathers an active part in Tradition.

When Schell, for instance, writes of the Fathers he sees them standing severely on their own. Active tradition in Schell's view of things, is twofold (conservative Tradition is in question rather than the constitutive Tradition of the Apostles): literary or documentary tradition and 'sachliche' or monumental tradition.[81] To this 'sachliche' tradition the activity of preaching belongs.[82] Of these two ways in which doctrine is conserved and handed on in the Church, the activity of the Fathers belongs to documentary tradition.

He is satisfied to say of the Fathers that when they teach unanimously that a truth is divinely revealed, then it does undoubtedly belong to the deposit of faith.[83] The only guarantee we have to support this claim for the Father's consensus is to be found in their natural and supernatural qualifications. The authority of one single Father is measured according to these natural and supernatural gifts which he possesses.[84] The more Fathers who agree in witnessing to a doctrine of faith, the higher the authority for it, until the highest authority is reached when there is unanimity. At that stage the teaching of the Fathers cannot be doubted.[85]

However, if the value of the Fathers' teaching is going to depend entirely on their own natural and supernatural equipment for the task, some clear account must be given of this equipment.

Clement Dillenschneider is not immediately interested in the Fathers of the Church or in their role in Tradition. His

---

[81] H. Schell, *Katholische Dogmatik*, vol. I. Paderborn, 1889, p. 161.
[82] op. cit., pp. 167, 168.
[83] op. cit., pp. 164, 165.
[84] op. cit., p. 164.   [85] ibid.

thesis has to do with the 'sens de la foi' in the universal Church
and it is in terms of this that he defines Tradition.[86] When
he does discuss briefly the Fathers of the Church it is in connection with the work of the Holy Ghost who is responsible
for the insights into the revealed truth which are attained
in the Church.[87] He refers to a common belief that the Fathers
of the Church benefited from a special inspiration of the Holy
Spirit.[88] It was not such an inspiration as would place the
writings of the Fathers on the same plane as Holy Scripture.
It was a gift in the order of knowledge given them with a
view to explaining the deposit of faith.[89] Beyond that Dillenschneider does not give any detail to help define the nature
of this gift. Some of the Fathers, he says, claimed this 'inspiration' for themselves, some attributed it to others.[90] The fact
that the nature of this "spéciale motion divine" is not properly
explained, he thinks, can be understood from the difficulty
of the subject.[91]

Muncunill gives the Fathers a place amongst the "secondary
means of preservation and transmission".[92] He speaks of a
special assistance of the Holy Ghost granted the Fathers when
they act as witnesses and doctors. He goes much further than
Dillenschneider when he writes that this special help confers
infallibility on the Fathers.[93] But he makes little attempt to
explain what this assistance of the Holy Ghost is, what form
it takes.

If we are to judge from these attempts, it becomes doubt-
ful if it will ever suffice to explain the value of the Fathers'

[86] P. C. Dillenschneider, *Le Sens de la Foi et le Progrès Dogmatique
du Mystère Marial*, Rome, 1954. Cf. p. 115.
[87] op. cit., pp. 278 ff.   [88] op. cit., p. 281.
[89] op. cit., pp. 281, 282. "Il reste . . . qu'on envisageait cette inspiration
. . . comme servant a l'élucidation du donné revelé primitif." Cf. Y. M-J.
Congar, art. 'Sainte Écriture et Sainte Église', in *R.S.P.T.*, 44 (1960),
p. 83 f.
[90] Dillenschneider, op. cit., pp. 281, 282.   [91] op. cit., p. 283.
[92] P. J. Muncunill, *Tractatus de Locis Theologicis*, Barcelona, 1916,
pp. 110, 129.
[93] op. cit., pp. 166, 167. "Imo Patres in hisce materiis (fidei et morum),
si accipiantur simul sumpti, sunt infallibiles propter assistentiam Spiritus
Sancti."

teaching by appealing to the natural and supernatural gifts of an isolated body of men. Schell merely refers to the characteristics of the Fathers and bases their authority on the qualifications which they indicate. Sanctity is one of these characteristics, one of the qualifications. It is a gift of the Holy Ghost. Is that all Dillenschneider means by inspiration: the understanding of divine truth that sanctity brings? And however great that sanctity was, would it render the Fathers infallible in unanimity, as Muncunill thinks they were? It is hard to see how the ordinary dispensation of grace and gifts and virtues could on its own explain the doctrinal authority which the Fathers enjoy. It appears that if the value of the Fathers' teaching is not satisfactorily explained solely by their relationship to the Magisterium, neither will it be explained only by their own gifts, for then it is impossible to see their teaching attaining the guarantee—theologians speak of infallibility—which would account for the role it is given in Tradition. The truth about the Fathers' teaching must lie somewhere between those two positions. Only on finding it can their role vis-à-vis Tradition be fully decided.

From this point of view the contribution of the German theologian, M. D. Koster, seems promising for he discusses the graces and gifts of the Fathers as a basis for their doctrinal value and he also links them with the Church—although specifically with the believing Church.

7. Gifted within the Church

To Koster's way of thinking the operative thing in Tradition is 'Glaubensinn'. Where there is this 'understanding of the faith' there will be Tradition. The Fathers have their active part in Tradition; they have their share of the 'Glaubensinn' of the Church.[94] The 'Glaubensinn'—the corresponding Latin term would read 'sensus fidei'—is the result of the supernatural virtue of faith, the supernatural light of faith, together with the three gifts of the Holy Ghost:

[94] M. D. Koster, *Volk Gottes im Wachstum des Glaubens*, Heidelberg, 1950, p. 107.

Wisdom, Understanding and Knowledge.[95] Whatever value the teaching of the Fathers has, whatever part it has in Tradition, must be traced to this. Such unanimity in doctrine as is found amongst the Fathers will not be explained by appealing to their powers of dialectic or to their general erudition. It is the result of the 'Glaubensinn', the work of the Holy Ghost.[96]

The 'Glaubensinn' is not peculiar to the Fathers. It is diffused in the whole Church. Between the 'Glaubensinn' of the Fathers and that of the faithful there is a difference of degree but not of kind. The difference of degree comes from a greater influence of the Holy Ghost on the Fathers—in conferring his gifts.[97] The unanimous teaching of the Fathers is not infallible as such. The Magisterium alone is infallible in its teaching.[98] The teaching of the Fathers is only "correct and certain".[99] The Fathers, then, belong with the faithful, with the believing Church. Their teaching is evaluated as that of believers, not as that of members of the Magisterium —although many of them were that, too.[100] The teaching activity of the Fathers which achieves unanimity belongs to Tradition. It is one of the ways of coming to know the content of objective tradition: a means for the Magisterium, too.[101] But infallibility will only belong to it when it gains specific recognition from the Magisterium.[102]

It is of primary interest to ask what Koster means when he says that the Fathers are to be regarded as part of the believing Church. Taken by itself, that statement could mean many things. It could mean, for instance, that the Fathers derived an added guarantee for their teaching from the fact that they taught in harmony with the universal belief of the faithful; that in their teaching this universal belief found expression, although in a more developed form. But it does not seem to mean that for Koster. He insists that they belong to the believing Church only because, as a body, they have not got the charism which the teaching Church alone has. They belong to the body of the faithful because of their lack

---

[95] op. cit., p. 92. These gifts will be discussed more fully in a chapter on the Faithful.   [96] op. cit., p. 108.   [97] op. cit., p. 110.
[98] op. cit., p. 109.   [99] op. cit., p. 108.   [100] ibid.
[101] op. cit., p. 112. Cf. p. 95.   [102] op. cit., p. 108.

of this charism rather than because of any organic bond between their teaching and the belief of the faithful. Their very
superiority in supernatural gifts over the main body of the
faithful induces Koster to evaluate their activity in isolation.
The teaching of the Fathers gains nothing from a common
heritage. Koster writes that there is one 'Glaubensinn' in the
Church, effected by the one Spirit; that Magisterium, Fathers,
Theologians and faithful all work together in unity,[103] but
he still insists on evaluating separately and according to its
own individual qualifications the particular contribution of
each group. And once again the value of the Fathers' teaching
is made to depend solely on their gifts.

It is fair to say, however, that Koster, although without
meaning specifically to do so, has illustrated the necessity of
sanctity as a quality of the Fathers of the Church. We must
assume that if sanctity is demanded as a characteristic of
Fathers of the Church, it has something to do with doctrinal
activity. But since sanctity is a complex matter of graces and
virtues and gifts, as a characteristic of men engaged in activity
such as the Fathers' activity it should be sanctity with a particular orientation that is in question. It seems reasonable enough
to assume that this orientation is achieved by a particular emphasis in the Holy Ghost's granting of the virtue of faith and
of the gifts that pertain to knowledge.

It is Koster's opinion that Heinrich, too, related the teaching of the Fathers to the belief of the faithful[104]—his *Dogmatik* appeared in 1873, the same year as that of his great
contemporary, Scheeben—but Heinrich's whole idea of the
position of the Fathers in the Church is different from that
just seen in Koster's work.

In a very full discussion of the Fathers and their place in
Tradition, Heinrich refers to them as "the richest and most
important source for the defence and explanation of the
Catholic faith".[105] His description of the Fathers is a detailed
description of their usual notes. He demands the 'Church
approval' first. It is because of this that the teaching of the

---

[103] Koster, op. cit., p. 111.   [104] op. cit., p. 107.
[105] Heinrich, op. cit., vol. II, p. 97.

Fathers can be definitive in matters of faith in the Church.[106] The recognition in question is given by the Church on the basis of the possession of the three other notes.[107] Orthodoxy in significant doctrine is required because the Church will only recognise as Fathers those who taught according to the mind of the Church, who represented in their own outstanding manner the Spirit of the Church.[108] Eminent sanctity is required as a guarantee of the purity of the Fathers' doctrine, not only because it guarantees that the Fathers have not used the deposit of faith carelessly, but because sanctity and fulness and purity of understanding of divine things are intimately bound up.[109] It is the holy man whom the Holy Ghost will use to produce the out-of-the-ordinary effects in the Church.[110] So God raised up the Fathers in the Church "equipped with extraordinary gifts and graces",[111] to defend and develop his doctrine. The gifts and graces conferred on them amounted to an enlightenment by the Holy Ghost.[112] That is not to say at all that the Fathers were inspired as the writers of Scripture were, or given a charism of infallibility such as the Magisterium enjoys.[113] If the Fathers were bishops, that is a non-essential circumstance that still lends more weight to their writings: for they would then have been in closest contact with the official mind of the Church, the 'mens Ecclesiae'.[114] Fathers and members of the Magisterium are always formally distinct, although they may in many cases be materially the same persons.[115]

[106] op. cit., vol. II, p. 100.
[107] ibid. Cf. also p. 108: "Durch die Approbation der Kirche wird festgestellt, dass ein Schriftsteller eben zu jenen rechtgläubigen, erleuchteten, heiligen und alten Lehrern gehört, welche wir Kirchenväter nennen."   [108] Heinrich, op. cit., vol. II, pp. 102, 103.
[109] op. cit., vol. II, pp. 106, 107.   [110] op. cit., vol. II, p. 106.
[111] op. cit., vol. II, p. 105.   [112] op. cit., vol. II, p. 104.
[113] op. cit., vol. II, p. 112.
[114] op. cit., vol. II, pp. 100—2. If a Father was a Pope, then a document containing a definition issued by him would no longer be counted simply as a writing of a Father of the Church—p. 101, footnote 1.
[115] According to Heinrich, it is not absolutely necessary that a Father of the Church be himself a writer provided that he have the other notes and that his teaching be recorded by some reliable person. Cf. op. cit., vol. II, p. 99.

There seem to be now in Heinrich's thought about the Fathers two closely connected but yet distinct themes. The first has to do with the authority of the Fathers as teachers in the Church. The second has to do with the quality or value of their unanimous teaching.

On the first theme—it has appeared before—Heinrich holds that the Fathers are public teachers in the Church precisely because of recognition by the Church.[116] In other words, whatever guarantees the Fathers' teaching may have had from their personal qualifications and their place in the Church, the universal Church cannot afterwards accept them as teachers until the Magisterium has officially assured the universal Church that their teaching is so guaranteed. Official recognition of them as Fathers of the Church, gives this assurance. Hence Heinrich says that the teaching authority which the Fathers enjoy in the Church—it is still not the authority of an official organ—is accorded them by the Magisterium, but accorded on the grounds of their possession of the other notes.[117]

It is on the second theme that Heinrich's real contribution is made. To him there is no absolute distinction between Fathers as witnesses and Fathers as doctors as if they were now one and now the other. Just as the faith is not a series of words and sentences but meaning for the mind, so the Fathers did not mechanically—"geist—und urtheilslose Zeugen" [118]—repeat or witness to propositions. Rather they gave us their own insight: they were witnesses and doctors together.[119] The result of this activity, the unanimous teaching of the Fathers, was infallible. The Church itself calls that teaching infallible.[120] This does not mean that the consensus of the Fathers is infallible because the Church has—'post factum'—regarded it so. Heinrich uses the Church's statements as a proof that the unanimous teaching of the Fathers is infallible, not as the reason for that infallibility. These statements form one of two proofs. The other proof is "from the

---

[116] Heinrich, op. cit., vol. II, p. 100.   [117] ibid.
[118] op. cit., vol. II, p. 129.
[119] ibid. "ist ihre Erklärung der Dogmen . . . unzertrennlich von ihren Zeugniss für dieselben".   [120] Heinrich, op. cit., vol. II, p. 119.

nature of things":[121] because of the Fathers' prominent position in the doctrinal life of the Church it is inconceivable
that they should have erred unanimously in matters of faith.
Therefore the unanimous teaching of the Fathers is not infallible because the Church regards it so: the Church recognises that it is so in fact. The question still remains: how is
the unanimous teaching of the Fathers infallible? Heinrich
suggests the answer.

The Fathers teach what is in fact the common teaching and
the common faith of the Church. As the teaching or as the
faith of the Church, it is infallible by reason of the infallible
authority of the Church. The unanimous teaching of the
Fathers is not infallible because the Fathers are infallible.
The Fathers are not infallible. But they teach the faith of the
Church, which is infallible.[122] Are we now back in the position
of those who explain the value of the Fathers' unanimous
teaching solely by relating them to the Church, to the Magisterium? We are not because we still have to take into account
the fact that the Fathers are witnesses and doctors at one
and the same time. To Heinrich that meant that the Fathers
were witnesses who, in the act of witnessing, clarified and so
enriched Church doctrine. If their teaching is now infallible
it can only mean one thing: it is the infallible faith of the
Church that is presented to us in the Fathers' teaching
although no longer in the form of magisterium. It comes to
us through the active minds of the Fathers, through minds
that are not only naturally but also supernaturally gifted. It
reaches us elaborated and enriched. It is still the faith of the
Church. It is as such that the Fathers teach it. But it is also
formally the teaching of the Fathers, the teaching of a
group of men providentially raised up and equipped to teach
Church doctrine with greater insight. Its ultimate value,
therefore, depends not only on the fact that it is the Church's
faith and not only on the fact that the Fathers' insight into
it is the work of the Holy Spirit through his graces and gifts,
but on a combination of these two factors. The Fathers,
living and working 'in medio Ecclesiae', gave their own
expression to the infallible belief of the Church, according

[121] op. cit., vol. II, p. 120.   [122] op. cit., vol. II, p. 118.

to the providence of the Holy Spirit and with the aid of his gifts.

The theological doctrine on the Fathers during our period is found in its most advanced form in the writing of M. J. Scheeben. Scheeben is undoubtedly amongst the greatest theologians of recent centuries. And the slight measure of his influence on subsequent theology is almost baffling. Only recently has a new and critical edition of his *Dogmatik* appeared. He was a pupil of Franzelin's at Rome when he lived at the Germanicum and attended lectures at the Gregorian University. A year after his ordination to the priesthood in 1858 he began to profess dogmatic theology in the seminary at Cologne, and he remained there until his too early death in 1888, at the age of 53. His thought on Tradition, we shall see, is a considerable advance on Franzelin. It is found mainly in the first volume of his massive *Dogmatik*. This is usually dated 1873, although the Preface to the volume is dated June 21, 1874.

The Fathers of the Church, according to Scheeben, are such as are naturally and supernaturally gifted to an eminent degree. Their particular calling they have from the Holy Spirit who placed them and equipped them in the Church.[123] Because of this providence of God and the gifts which it implies, the Fathers have their place in Tradition. Just as the 'Sedes Apostolica' is the principal bearer of Tradition in the heart of the Magisterium; so the Fathers are principal bearers within the general stream of Tradition in the whole Church.[124]

What form does their activity take? So far from being only historical witnesses who reflect the actual teaching or belief, the actual Tradition, the Fathers are the 'eyes' enlightened by the Holy Spirit, the agents through whom the inner meanings of the deposit of faith become known and are preserved in the Church.[125] Through them development of doctrine takes place.[126] Their teaching, then, is not confined to that which is currently and formally taught or believed in the

---

[123] Scheeben, op. cit., p. 95.   [124] op. cit., p. 166.   [125] ibid.
[126] op. cit., p. 167. "gerade durch ihre Einsicht und Tätigkeit die etwa latent gewordene Tradition wieder in Fluss gebracht und das Keimartig um Depositum enthaltene entwickelt werden soll".

Church. The Fathers are instruments of the Holy Spirit in development, too.[127] Their teaching will represent both what was explicitly believed or taught in the Church and that which was implicit in that teaching or belief.[128]

The teaching of the Fathers must be unanimous over a long time in order to have its full value. Only when it is so will it definitely represent the common Church Tradition and be surely the product of the one Holy Spirit.[129] Scheeben, too, will speak of the infallibility of this unanimous teaching of the Fathers.[130] For the 'inner grounds' of the infallible character of this teaching he simply refers us to what he has already written about the Fathers.[131] We can see these inner grounds best from the following passages.

It is primarily because they witness to the faith of the Church that the teaching of the Fathers is infallible. This does not mean that their witness must be mere repetition, historical witness to formally believed truth. They are witnesses to Church belief also—we have noted already—in their very clarifying and developing of Church doctrine. The activities are inseparable.[132] It is primarily and principally because their teaching is a reflection—although, we must not let the word 'reflection' give the impression of a mechanical witness —of the teaching of the Church that it is an infallible teaching. The infallibility, like the doctrine itself, comes from the Church. Yet it is relatively autonomous, this teaching of the Fathers with its character of infallibility, because of the fact that the Fathers are instruments of the Holy Spirit and not of the Magisterium.[133] Because of this relative autonomy it can act as a guide and a confirmation or corroboration for the faithful and for the Magisterium in its doctrinal decisions.[134]

---

[127] Scheeben, op. cit., p. 167.   [128] ibid.
[129] op. cit., pp. 166, 167.   [130] op. cit., p. 180.   [131] ibid.
[132] op. cit., pp. 178, 179. "Demgemäss ist das Ansehen der Väter, formell betrachtet, allerdings zunächst und hauptsächlich zu finden in ihrer Eigenschaft als Zeugen der Glaubens der Kirche, aber nicht so, dass es auf das formelle, nämentlich das historisch referierende Zeugnis von dem öffentlichen Glauben der Kirche zu ihrer Zeit beschränkt werden dürfte. Es kommt ihnen zu als erklärenden und entwickelnden Lehrern der religiösen Wahrheit."   [133] op. cit., p. 95.
[134] op. cit., pp. 95, 96.

For the Magisterium itself will recognise that the teaching of the Fathers is infallible; it is a deeper reflection of its own infallible teaching.[135] Of course only the Magisterium is finally entitled to say what men were qualified to act as Fathers in the Church.[136] But the relative autonomy of their contribution is decided before that recognition is taken into account.

Scheeben relates the Fathers particularly closely to the Magisterium.[137] They are 'Helpers Extraordinary' to the Magisterium. He uses the term 'Hilfsorgane',[138] but he obviously does not mean that the Fathers' teaching is commissioned by the Magisterium, or supervised or concomitantly approved by the Magisterium so that the teaching would derive all its value from one of these relationships. The link between the Fathers and the Magisterium is forged mainly through the doctrine which they, like all members of the Church, received from the Magisterium. It was the business of many of them to present and defend it as members of the Magisterium. But it was the vocation of all of them as divinely equipped Fathers of the Church to present and defend it with a greater clarity and depth.

8. SUMMARY

The Fathers of the Church were a body 'sui generis', membership of which was confined to those possessing four marks or characteristics. They were men of considerable natural gifts of mind. But the important thing to note amongst their

[135] op. cit., p. 96. Note that Congar takes these two paragraphs of Scheeben's—pars. 166, 167 on pp. 95, 96—on their own and comments: "Scheeben is one of the very rare theologians who gives their place to charismatic organs of teaching" (Y. M-J. Congar, *Lay People in the Church*, trans. Attwater, London, 1957, p. 285) having himself instanced St Theresa and Pascal (op. cit., p. 284). It is better to regard Scheeben as writing here of Fathers and 'Lehrer per excellentiam', for his section on the Fathers refers back to this place—cf. op. cit., p. 166. He does not seem to have in mind any persons that could be called charismatics beyond those we normally refer to as Fathers of the Church and the Great Theologians. [136] op. cit., pp. 95, 96.
[137] op. cit., p. 166. They are almost all members of the Magisterium.
[138] op. cit., p. 96.

D

qualifications is rather their supernatural equipment. This is indicated by the mark of 'sanctity'. It does not mean only that sanctity in general gives a certain aptitude for divine truth, just as vice involves a certain blindness. It means that the Holy Spirit in sanctifying these men equipped them particularly for the task of expounding the revealed truth—and that presumably by a generous grant of these gifts that pertain more to faith and knowledge. 'Orthodoxy' implies that the Fathers remained true to the faith of the Church which it was their task to expound. The Church recognises that she had such outstanding men amongst her members. Her recognition of them—whether explicit or implicit—assures us of their nature and role in the Church. To that extent it recommends their teaching, indirectly and in general, and so augments the role which that teaching plays now in Tradition. But the teaching of the Fathers had its own value and its own guarantees prior to that. It was, in fact, infallible. And the Church itself treats it as such.

The Fathers of the Church were subject to the Magisterium like other members of the Church. They received the faith from the Magisterium. Most of them were bishops. Therefore they received the faith of the Magisterium more immediately, from within. Precisely as Fathers of the Church, however, their membership of the Magisterium is accidental. The faith they received bound them as infallible doctrine coming from the authoritative Magisterium, as every bishop is bound to believe the doctrine taught by the Magisterium.

The Fathers did not receive the faith in mere passivity. Those who were bishops had at least to articulate it and to present it to their individual flocks. But it was not that which made them Fathers of the Church. What made them Fathers of the Church was their deeper insight into the faith they received—or, rather, the qualifications that implies—and the incorporation of that in writing towards the benefit of the whole Church. This deeper insight was the result of enlightenment by the Holy Spirit. It was not by accident that the Church was blessed with Fathers.[139] There is no need to cry

[139] Scheeben, op. cit., p. 166. They were "divinitus per tempora et loca dispensati".

'Protestantism' the moment such enlightenment is mentioned. It has nothing equivalent to revelation or inspiration in the strict sense and it implies no charism of infallibility. It is simply a way of expressing a special effect of eminent sanctity. The gift of faith is normally referred to as the light of faith, 'lumen fidei', and some of the gifts of the Holy Spirit have to do with perception and understanding. It is because the Holy Spirit was generous with some writers in the Church that we have Fathers of the Church. If that is all Protestantism means by enlightenment it is quite orthodox.[140]

Since the Fathers were separated by time and space they communicate with each other and establish a unanimity of doctrine through writing. It is in this unanimity over ages and places that the full value of the Fathers' teaching is found. When the teaching is unanimous in these circumstances it can only be the teaching of the perennial Magisterium in the form now of Patristic doctrine and the effect now of the influence of the 'one Spirit' on the Fathers.

There are other ways—according to the common run of Catholic text-books—in which a teaching of the Fathers may be known to represent the teaching of the Church and to be the effect of the work of the Holy Spirit. Other ways, that is, besides the fact of unanimity. So, for instance, the text-books say that for practical research it is sufficient to ascertain the teaching of the Western Fathers or of the Fathers of one particular century on any point of faith since these will not be found at variance with the remainder of the Patristic body. In very particular cases, too, when one Father appears as the spokesman of the Church against heresy—the case of Augustine against the Donatists and Pelagians is usually quoted—it can be taken that his teaching coincides with that of the whole Patristic body. But it is not desirable to discuss here the possible justification for each of these practical pointers to Patristic teaching. The more theoretical question

[140] Pinard de la Boullaye, art. cit., p. 864. "tout ce que affirme l'action incessante du Saint-Esprit dans les ames, la necessité de son concours pour pénétrer le sens des Écritures et pour arriver a la foi . . . tout cela ne peut que rejouir, avec les catholiques, les croyants de toutes les Églises encore attachées a la vieille foi".

of the value of Patristic teaching itself is a more fundamental
question and it is best discussed where the value of that teaching is most obvious—in moral unanimity.

This unanimous teaching is very often termed infallible by
theologians. It is better to say that the unanimous teaching
of the Fathers is infallible than to say that the Fathers in
unanimity are infallible. In the latter case there is always the
suspicion that one thinks the Fathers to be infallible ex officio.
In the case of the teaching of the Magisterium infallibility is
the direct effect of the charism of infallibility given in view
of the office and function. In the case of the teaching of the
Fathers infallibility is the effect of the teaching of the Magisterium primarily and the effect of the gifts of the Holy Spirit
secondarily.

It is because the value of the teaching of the Fathers cannot
be fully explained by the fact that they receive their faith
from the Magisterium that Scheeben writes of a 'relative
autonomy' in their teaching. It is because of this relative
autonomy in turn that the teaching of the Fathers is regarded
as part of active tradition in its own right—an activity that
is of its very nature secondary to the primary activity of the
Magisterium. It is not sufficient to be right in saying that the
Fathers have their part to play in the activity of tradition. It
is necessary to be right for the right reasons, as Heinrich and
Scheeben were.

9. The Great Theologians

It is really in treating of Theologians that the mark of the
Fathers known as 'antiquity' must be discussed.

To Scheeben's way of thinking there need be no fundamental distinction between the Patristic age and the period
which followed it, the age of Theologians. The note of antiquity, he writes, was only introduced in the eighteenth
century to the discussion on outstanding teachers of the
Church. The Church itself has not confined the title 'Doctor
Ecclesiae'—a title with which men who had the qualifications
of a Father to an outstanding degree were honoured—to the
Patristic period. She has named Doctors from amongst the

later Theologians, too. And apart from the Doctors there have been in the Church since the Patristic age holy men who have left outstanding contributions to theology.[141] Scheeben himself, when he is writing about the "Helpers Extraordinary" does not confine membership to Fathers of the Church. He writes of "the Fathers and teachers par excellence . . . raised up by divine Providence at different times and in different lands".[142] Ideally, all that he has written about the Fathers should be applicable to that extension of their gifts and calling which is seen in the "Teachers par excellence". But there is a difference in the circumstances of the times of which he is very conscious. In a slightly pungent statement, Scheeben remarks that, when the authority of Theologians and the dogmatic worth of their teaching is in question, not any and every writer of theology who happens to have a Catholic name can be counted.[143] And yet it is a great deal easier to draw the boundary in Patristic times that would separate Fathers of the Church in the full and proper sense from others who would be called only ecclesiastical writers than it is today to segregate the "weighty and approved authors" from the rest of theological writers.[144] And that is one of the differences between the Patristic and post-Patristic periods: the difficulty of pointing to a clearly delineated body of men in the latter period who would correspond by gifts and calling to a body such as we have examined in the former.

Despite those differences and that difficulty, Heinrich is more inclined to dwell on the similarities between the periods: "The Church has great and divinely enlightened teachers in every period of her existence." [145] But he does say that in the Patristic period, when the fundamental truths of faith were more in question, God gave more special grace and enlightenment.[146] He knows, as Scheeben does, that a very much higher

---

[141] Scheeben, op. cit., p. 177, par. 372. [142] op. cit., p. 166.
[143] Scheeben, op. cit., p. 184. "Man darf folglich das, was von dem theologisch-kirchlichen Ansehen der Theologen gesagt wird, nicht ohne weiteres auf alle beliebigen Schriftsteller mit katholischem Namen anwenden."   [144] ibid.   [145] Heinrich, op. cit., vol. II, p. 107.
[146] op. cit., vol. II, p. 108.

percentage of the Fathers were also official teachers, bishops in the Church, than were Theologians (although many of the great Theologians have been bishops or Cardinals, too).[147] He writes that the same sanctity is not demanded even of the weightier Theologians that was demanded in the Fathers of the Church.[148] Yet in discussing the worth of the unanimous teaching of Theologians, he is inclined to dwell on the Doctors of the Church—who belong to all ages[149]—and on those who with them would be termed "the great Teachers", and to claim that "what we said of the Fathers is true also of the great Theologians of later times: that God himself grants the Church great Teachers, great Lights of the Sacred Science according to the needs of the times and the good pleasure of his Providence".[150]

It is still very noticeable, however, that he will not speak specifically of Theologians clarifying or developing doctrine on anything like the same plane as the same activity of the Fathers.

More conscious perhaps of the differences between the periods, of the difficulty of pointing to a group of teachers clearly corresponding to the Fathers of the Church, Scheeben more explicitly limits the scope of Theologians' doctrinal achievements when he comes to deal expressly with them. Where the Fathers' teaching represented more the mind of the Holy Spirit, "sensus Spiritus Sancti", the Theologians more immediately represent the mind of the Church, the "sensus der Kirche".[151] Taken in general, the Theologians are more characterised by natural erudition and industry where the Fathers in general were more consistently characterised by the influence of the gifts and graces of the Holy Spirit. Hence he means to say that the value of the Theologians' teaching will be traced far more exclusively to the teaching or belief of the Church which they present, and not, to the same extent as the Fathers' teaching, to the influence of the Holy Spirit. Yet Scheeben *will* still speak of the influence of the Holy Spirit

[147] op. cit., vol. II, p. 142.
[148] op. cit., vol. II, p. 138. Cf. Scheeben, op. cit., p. 169.
[149]Heinrich, op. cit., vol. II, p. 110.
[150] op. cit., vol. II, p. 142.   [151] Scheeben, op. cit., p. 169.

as a factor in preserving the unanimous teaching of Theologians from error. Basing his teaching on the Brief 'Gravissimas inter' of Pius IX, he grounds the value of the unanimous teaching of Theologians in the natural guarantee of a consensus of such learned men, the teaching of the Magisterium which they receive and present and the help of the Holy Spirit.[152] At this stage it is to be presumed that what has been said before of the Fathers concerning deeper penetration and development of doctrine applies also to Theologians, but to a lesser and lesser extent according as the body of Theologians extends beyond those who could be placed on a par with the Fathers by reason of their place in the Church and the wealth of their natural and supernatural gifts.

Again in discussions of the nature and worth of the teaching of Theologians there are authors who base that worth only on gifts or qualifications of the men themselves and authors who base it only on a relationship with the Magisterium. Amongst the former Koster is found again writing of the 'Glaubensinn' of Theologians. In fact, Fathers and Theologians are usually mentioned together. Their 'Glaubensinn' is evaluated similarly.[153] But it must be more difficult with Theologians—taken en masse, as they are generally quoted today—to point to a significant influence of the Holy Spirit on them above that on the general faithful. Perhaps that is why Schell, who relies on personal gifts to explain the value of unanimous teaching in the case of Theologians also, only speaks of their natural qualifications.[154]

If the main difficulty with Theologians is that it is much harder now to point to a group of teachers whose supernatural qualifications must be taken into account in evaluating their teaching, it is easy to understand why in actual fact arguments drawn from the consensus of Theologians do not confine themselves to such men. There is much more justification, therefore, for those who refuse to envisage the developing activity amongst Theologians as at all on a par with simple witnessing. So Dorsch, to give one instance, will not distinguish Theologians as witnesses and Theologians as doctors at all.[155] It is

---

[152] Scheeben, op. cit., p. 185.
[153] Koster, op. cit., pp. 107 ff.
[154] Schell, op. cit., p. 166.
[155] Dorsch, op. cit., pp. 748 ff.

much easier now, and perhaps of much more practical value, to write: "The authority . . . of Theologians refers simply to an argument that leads from theological teaching . . . to the formal teaching of the magisterium." [156] It is easier and more practical to regard Theologians as historical witnesses, to give their doctrine full authority solely on the basis that it is the formal teaching of the Magisterium which they present. That is essentially the position of Franzelin who, when he comes to write of Theologians, will no longer write of witnesses and authentic doctors, but only of those by whom we can be brought into contact with the teaching of authentic guardians of the faith.[157] And even Scheeben, in one particular passage, describes a function of the teaching of the theological schools as that of giving an expression, not otherwise easily attainable, to the ordinary and universal magisterium.[158]

Of course, even as mere witnesses Theologians must have qualifications. We must be sure that they relay true Church teaching accurately. To assure this Franzelin observes that Theologians are commissioned by or, at least, under the authority and supervision of the Magisterium.[159] If there must be question of their developing doctrine, Franzelin will regard that as a purely human preparation for a possible definition by the Magisterium. If a development became common it would be temerarious to deny it.[160] It is never by itself infallible.

From these contributions, with their gradual grading down of the admitted value of theological teaching, two facts come to light. First, there is undoubtedly after the Patristic age a body of men equipped to take the place of the Fathers of the Church. These may be called the Great Theologians. Apart from the Doctors of the Church, who have been officially

---

[156] Michel, art. cit., col. 1348. Cf. Burghardt, op. cit., p. 26.

[157] Franzelin, op. cit., p. 187. Following his treatment of the Fathers, it is significant that he writes here: "A monumentis quae *immediate exhibent* authenticum judicium vel consentientem doctrinam successionis apostolicae, distingui debent documenta privatae auctoritatis, quae mediate deducere possunt in cognitionem doctrinae traditae in Ecclesia."   [158] Scheeben, op. cit., p. 162.

[159] Franzelin, op. cit., p. 188. So he prefers to write of the papally instituted schools and universities of the twelfth to the eighteenth centuries when discussing the consensus theologorum.   [160] op. cit., p. 191.

named, we cannot as yet name the Great Theologians who would form a body equivalent to that found in the Patristic age. We suspect that there is a consensus of teaching equivalent to Patristic teaching. We have no reason to believe that the Church is less well equipped later on than it was in the first eight centuries.

We can see, too, some grades in theological writing. The theological text-book at least is a recognisable form. Its purpose is more to lay out accepted doctrine in theses than to attempt the deeper explanations and syntheses. We can see that works like those we have discussed from Franzelin or Billot or Scheeben are on a different level. If we cannot now name the Great Theologians with the same success as we can name the Fathers it may be because we are too near them. If we must content ourselves now with drawing a consensus of doctrine from all theological writers of evident orthodoxy, we can only regard its value as derived totally from the Magisterium whose doctrine it teaches and theological teaching as such cannot as yet establish fully its claim to an active part in Tradition.

'Antiquity', then, as a note of the Fathers will not mean that no outstanding teachers have appeared in the Church after the Patristic age. It will indicate the men who expounded the great fundamental truths of the Christian religion and the period in which that task was performed. Since all future development of doctrine is based on this first great exposition of the oral deposit, the men responsible for it are very aptly called 'Fathers of the Church'. It may be too that they received a greater help from the Holy Ghost to perform their task, without prejudice to the great gifts undoubtedly conferred on some Theologians of later ages.[161]

10. CONCLUSION

What we say now about the Fathers can be applied to that as yet largely unnamed body of men—the Great Theologians.

The teaching of the Fathers is a record of the Magisterium of their time, an echo of official teaching, but it is more than

[161] cf. Scheeben, op. cit., p. 169.

that. The Fathers can be called the voice of the Magisterium, an organ of the Magisterium in teaching because they do hand on the truth they received from the Magisterium, but it is better to use another metaphor and to call them the 'eyes' of the Magisterium or of the Church, for they see deeper into that truth.

The Fathers exercised an activity that is not formally identical with magisterium just as its object, the material doctrine, does not completely coincide with the material object of magisterium in every respect. Yet the Fathers *are* active in handing on truth and their teaching is guaranteed, infallible. If they are now denied an active part in Tradition it can only be because the guarantee demanded for active tradition is the charismatic infallibility that goes with divine mission and authority in the agents. Franzelin looked specifically for such authority for Tradition and Billot, looking for charismatic infallibility for the agents in Tradition, found the same authority and declared it to belong to Tradition when explaining how Tradition is a rule of faith.

When one has travelled the way of this second chapter one finds it hard to see why the Fathers' activity should be excluded from Tradition, once that is seen to be an activity proper to Fathers of the Church, not identical with magisterium, and yet infallible. It is hard to see why this is not sufficient for Tradition, though there be only derived infallibility. In short, the exclusion of the activity of the Fathers from Tradition—once that activity is properly described—is a completely arbitrary thing.

Chapter Three

THE FAITHFUL

"Someone has used the expression 'the faithful teach, in a way, by their very believing'."
Riudor, *Est. Ecl.*, vol. 31, p. 198

THE term most in evidence wherever the contribution of the faithful to Tradition is discussed is the term 'sensus fidelium' or an equivalent such as 'sensus fidei', the French 'sens de la foi' or the German 'Glaubensinn'. It is difficult to find an English equivalent: perhaps 'understanding of the faith'. As the term itself stands 'sensus fidelium' or any of its equivalents could refer to the internal intuition, knowledge or grasp of the truths of faith or to that grasp when it is expressed in some way. The term will always be used in this chapter in the latter sense unless the former sense is clearly indicated. 'Consensus fidelium' obviously refers to the unanimous belief of the faithful, all of one mind in the universal Church.

The term is more than ever in evidence since the definition of the Assumption. Yet its orthodoxy or, at least, the orthodoxy of its implications has been called in question. To Schell's mind, for instance, the term 'sensus fidei' belongs to a modern tendency to speak of Tradition as something occult, as something the limits of which are really unknown. He thinks it is such a term and such a usage that gives Protestants like Harnack the opportunity to pronounce that the Catholic Church can very easily claim to define only what is in Tradition when Tradition for the Catholic Church involves something as vague as the 'sensus fidei'.[1] He believes that to follow this 'sensus fidei' as a determinant of doctrine and an expression of Tradition can only involve us in an objective or quantitative increase in the deposit of Christian truth.[2] And

[1] Schell, op. cit., p. 161. [2] op. cit., pp. 171, 172.

later on, using now the term 'sensus fidelium', he clarifies what he means by this criticism when he indicates some of the less prudent devotional movements that found favour among the faithful—there was a devotion to the immaculate conception of St Joseph, a cult of the heart of St Joseph and a cult of Our Lady's blood. These, he writes, were all due to misunderstandings of Church Tradition;[3] and if the 'sensus fidelium' were seriously taken to be a constitutive part of Church Tradition, these devotional movements would have resulted in new dogmatic beliefs.

A somewhat similar line of thought is found in an article by Bennett, for whose allegiance to the Church the definition of the Assumption proved a final stumbling-block. The stress of his objection, however, falls on the 'sensus' rather than on the 'fideles'. For the term 'sensus fidelium' implies more than the fact that the faithful have a part in Tradition; it implies that the process of seeing deeper into the faith, of developing Christian truth, is not confined to theological reasoning of a strictly formal type. And this 'sensus fidelium' is one basis for the doctrine of the Assumption pointed to by Papacy and theologians alike. So Bennett attacks the type of doctrinal development which is claimed in the case of the Assumption by Canon G. D. Smith. Fixing on the words "not a purely logical process by which one abstract idea is deduced from another" and perhaps most influenced by the sentence: "There is nothing quite like it in any department of human knowledge" [4] he maintains that the idea of a "mystical process" is being advocated by Catholic Theologians which must destroy the older doctrine of the closed deposit.[5]

De San is more concerned about the influence of the Holy Ghost, which is one of the factors used to explain the dogmatic value of the 'sensus fidelium'. To him that only suggests the unorthodox doctrine of the 'intrinsic taste, the godly relish, the divine illumination' which the faithful are supposed to receive to help them understand the Scriptures. Such a doc-

---

[3] op. cit., p. 180.   [4] Quotation from *The Tablet*, 28 Oct., 1950.
[5] V. Bennett, art. 'The Assumption: a Postscript', in *Theology*, vol. 54 (1951), p. 410.

trine must be completely rejected for he thinks it provides something akin to new revelation.[6]

It is with these highly unfavourable views of the 'sensus fidelium' in mind that we must examine the term and the doctrine connected with it amongst modern theologians.

1. HAVE THE FAITHFUL A PURELY PASSIVE ROLE IN TRADITION?

Much the same division of opinion is found here as was already found in discussing the teaching of Fathers and Theologians. To Burghardt and Michel, ever meticulously consistent with their Tradition-magisterium position, the faithful simply manifest in their beliefs the mind of the Magisterium and these theologians judge the worth of their witness solely on that factor.[7] In this context, too, the images of 'instrument' and 'echo of the Teaching Church' reappear. With Van Noort, for instance, "the communal belief of the Churches is the inevitable response to the clear and articulate preaching of the Roman Catholic Episcopate, like the echo of its voice".[8] When he writes of the dogmatic value of this unanimous faith, it is infallible. But its infallibility derives solely from its obedience, from its material correspondence with the preaching of the Magisterium.[9] When Deneffe is discussing the various concepts of Tradition found in theological usage he agrees that one could apply the name Tradition to the handing on of doctrine in the whole Church, by bishops, priests and people.[10] This is a less proper usage of the term, however, and is only allowable because the faithful are "instruments of the Magisterium", because they reflect or echo in their beliefs the teaching of the Magisterium.[11]

To all those authors one persuasion is common: the faithful have no active part in Tradition. Their function in Tradition is the passive one of mirroring or reflecting the preaching of the Magisterium. Any activity they may exercise has no

---

[6] De San, op. cit., p. 10.
[7] Burghardt, op. cit., p. 23. Michel, Dict. art. cit., col. 1347.
[8] Van Noort, op. cit., p. 108.   [9] ibid.
[10] Deneffe, op. cit., p. 137.   [11] op. cit., pp. 137, 138.

guarantees of its own; any qualification their belief has belongs only to the material doctrine precisely in so far as it comes to them from the Magisterium. It is necessary to insist that this is Franzelin's position, too, for that is not always recognised.

Although Franzelin's chapter on the 'consensus fidelium' [12] appears very curiously in his section entitled 'Concerning Divine Tradition considered in itself', instead of appearing, as it normally does, in the section entitled 'Concerning the Instruments and Documents of Tradition', there can be little doubt from the general argument in the chapter that the faithful, to Franzelin's mind, have no active part in Tradition and that the value of their belief derives solely from the fact that they receive obediently the infallible doctrine of the Magisterium.

As he puts it: the Holy Spirit preserves the integrity of the faith in the body of believers. But he does so through the ministry of the authentic Magisterium.[13] Through this ministry the Holy Spirit is present ('adest') to the faithful, not allowing them to believe anything outside the apostolic deposit. He operates always through the visible ministry of pastors and doctors.[14] To prove his point he simply repeats what he has already written about the nature and authority of the Magisterium and remarks that Christ and the Apostles never envisaged a teaching authority without an obedient people whose faith would be an effect of that teaching.[15] He means to add nothing to this when he writes that the charism of infallibility was conferred on the Magisterium "towards the needs and for the benefit of the whole body".[16] The net result of this mediated influence of the Holy Spirit is infallibility of belief in the believing Church. But that infallibility derives solely from the Magisterium. It is an infallibility altogether conditioned by obedience.[17] Franzelin does refer in this context to that immediate and direct effect of the Holy Spirit on the faithful by which he confers the internal graces.[18] His only concern in mentioning this, however, is to point out that such

---

[12] Franzelin, op. cit., pp. 96 ff.   [13] op. cit., p. 96.
[14] op. cit., p. 99.   [15] op. cit., p. 97.   [16] ibid.
[17] op. cit., p. 97 footnote.   [18] op. cit., pp. 99 ff.

an activity does not in any way rule out the external ministry of a teaching apostolate. He nowhere discusses any possible guarantees which it might lend the beliefs of the faithful as such. To Franzelin's way of thinking, the divine help given for the propagation and preservation of the deposit of faith is given only to the Magisterium. Tradition can only belong to an organ with charismatic infallibility and divine authority. In describing the organ of Tradition he has only described such an organ and he has always emphasised the charism. On the question of the 'consensus fidelium', therefore, he is in the same position as Van Noort above.[19]

Even Dillenschneider, whom we shall see makes more of the 'sensus fidelium' than most authors, will bear out this interpretation of Franzelin: "We believe that it would be wrong to identify the 'sens chrétien' with the simple obedience of the faithful to the teaching of the Magisterium. So it was understood by a number of theologians of the nineteenth and twentieth centuries, principally by Franzelin."[20] And

[19] cf. p. 3 above. It is not, then, an accurate paraphrase of Franzelin's thought to write, as Müller does, that Franzelin recognised that the charism of infallibility was conferred on the Magisterium towards the benefit of the whole Church and *therefore* he recognised alongside the Magisterium another organ or bearer of Tradition—the faithful in their acceptance and profession of the faith (O. Müller, art. cit., p. 168). Then Müller goes on to quote Franzelin: "spiritus veritatis adest toti fidelium coetui", without adding the qualification which Franzelin himself adds: "sed hoc exequitur suavi providentia per visibile ministerium pastorum et doctorum" (Franzelin, op. cit., p. 99) and Müller links the infallibility of the faithful directly with that first partial quotation, giving the impression that this infallibility is at least partly explained by a direct influence of the Holy Spirit on the faithful, in Franzelin's thought. Müller's account of Franzelin's doctrine is repeated by Schmaus in his *Dogmatik* (III, I, p. 770). And a similarly unsatisfactory treatment of Franzelin's statement of his twelfth thesis is found in the article of Ternus already cited, *Beiträge*, p. 49.

[20] Dillenschneider, op. cit., p. 320. And yet as if he had not realised this fact or as if this passive role of the faithful did not preclude them from being regarded as bearers of tradition, Dillenschneider writes earlier: "D'après Franzelin . . . la Tradition est le sens chrétien vivant dans toute la communauté des fidèles sous la dépendance du magistère et en communion avec lui" (op. cit., p. 113). That may well be a defensible notion of Tradition and one that appeals to Dillenschneider himself, but

Diekamp echoes Franzelin's position on the 'sensus fidelium' perfectly when he writes that it is a criterion of true Tradition since it possesses a passive infallibility which is caused by the Holy Spirit, but only through the ministry of the official Church teachers.[21] The strong words of a contemporary theologian could well be applied to this view of the doctrinal position of the faithful (without disrespect to a classical Christian metaphor): "the faithful are sheep to be fed regularly and to be sheared at times".

But Catholic theology has much more to say about the 'sensus fidelium'. First in Mazzella we meet a theologian who is prepared to allow an activity in Tradition to all the faithful while he does not, explicitly at least, grant them any more prerogatives than do the theologians we have just discussed. He enumerates the faith and practice of the Christian people amongst the activities by which tradition is transmitted.[22] Yet when he formally treats of the 'sensus fidelium' he simply states that the Christian people are infallible in their beliefs because the Magisterium is infallible (in order to preserve the integrity of faith in the whole Church)—and the whole Church is indefectible.[23]

It is an unsatisfactory position when left at that. No one is going to have a part in active tradition who has not got some guarantee in some way proper to himself. An unbeliever might very well acquire a knowledge of our faith from the teaching of the Magisterium, might write it down accurately and so transmit it. It can be said now that the Magisterium preserves the integrity of the faith in his mind, since he acquired it from the Magisterium. He does not believe it, of course. But then what difference does faith make to transmission? It is on the answer to that question that hinges at once the filling out of Mazzella's position and the case against those who allow the faithful no activity in Tradition proper.

---

it is not the notion of Tradition that Franzelin adopts when he goes about defining the term.

[21] F. Diekamp, *Katholische Dogmatik*, vol. I, Münster i. W., 1938, p. 60.

[22] H. Mazzella, *Praelectiones Scholastico-Dogmaticae*, vol. I, ed. 4, Rome, 1908, p. 494.

[23] op. cit., p. 507.

2. They Bear Active Witness with the Help of the Holy Spirit

One of the most significant things encountered in tracing the development of teaching on the 'sensus fidei' in the period is Michel's slight change of heart; or, better, the reason for it. The context of the change is a comment on the theology of Pius XII, and particularly on his theology on the occasion of the Assumption definition. It is in view of this that Michel thinks a more definite role in the argument of Tradition must now be accorded to the belief of the faithful.[24] In elucidating this statement Michel writes that, although the 'sensus fidelium' is never on the same level as magisterium—which watches over it and guides it—it is a living witness to traditional faith and the Magisterium can ask of it a proof of the continuity of current belief with apostolic doctrine.[25] Because the same Holy Spirit is the principle of living faith in bishops and faithful alike. Every faithful member of the People of God in virtue of his Baptism and Confirmation is dedicated to the witnessing of his faith in profession and action before the world.[26]

We cannot conclude that Michel will now concede fully that the faithful are active in Tradition. He certainly recognises that they are active witnesses, that they have a direct influence of the Holy Spirit to help their witness; but we shall see that Filograssi allows them as much without yet allowing them a proper part in active tradition.

Cardinal Tisserant spoke of the 'sensus fidelium' in relation to Mariology, too, at the Mariological Congress at Lourdes in 1958. We gather from his words that it is mainly to help explain the development of dogma that the role of the 'sensus fidelium' in Mariology is discussed. We gather that the gifts which fit the faithful for this role are neither reducible to the illumination of some Protestantism nor to the rather

[24] A. Michel, art., 'Pie XII, Lumière de la Theologie', in A.Cl., 7th series, n. 45 (6 Nov., 1958), p. 656. In 1956 Michel had simply repeated his position as that is outlined in his *Dictionnaire* article. Cf. his art. 'L'Église, l'Écriture et la Tradition', A. Cl., n. 8 (1956), pp. 119 ff.

[25] art. cit., Pie, p. 657.   [26] ibid.

indefinable 'religious experience' of Modernism.[27] He says: "it can happen that some truth be detected, strengthened and developed by that believing body, i.e. by the simple faithful under the guidance of their pastors".[28] For the faithful are not merely passive recipients of doctrine taught by the infallible Magisterium.[29] They, too, have the influence of the Holy Spirit upon them.[30] That is how he accounts for the importance accorded to the faith of the universal Church by Pius IX in defining the dogma of the Immaculate Conception and by Pius XII in defining the Assumption.[31]

This 'sensus fidei' is no blind intuition or special illumination. It belongs to the ordinary dispensation of grace in the Catholic Church.[32] In Baptism and Confirmation especially the faithful receive the Spirit of Truth. Whatever illumination of intellect or inclination of will, whatever consequent intuition of truth they receive, is the result of the graces and gifts conferred on them by the Holy Spirit. Equipped with these they detect the Marian privileges.[33]

Cardinal Tisserant is careful to stress the teaching of 'Humani Generis' that the authentic interpretation of the deposit of faith belongs to the Magisterium alone.[34] He writes that final and authoritative certainty for theology comes only with a definitive decision of the Magisterium. But there is certainty from the universal faith of the Church before that.[35]

Nowhere in his address was Cardinal Tisserant concerned with what was or was not active tradition. But Filograssi, who describes the part of the faithful in the development of Marian dogma in much the same terms, is also concerned with the definition of Tradition. Filograssi applies the words of Vincent of Lerins—by claiming that the Vatican Council does so—to the faithful, to bear out his point that understanding of the faith grows in the whole Church and in each member.[36] He, too, describes the basis of the value of the

[27] E. Card. Tisserant, art. 'De Mariologia in ambitu sacrae Theologiae', in *Nuntia Periodica*, n. 6, Rome, 1959.

[28] art. cit., p. 15.   [29] ibid.

[30] ibid.   [31] art. cit., pp. 13, 14.   [32] art. cit., p. 17.

[33] ibid.   [34] art. cit., p. 14.   [35] art. cit., p. 18.

[36] I. Filograssi, art. 'Constitutio Apostolica "Munificentissimus Deus" de Ass. B.M.V.', in *Greg.*, vol. 31 (1950), p. 524.

'sensus fidei' in much the same way as Cardinal Tisserant. When the 'sensus fidelium' contains a certain belief before that has been defined by the Magisterium, he writes, its dogmatic value is based on the supernatural gifts of the Holy Spirit. These give a certain instinctive perceptiveness into the truths of the deposit of faith received from the Magisterium. The 'sensus fidelium' grows by the influence of life and example of faithful on faithful, of priests and bishops on faithful, and it is always under the direct guidance of the Magisterium.[37]

What directly interests us here is the fact that, as far as we can gather, this developing activity of the faithful is not part of Tradition. Only the activity of the Magisterium is active tradition. Its developing activity alone is a direct preparation for definition.[38] The developing activity of the faithful is only an indirect preparation.[39]

This attitude is an echo of Franzelin's view of the development of dogma. He, too, thinks of development of dogma mainly in terms of preparation for a definition by the Magisterium. He writes then of what he terms the human element in this preparation. The whole sequence of preparation, he says, is under the guidance of the Holy Spirit. But only the activity of the Magisterium is directly under that guidance; the activity of any other agent only indirectly, in so far as it serves under the authority and guidance of the Magisterium.[40]

Already because of the fact that he demands charismatic infallibility and ecclesiastical authority wherever Tradition is admitted, there is small possibility of Franzelin admitting that the faithful play an active part in Tradition. But there is even less possibility of this when we remember that he never seemed to think of the internal graces and gifts granted to all the faithful by the Holy Spirit as having any connection with the value of their witness to the truths of faith. His thought here is consistent at once with his Tradition-magisterium theory and with his attitude to the 'consensus fidelium' in his chapter on that subject. It is clear, too, from the fact that Filograssi follows Franzelin in the Tradition-magisterium line

---

[37] Filograssi, art. cit., 'Traditio Divino-Apostolica', pp. 468 ff.
[38] art. cit., p. 464.   [39] ibid.   [40] Franzelin, op. cit., pp. 277, 278.

of thought, that he will not be prepared to allow the faithful an active part in Tradition. But in his case, once he has recognised some supernatural equipment behind the 'sensus fidelium' and proper to it, it is less obvious that he is not guilty of the arbitrary exclusion of an admitted doctrinal activity from the sphere of active tradition. The key to Filograssi's attitude on this point is to be found in his opinion that the 'sensus fidelium'—the "via affective", as he terms it—never of itself achieves enough certainty in a doctrine believed to make that doctrine definable.[41] It is Balic's opinion, on the contrary, that such certainty is reached by the unanimous belief of the whole Church: the 'sensus fidelium' of all the members of the Church, clergy and laity together.[42] At this stage at least and still before it becomes magisterium, the 'sensus 'fidelium' should be regarded as part of active tradition. This difference of opinion can only be resolved by a closer examination of the supernatural guarantee which the belief of the faithful possesses.

3. THE SUPERNATURAL GROUNDS FOR THE VALUE OF THE 'SENSUS FIDELIUM'

Koster's division of the members of the Church into groups was numerical and exclusive. So the faithful, to his mind, are the simple faithful. They are not also members of the Magisterium, not Theologians and they were not Fathers of the Church. The 'sensus fidelium'—the 'Glaubensinn' of the faithful, to use his own term—is the faith of the simple faithful. Its dogmatic value is measured according to the measure of the gifts and graces which the faithful receive for the benefit of their faith. Therefore, Koster maintains, whereas the 'Glaubensinn' of the appointed teachers is endowed with infallibility, the 'Glaubensinn' of the simple faithful never can provide us with more than reliable assurance.[43]

It is legitimate enough in speaking of the 'consensus fidelium' to confine one's attention to the simple faithful. Before

[41] Fillograssi, art. cit., 'Traditio', p. 470.
[42] C. Balic, art. 'Il Senso Cristiano e il progresso del dogma', in Greg., vol. 33 (1952), p. 130.   [43] Koster, op. cit., p. 107.

we have reflected very much on the subject it is probably in this confined sense that the term first strikes us. It is more questionable when one's attention is confined—within this already confined sphere—to the graces and gifts which the simple faithful receive from the Holy Spirit and when the dogmatic value of the 'consensus fidelium' is based on these alone. For the word 'infallible' is applied to the 'consensus fidelium', too, just as to the unanimous teaching of Fathers and Theologians. If the application of that term—where it is not explained only by the material coincidence of beliefs of the faithful with the teaching of the Magisterium—is at all justified, then Koster's position in this question must be as unsatisfactory as his position on the unanimous teaching of the Fathers.

Yet mention of gifts and graces of the Holy Spirit, since they are part of the ordinary and universal dispensation of supernatural gifts, suggests a point which is made explicitly by so many theologians of the period: the body of believers involves every member of the Church whether he be bishop, Father of the Church, Theologian or simple believer.[44] That is what Mazzella had in mind when he describes the faithful as those "who belong to the Church in so far as they believe and profess their faith, and therefore, not only ordinary believers are indicated but the bishops and the Pope, in so far as they believe and profess in their private capacity what they teach in their official capacity and thus belong to the believing Church".[45] For all receive the faith obediently and yet actively in their private lives. It is easy to see that every ordinary bishop—since he is not the Magisterium in person—receives the teaching of the Magisterium in obedience. But Mascall, an Anglican who has more in common with the Roman Catholic faith than most of his co-religionists, has objected that the Catholic theory of Papal prerogatives divides the Church into two completely distinct classes. One class, of course, consists of one member only, but that plea does not escape the objection. A division is made since all other members of the Church hold their faith in obedience but the Pope cannot make an

[44] cf. C. Journet, *L'Église du Verbe Incarné*, vol. I, Desclee, De Brouwer, 1941, pp. 36 ff.　　　[45] Mazzella, op. cit., p. 506.

act of submission to himself. To this C. Davis replies by describing the Pope's act of Faith "as an act of divine and catholic faith, it does not differ from the act of faith of the ordinary Catholic. His faith is mediated, like ours, by the living testimony of the Church. The Pope must humbly and docilely believe, as we beileve, what he discerns to be the faith of the Church." [46] If we take the body of believers in this widest sense, then, we can examine the nature of their gifts and the extent of their activity: always precisely as believers.

The sacraments of Baptism and Confirmation have already been mentioned in connection with the doctrinal activity of the faithful. Congar writes: "Through baptism each one of the faithful belongs to the people of God, set apart and consecrated to bear witness before the world (1 Peter ii. 9)." [47] For through Baptism we are not only enabled but expected to take part in the Church's sacraments and sacrifice and in the general life dictated by our faith. Such participation in such a life and activity we shall later see described as part of the 'witness before the world' for, as Congar has also remarked, "Teaching through witness is not given through words alone." [48] With Confirmation our ability to witness and our commitment to witness become more complete. "Confirmation is a very special development of the baptismal character with reference to the Christian's strengthening and activity in the social life of the Church and of the world." [49] Dabin sees in these two sacraments the source of a certain prophetical function just as the source of a certain priesthood of the laity is often seen in them. [50]

In these sacraments commitment to a task and the ability to perform it go hand in hand. Indeed the graces and privileges given in the sacraments carry obligations to activity. [51]

Undoubtedly the graces which enable a member of the Church to live the life of the Church are given more often

---

[46] C. Davis, art. cit., p. 487. E. L. Mascall, The Recovery of Unity, London, 1958, p. 209.　　[47] op. cit., Lay People, p. 289.
[48] op. cit., Lay People, p. 290.　　[49] op. cit., Lay People, p. 289.
[50] P. Dabin, La Sacerdoce Royal des Fidèles, Paris, 1950, p. 52.
[51] cf. J. R. Geiselmann, art. 'Die Tradition', in Fragen der Theologie Heute (eds. Feiner, Trütsch, Böckle), Einsiedeln, 1958, p. 106.

than on the occasion of receiving these sacraments. But the reception of the gifts of the Holy Ghost is connected in a special way with Confirmation. And three of these we find mentioned quite often as a basis for the 'sensus fidelium'. It is not part of our task to try to ascertain how Knowledge, Understanding and Wisdom should be defined and distinguished from one another. Beumer has accused Koster of being over-confident in his definitions of these three gifts. He maintains that Scheeben wrote of them too, but described them differently and that both Koster and Scheeben still appeal to St Thomas.[52] And there is no doubt that Catholic theology is still far from the last word on the subject. But it is sufficient for our purpose if it be granted that these three gifts refer to an influence of the Holy Spirit by which a member of the Church is led to a better grasp of the faith. For the rest, at least Koster and Dillenschneider are fairly well agreed on the general nature of the three gifts. Knowledge they regard as the gift that helps one to see if a proposition is connected with the deposit, to distinguish those that are from those that are not. Understanding is more a penetration of the deposit truths themselves to see their deeper implications and Wisdom is the gift by which one sees the truth in its relation to God who revealed it—it tends to present truth more from the divine viewpoint; it is linked with Charity and divine intimacy.[53]

Prior to these special gifts of the Holy Spirit there is a more fundamental basis for the 'sensus fidelium', the grace or virtue of faith which is often referred to in terms of enlightenment.[54] For this grace or virtue of faith is not a mere supernaturalising of an act of believing. It affects the knowledge itself. There is all the difference in the world between the grasp of the Catholic faith possessed by a non-believer who has been instructed in the truths of that faith and the grasp on the Catholic faith by a believer who has been instructed in the same truths. The virtue of faith provides a firmness of assent

[52] J. Beumer, art. 'Glaubensinn der Kirche', in *T.T.Z.*, 5/6 (1952), p. 135.
[53] cf. Koster, op. cit., pp. 78 ff. and Dillenschneider, op. cit., pp. 323 ff.
[54] Heinrich, op. cit., vol. II, p. 17.

so that the possession is no longer a dead possession of abstract theories but becomes a vital committment to truth.

When discussion centres on these graces and gifts of the Holy Spirit which support the 'sensus fidelium', the impression must not be given that this is a case of particular gifts possessed by separate individuals so that the 'sensus fidelium', at least in so far as it is the effect of these graces and gifts, would not of itself promise any great unity. The giving of these gifts is part of the vivification of the whole Church by the Soul of the Church, who is the Holy Spirit. This is a point well emphasised by Ternus in the discussion of the 'sensus fidelium' as a factor in Tradition.[55]

Ternus first concentrates on the fact that a deposit of Revelation was completed with the death of the Apostles and that it is still in the Church today, unchanged and held in the faith of the members of the Church. He wonders if some kind of community faith or common faith (faith in the subjective sense of virtue or act) is demanded to explain the unity and integrity of this deposit in the Church today.[56] He thinks that, since the deposit of Revelation has always been believed by the members of the Church and has come down in its integrity from generation to generation through this faith, the subjective faith of the Church must have an internal unity proper to it.[57] He finds a unity that is more than a unity of similarity in distinct individuals. He traces the unity of faith to the principle, the Soul of the Church.[58] He links the 'sensus fidelium' to the doctrine of the Mystical Body. In so far as the 'sensus fidelium' is based upon supernatural gifts and graces, these gifts and graces are the work of the one Spirit, the life-giving Soul of the Church. The subjective faith of the individual goes to build up the faith of the Church, but that subjective faith presupposed a believing Church, too, for only through the Church is such faith given.[59] So, as Baptism

---

[55] In his article on Tradition—art. cit., *Beiträge*, p. 40—Ternus deliberately refers us to another article, on the 'sensus fidelium': J. Ternus, art. 'Vom Gemeinschaftsglauben der Kirche', in *Schol*. X (1935), pp. 1 ff.
[56] art. cit., Vom Gemein., p. 8.   [57] art. cit., Vom Gemein., p. 7.
[58] art. cit., Vom Gemein., p. 13.
[59] art. cit., Vom Gemein., p. 4. Cf. also p. 11.

and Confirmation have committed a man to a community which believes and professes its faith, his faith is an integral part of the faith of that community. It comes to him from the Soul of that community, from the principle of unity. The 'consensus fidelium' is the result of this unified supernatural life of the Mystical Body of Christ.

Apart altogether from the fact that gifts and graces of the Holy Spirit are given towards a better grasp of revealed truth, the truth itself presents a challenge. The faithful Christian who hears it will wed it to his own thinking and experience.[60] It will not lie dormant in the mind. There is too much depth in it and too much mystery about it for that. From the very nature of the truth and the challenge it presents, the 'sensus fidelium', must grow in understanding.[61] Further, this Christian truth has a practical aspect. It affects the whole lives of men. It does not come to men fully prepared to accept it—but almost to enemies.[62] It changes lives. In this way it is put into practice and expressed. And often its implications can only be fully seen when it is lived.[63] Or, to view it from another angle, a depth of truth can be handed on for a long time in practice before it is apprehended by the mind. Bavaud provides an example: "Development of dogma takes its point of departure from the whole sacramental and 'institutional' life of the Church. For a long time Christians had 'lived' their seven sacraments before the Church defined the nature and the number of them." [64] It was in this sense that Congar quoted Blondel to say that a man can carry more truth implicit in the practice of his life than he can at first fully comprehend: that it is often by becoming conscious of the fuller implications of his practice that he finally becomes conscious of the fuller implications of his faith.[65]

But even when one has described the depth and vitality of

[60] Semmelroth, art. cit., p. 9.   [61] ibid.
[62] Semmelroth, art. cit., p. 6.   [63] Semmelroth, art. cit., p. 9.
[64] G. Bavaud, art. 'Écriture et Tradition selon M. Cullmann', in N.V., n. 2 (1953), p. 137.
[65] cf. Y. M-J. Congar, Jalons pour une Théologie du Laicat, Paris, 1954, p. 405. He quotes from Blondel: "ce que l'homme ne peut comprendre totalement, il peut faire pleinement, et c'est en le faisant qu'il

the truth with which the 'sensus fidei' is concerned one has still not exhausted the possibilities of the 'sensus fidei'. A factor still remains to be considered which is brought forward explicitly by Schmaus when he writes: "In his faith the believer does not merely give his assent to true propositions. Much more, through his faith he comes in contact with the one in whom he believes." [66] The believer's act of faith does not terminate in a proposition but in a reality.[67] By faith one is brought into living contact with God. God is the formal object of his faith; God and God's activity are also the material object of his faith. Such contact is the condition of the growth of all understanding. In everyday action the mind of its very nature abstracts knowledge. We know in part. Yet the knowledge abstracted is only rich or deep in so far as the mind is always in contact with the actual object or existing reality which it seeks to know. So it is with faith, too. Truths are presented to the mind to be believed. They are truths about a person, truths believed on the authority of a person, and through them a person is known, a person who is present. The Magisterium can teach infallible truth but only the individual can contemplate the person described in his own personal communings. In this contact with a person, particularly a divine person, there is a dynamism, a necessary enriching of knowledge.[68]

The point made here is a point put forward by Bacht, especially in connection with the notion of Tradition. Bacht maintains that some concepts have to be clarified before the nature of Tradition can be fully discussed.[69] Amongst these he

---

entretiendra vivante en lui la conscience de cette realité encore a demi-obscure pour lui".

[66] Schmaus, op. cit., p. 778.

[67] To say this is not to say with Emil Brunner that dogma obscures and even distorts the true character of faith (cf. *The Misunderstanding of the Church*, London, 1952, p. 88). Faith is one kind of knowledge and as such it has a content that can be expressed. But its content concerns a person and his authority recommends it.

[68] Schmaus, op. cit., p. 778.

[69] H. Bacht, art., 'Tradition und Lehramt in der Diskussion um das Assumpta-Dogma', in *Die Mündliche Überlieferung* (ed. M. Schmaus), Munich, 1957, pp. 39 ff.

dwells mainly on the concepts of Revelation, the closing of
the deposit and the development of dogma. He takes his concept of Revelation from Rondet and De Lubac but principally
from Karl Rahner. From Rondet he derives the idea that
Revelation did not come only through teaching truths but
also through the coming of a person and the living of his
life.[70] The very presence and activity of Christ was essential
to Revelation. From Rahner he derives the same notion of
Revelation with an addition.[71] For Rahner is quoted to say
that this Revelation does not only pass over intentionally into
the faith of the believing Church. The believing Church
possesses the reality (presence and activity) as well as the
teaching.[72]

At first glance it seems as if this position falls directly under
a criticism similar to this one by Dillenschneider:

> If at the source of all dogmatic development there is simply
> the infinite mystery which exists integrally from the beginning
> in the Church by the very presence of Christ in it, and if this
> infinite mystery becomes more intelligible and explicit by the
> action of the Holy Spirit who animates and perfects the Church,
> then we are faced, not with a revealed truth becoming more
> explicit but with continuous revelation.[73]

Undoubtedly, if Revelation came partly through an existential situation such as that created by the presence and
activity of Christ, and if there was then a part of Revelation
which was not communicated by teaching or its equivalent
(e.g. by infusion or illumination); if, further, that presence
is still with us, still communicating truth as it did in the
apostolic age,[74] we are, as Dillenschneider says, confronted
with continuous revelation. In order to avoid the objection
it would need to be stressed explicitly that all the truth of

---

[70] art. cit., p. 43. "Offenbarung ist Rede und Leben, Gespräch und
Gebärde . . . auf ihre Höhepunkt ist also die Offenbarung Gott selbst,
so wie ere inmitten der Menschen lebt und lehrt."

[71] Bacht, art. cit., p. 43.   [72] cf. Bacht, art. cit., p. 44.

[73] Dillenschneider, op. cit., p. 53.

[74] It would, of course, communicate truth very much to a lesser degree
in the post-apostolic Church since Christ's physical presence and activity
was more directly calculated to arouse an appreciation of the truth than
his invisible presence and activity today.

Revelation was communicated by teaching or its equivalent. The presence and activity of Christ certainly had something essential to do with Revelation. It was 'revelation' in the sense of a living actualising of the teaching—but revelation itself was "God's teaching about his economy of Salvation",[75] and that was necessary in order that the significance of the work be known. Christ's activity and presence provided an existential situation in which this teaching could be appreciated and in which it was verified. There is all the difference in the world between saying that Christ revealed truth by his life and presence amongst men and saying that Christ's Revelation or teaching was given the Apostles in the very context of its fulfilment.

It is clear enough that with Bacht only the latter is meant.[76] When he comes to describe, in Rahner's words again, the present situation in the Church, it is clear that he is not saying that the presence of Christ and His Spirit in the Church reveals truth to us but, rather, that the truth once revealed and now passed on to us is deepened in our understanding by the presence of its object in the Church, with which it puts us in contact: "the hearing of the Word by the Church and its meditation on it is not a mere logical task which seeks to derive gradually from the Word, understood as a sum of propositions, all the consequences and all that is virtually contained in it, but rather . . . (is it) meditation on the truths heard, in vital contact with the Object itself".[77] And Rahner goes on to unite this point of view with another already discussed here when he reminds us that the same Holy Spirit who is an object of our faith is also the dynamic principle of that faith by which we come to know him.[78]

This same contribution of Rahner's is taken over by Schmaus, too, and related to the 'Glaubensbewusstsein'— another equivalent for 'sensus fidei'—in the Church. The Apostles' experience of Christ, he writes, formed the living context for the express teachings of Christ. They could always

[75] Semmelroth, art. cit., p. 4.
[76] Bacht, art. cit., p. 44. "Das darf nicht im Sinne einer falschen Unmittelbarkeit verstanden werden, welche die Vermittlung der Wortbotschaft überspringt."   [77] ibid.   [78] cf. Bacht, art. cit., pp. 44, 45.

reflect on these teachings with memories of this living context and see them more vividly for that. A similar experience is granted the faithful of the post-apostolic Church. For, as well as the words, they have the reality—and an active reality, too, that works towards a fuller knowledge of itself.[79]
It was not precisely this viewpoint that H. F. Davis had in mind but we can still apply his words: "Men, whether collectively or singly, do not normally grow in understanding through formal syllogistic argument";[80] for "the faith and love of Christians will sometimes reach a deeper understanding of Christian truth without formal theologizing",[81] and so "in matters of revealed truth, as in many other matters, the process of growing in one's understanding of the truth one possesses is not confined to either leaders or experts".[82]

4. THE 'TEACHING' OF THE FAITHFUL

At this stage of the discussion of the 'sensus fidelium'—having considered the supernatural basis for this 'sensus': the gifts and graces of the Holy Spirit, the truth with which it is concerned, a truth that challenges the mind, that affects the whole living of lives, that puts men in contact with Divine Reality—it is obvious that the 'sensus fidelium' involves its own synthesis, its own insights, its own peculiar possession of the truth.[83] It may be remarked also that this developing insight is not solely the result of purely supernatural factors. In any community of men there will be development of the truths that affect the life of the community. In the Church, in doctrinal matters also, grace builds on nature. The natural operations of minds living in community are not suspended but perfected, supernaturalised and made part of a higher providence.[84]
"The faithful teach in a way—'quodammodo'—by their

[79] Schmaus, op. cit., pp. 783 ff.
[80] H. F. Davis, art. 'Our Lady's Assumption', in *Mother of the Redeemer* (ed. McNamara), Dublin, 1959, p. 201.
[81] idem, art. 'The Immaculate Conception', in op. cit., p. 88.
[82] idem. art. 'Our Lady's Assumption', p. 201.
[83] cf. Semmelroth, art. cit., p. 7.   [84] cf. idem, art. cit., pp. 7, 8.

very believing." [85] It is time to make that 'quodammodo' a little more explicit. To Congar's mind the faithful teach in so far as they develop their particular insight into the truth communicated to them.[86] Geiselmann relates the witnessing activity of the faithful again to their own particular grasp of the faith, and also to their profession of it.[87] For the word 'teaching', when applied to the faithful, implies a particular external witnessing to the truth which they possess in their own way. It implies no part in magisterium. Yet it can well be called teaching in a sense, because it has its own contribution to make and its own ways of expressing that contribution. The expression of the grasp on the faith which the body of believers possesses, on which its claim to a part in Tradition is based, takes many forms. Very often in this connection works of literature and art are mentioned. And here alone is indicated a very wide field of lay activity that covers journalism, apologetic writing (e.g. Chesterton), 'spiritual writing' (e.g. Pascal), Christian Philosophy or Christian Wisdom (e.g. Maritain, Gilson) and a hundred other activities like that of the Catholic Evidence Guild and other Catholic associations, all over and above activity that belongs more specifically to creative literature and to the arts. But more important still is the common, everyday profession of faith.[88]

The faithful as a body cannot be classified as writers as the Fathers of the Church can, nor are they usually very vocal about their beliefs apart from their prayers. Their expression of their beliefs is, therefore, normally seen best in their practical living—in their participation in the Liturgy, in

---

[85] Almost the exact words are found in Bainvel, op. cit., p. 98: "sed credendo etiam docent quodammodo, magistrisque viam indicant; fides enim prior est fidei definitione". This is curious since Bainvel takes his definition of Tradition from Franzelin—cf. Bainvel, op. cit., pp. 39, 40 —and should not then be inclined to speak of the activity of the faithful in this way. A similar change of emphasis is found in his article 'Tradition and Living Magisterium', in *The Catholic Encyclopedia*, vol. 15, New York, 1912. Cf. pp. 6, 10.

[86] Congar, op. cit., Jalons, p. 405.

[87] Geiselmann, art. cit. 'Die Tradition', p. 105.

[88] cf. I. Riudor, art. 'Mision de los laicos en la Iglesia, segun las ensenanzas del Papa Pio XII', in *Est. Ecl.*, vol. 31 (1957), p. 198.

the popular forms of piety, in their general practice of the Christian life. The development of Mariological doctrine in particular bears witness to this fact.[89] It was in orientation and emphasis in practical devotion to Our Lady that the believing Church revealed its growing perception of her prerogatives. Because this activity is activity within a community, insight and expression act and re-act on each other as one member of the community influences another. In the words of C. Davis: "The Holy Spirit dwells within the members of the Church. Their faith is a personal reality. By living the life of faith, they can pass on the faith to some, help the faith of others and by insights granted to them enrich the life of faith within the Church." [90] Balic, in fact, regards not only the internal gifts but also these external expressions of faith as graces of the Holy Spirit and part of his providence.[91] When one becomes a member of this Church which bears witness to Christ before the world, one benefits not only from the internal activity of the Holy Spirit towards sanctification but also from the inter-activity of member on member. We are members of one Body.[92]

All this amounts to the fact that, firstly, because of the factors mentioned in the last section above, the whole believing Church has its own particular grasp of revealed truth, and, secondly, because it expresses this in its own way, it hands on revealed truth in the Mystical Body. For truth is handed on by expression, from one member to another. If it can be shown that the 'consensus fidelium' as such is infallible, it will be as arbitrary to rule it out of a definition of Tradition as to rule out the teaching activity of the Fathers of the Church

[89] cf. J. R. Geiselmann, *Die Lebendige Ueberlieferung als Norm des Christlichen Glaubens,* Freiburg i. B., 1959, p. 296.

[90] C. Davis, art. cit., p. 485. Cf. also H. F. Davis, art. cit. 'The Immaculate Conception', p. 101, for this "interplay of mind on mind, until the Holy Spirit brings to all a deeper understanding".

[91] Balic, art. cit., p. 117. "lo Spirito Santo . . . predendo l'occasione per illuminare l'anima dalle circonstanze esteriori che eccitano i nostri pensieri".

[92] Geiselmann, art. cit. 'Die Tradition', p. 107, points out that only in this Body could the 'sensus fidelium' grow towards perfection as it does.

and of the Theologians. Needless to say, the theologians whose contributions have been examined in the last section above and in the present section allow the faithful part in active tradition.

5. THE INFALLIBILITY OF THE 'CONSENSUS FIDELIUM'

When we say with Geiselmann that the 'consensus fidelium', the express and unanimous belief of all the faithful, is infallible[93] we immediately raise the question of the relationship of 'sensus fidelium' to magisterium. Is the 'consensus fidelium' infallible from its own supernatural equipment and inherent vitality? And is there then an infallibility in the Church independent of the Magisterium?

From the manner of describing this matter used by Ortigues one can too easily get the impression that such infallibility as is possessed by the 'consensus fidelium' is completely the result of a direct and immediate action of the Holy Spirit on the faithful.[94] Ortigues prefers to speak of the indefectibility of the universal faith of the Church and to reserve the term 'infallibility' to the teaching of the Magisterium. He relates both directly to the assistance of the Holy Spirit. This assistance of the Holy Spirit has a positive and a negative side. As a positive assistance it involves the dispensing of graces in the sphere of knowledge and action, to every member of the Church, bishop and simple faithful alike.[95] In its negative aspect the assistance of the Holy Spirit guards against error. It protects the universal faith of the Church from error and renders that faith indefectible. It prevents the teaching of the Magisterium from error and thereby renders the Magisterium infallible.[96]

It is true that the 'consensus fidelium', the universal belief of the Church, is infallible—or indefectible: a term that indicates infallibility together with the impossibility of defect or

[93] Geiselmann, art. cit. 'Die Tradition', p. 106.
[94] E. Ortigues, art., 'Écritures et Traditions Apostoliques au Concile de Trente', in *R.S.R.*, vol. 36 (1949), p. 294.   [95] ibid.
[96] E. Ortigues, art. cit., pp. 294, 295.

loss of truth. But this explanation of the matter by Ortigues leaves out of account a factor which goes to explain that infallibility. And without express mention of this factor the impression can be given that the body of believers as such has a charism of infallibility direct from the Holy Spirit. The factor in question is mentioned by Liege but yet its full implications are not brought out.

Liege does advert specifically to the fact that the Magisterium controls the communal faith of the Church: that it has a priority over that communal faith by reason of the fact that it teaches with authority.[97] Presumably he means to indicate that the faithful get the doctrine of the deposit from the teaching of the Magisterium. Yet he does not use this factor to help explain the infallibility which he, too, attributes to the faith of the People of God.[98] In fact he commits himself to the statement: "the first infallible criterion of Tradition consists in the unanimity of the Christian understanding of the faith".[99]

Dillenschneider is even more explicit on the point that the truth of Revelation is communicated to the faithful by the Magisterium,[100] and yet he writes of an infallibility in the body of believers that derives directly from the Holy Spirit. In the context he is refuting a position which maintains that there is no infallibility in the 'consensus fidelium' until after definition of truth by the Magisterium. Before that the 'consensus fidelium' has only got, according to this theory, whatever certainty its own intuitions allow it.[101] In seeking to refute this position Dillenschneider claims that the believing Church is infallible prior to any normative decision of the Magisterium and by an infallibility direct from the Holy Spirit.[102] Admittedly he does quote in the context a passage from Congar which describes the communication of infallibility to the faithful as follows:

> In the first case, the Holy Spirit makes the hierarchy infallible, and the hierarchy, by subjecting the faithful to itself, communicates the benefits of its infallibility to them; in the second case,

[97] Liege, art. cit., p. 33.
[98] art. cit., p. 31.
[99] art. cit., p. 33.
[100] Dillenschneider, op. cit., p. 359.
[101] op. cit., p. 339.
[102] op. cit., p. 340.

E

the Holy Spirit makes the Church as a whole and as such,
infallible, and in her each organic part according to what it is—
the whole body in order that it may believe and live, the apostolic and magisterial hierarchy in order that it may transmit
the apostolic deposit to the body and declare its authentic
meaning.[103]

But this passage taken by itself is not as satisfactory as it
might be. It does not explain precisely what is intended by
saying that the Magisterium communicates the benefit of its
infallibility to the faithful by subjecting them to itself. In the
context in which Dillenschneider quotes it, that seems to
mean no more than that the Magisterium exercises authoritative vigilance over the developing activities of the faithful.[104]

It is much better, when speaking of the infallibility of
the 'consensus fidelium', to refrain from speaking of an infallibility direct from the Holy Spirit. For then the infallible
teaching activity of the Magisterium cannot be given the part
which we shall see it given in more precise accounts of this
matter and which it ought to be given in explaining the
infallibility of the 'consensus fidelium'. When the passage
quoted from Congar is seen in its own proper context, it is
less likely to give the impression of an infallibility directly
applied to the faithful by the Holy Spirit. For Congar had
written just before the passage quoted above: "The loving
and believing Church is infallible only when it listens to the
teaching Church and thus partakes of the teaching Church's
infallibility." [105]

Scheeben writes that infallibility belongs immediately to
the body of believers.[106] But that does not mean that infallibility is given directly to the faithful by the Holy Spirit. For
Scheeben elaborates his thought as follows: God wills that it
be impossible for the whole Church to err. In view of this
fact the body of believers has a direct claim that its faith
be preserved from error.[107] But what it claims is effected
first through the Magisterium. In the order of intention

[103] Congar, op. cit., *Lay People*, p. 277.
[104] Dillenschneider, op. cit., p. 340.
[105] Congar, op. cit., *Lay People*, p. 277.
[106] Scheeben, op. cit., p. 102.   [107] ibid.

infallibility belongs first to the faithful. It is intended for the believing Church. It belongs to the believing Church 'finaliter' in other words, and for the faithful it is a 'gratia gratum faciens', for the benefit of the faithful themselves. In the order of execution, however, infallibility is given first, immediately and directly to the Magisterium. It is given as a charism, a 'gratia gratis data', for the benefit of the whole body, the body of believers. Infallibility is the gift of the Holy Spirit to the faithful; but he makes the whole body of the faithful infallible by making the Magisterium infallible.[108]

To say, however, that the infallibility of the faithful as such comes from the teaching of the Magisterium does not imply for Scheeben that the 'consensus fidelium' has a purely passive role, that its whole value is explained solely by the fact that it happens to echo Magisterium teaching. We have seen that it never echoes the teaching of the Magisterium mechanically. Scheeben realises that too. Müller did him less than justice when he wrote of Scheeben's position: "The activity of the Magisterium appears as a repetition of God's Word, that of the body of believers as an echo of this." [109] The impression of a mechanical echoing of official teaching is too easily given here, whereas in the passage referred to by Müller, Scheeben adds immediately: "since however this echo is also animated by the Spirit of God in its own right, so it must also be regarded as a repetition of God's Word in its own way".[110] For even though the infallibility of the 'consensus fidelium' is derived from that of magisterium, its value cannot be completely accounted for without adverting to the fact that it has its own direct influence of the Holy Spirit upon it.

It is really a question of different forms of existence for the one deposit of revealed truth. It exists in the form of infallible and authoritative teaching in the Magisterium and it exists in the form of infallible belief in the whole Church. In that second form are found possibilities for new syntheses, a new emphasis on different aspects of the truth, a new depth of insight into some part of it. This is most noticeable when a solemn definition has in fact taken place and one can look back on the gradual growth of faith, revealed in its different

[108] ibid.   [109] Müller, art. cit., p. 169.   [110] Scheeben, op. cit., p. 98.

modes of expression, that preceded the definition. But the contributions of that second form are not confined to preparation for a solemn definition. Solemn definitions and General Councils of the Church are few and far between. The ordinary magisterium and the corresponding faith of the Church carry on from day to day. Even when no new definition can be pointed out, every age has its own insights.

Three things are true. The Holy Spirit uses the Magisterium as his instrument to teach infallible truth to the faithful. The Holy Spirit works directly on the body of believers towards the interiorisation of this truth.[111] The 'consensus fidelium' is infallible. One can say clearly little more than was said vis-à-vis the unanimous teaching of the Fathers. The infallible teaching of the Magisterium does not lose its infallibility by becoming the faith of the Church, for its entry into this new form is also under the influence of the Holy Spirit. At this stage the infallibility of the 'consensus fidelium' has not been attributed to direct action of the Holy Spirit. No charism is demanded for the faithful. And yet the action of the Holy Spirit has been recognised in translating infallible teaching into infallible belief and profession of faith—with any particular insights or synthesis which that may involve in the course of time.

This action of the Holy Spirit is manifold. A brief attempt has been made to describe it above under the section on the supernatural grounds for the value of the 'sensus fidelium'.[112] Yet, manifold and mysterious as it is, it is perhaps easier to give a positive account of it than to give a positive description of that charism of infallibility with which the Magisterium is endowed. It is easier to describe the influence of the Holy Spirit on the faithful by which he helps them to receive and assimilate the infallible teaching of the Magisterium than it is to explain how in fact the Holy Spirit renders the Magisterium infallible. We simply repeat here the Catholic doctrine that the Magisterium is infallible—it is a scriptural truth—and we do not have to decide how exactly the Holy Spirit goes about keeping it so. We simply affirm that because the Magisterium teaches the revealed truth infallibly to the faithful and

[111] cf. Baumgartner, art. cit., p. 174.   [112] cf. section 3, this chapter.

because the Holy Spirit is active in their reception of this infallible teaching by his manifold gifts and graces—principally,
of course, by his gift of faith—the belief and profession of faith
by the whole believing Church is infallible. That is obviously,
then, a derived infallibility as distinct from a direct or charismatic infallibility.

Because "the profession of faith by the body of believers is
not of value *only* by reason of the influence of the Magisterium, which begets it, but possesses its own intrinsic, relatively autonomous value as a result of the direct working
of the Holy Spirit on the faithful",[113] it can act as a guide or
"orientierendes Moment" [114] for the teaching of the Magisterium and in this way re-act on its source. This is not at all
to say that the authority of the Magisterium is a result of
or a reflection of the value of the witness of the faithful.[115]
The Magisterium has its own autonomous qualifications and
authority as supreme judge in matters of faith: it is the
appointed and authentic witness of the faith for the whole
Church.[116]

Now this 'consensus fidelium' obviously has a part in active
tradition. It is like the unanimous teaching of the Fathers in
this: that it is an activity with a relatively autonomous value
of its own. But it differs from the unanimous teaching of
Fathers and Theologians in that the scope of its effectiveness
is more limited. The value of the 'consensus fidelium' as a
witness to tradition has always been limited, as it is by Scheeben, to those truths "which do not lie beyond popular understanding" [117] and even with these to their more substantial
rather than to their more subtle aspects. Because they express
their beliefs mostly in the practice of their lives, it is to the
fundamental truths that affect their lives that the value of the
unanimous belief of the faithful is confined. A Father of the
Church was a member of the faithful, too, but he only took
part in the 'consensus fidelium' in so far as he expressed, in
the life and practice which he had in common with all the
faithful, his own personal faith. In so far as he engaged in
other activity, in so far as he was also a teacher, a member of

[113] Scheeben, op. cit., p. 98.   [114] op. cit., p. 99.   [115] ibid.
[116] ibid.   [117] cf. Scheeben, op. cit., p. 161.

the intellectual elite of the Church, a man whom the Holy Spirit especially endowed and used and one who was in close intellectual communion with the official teaching body, his teaching is counted not as part of the 'consensus fidelium' but as part of the 'consensus Patrum'. Much the same distinction must be made in the case of members of the Magisterium and in the case of Theologians. For these belong by reason of special endowment and special activity to particular classes or organs in the Church, but they are all faithful believers in the Church, too, with endowments and activity common to all the faithful.

Chapter Four

WIDER NOTIONS

"Like a broad stream."
SCHEEBEN, *Dogmatik I*, p. 210

IT is fairly well established now that the activity in Tradition is not confined to the infallible teaching of the hierarchy and is not exclusive to the Magisterium at all. Every member of the Church takes part in Tradition. To say that much, however, and even to prove it, is not to exonerate oneself from any further attempt to define or describe Tradition. Even when it has been proved that Fathers and Theologians and Faithful share active tradition with the Magisterium one important question still remains. Can a comprehensive description of Tradition be given and how should it read? This chapter is to describe attempts made by theologians to present such a comprehensive account of a concept that is wider than the Tradition-magisterium concept.

1. THE FACTUAL DESCRIPTIONS OF TRADITION

The first approach to a comprehensive concept is a very realistic and factual one and there is this much at least to be said about it: it betrays no predisposition to seek Church Tradition in any one particular agent or in any one particular form of activity, it shows no 'a priori' tendency to seek Tradition only in a particular organ because of an 'a priori' conception of the guarantees that organ must have. On the contrary, it is determined to look at reality first. Its aim is to see how truth is in fact handed on in the Church. Guarantees can be discussed afterwards.

These are the characteristics of Schultes' approach to

123

Church Tradition. When he looks at the actual transmission of truth in the Church he finds that it is an activity in three forms. The oral form of transmission is exercised not only by members of the Magisterium but by Fathers and Theologians, too. The practical form of transmission is the Christian life itself for that life is lived according to divine teaching and Christian worship in particular is equivalent to profession of doctrines of the faith. The written form of transmission comprises official documents of the Magisterium, the written liturgies, the writings of Fathers and Theologians.[1] Of course the same truths are transmitted orally and in writing and leave their stamp on daily life and practice. And when such a factual description of Church Tradition is complete, Schultes dispenses with any fears for the integrity of doctrine in transmission by simply reminding us that the Church is infallible in her faith and possesses a Magisterium which is infallible in dealing with divine truths.[2]

A similar factual description is provided by Schell. To him Church Tradition is either documentary or practical. By 'practical' he indicates (1) preaching, as that is exercised by official preachers, by catechists and by all those who have care of souls, (2) cult or worship, (3) divine positive law as it is seen in practice in the Church.[3] Bartmann was concerned more with the objective tradition that came from the Apostles and that exists in the Church as a rule of faith. So he simply describes active tradition in the Church as the outward expression or 'clothing' of the Christian faith.[4] This outward expression is seen in many forms—"in habit and devotion, in usage and practice"—some of them essential and immutable, some optional and changing with time and place.[5] Bartmann indicates the grounds for trust in the present integrity of the truth simply by pointing out that the Church possesses a power to define the content of the faith.[6]

[1] R. Schultes, *De Ecclesia Catholica*, Paris, 1925, pp. 588, 589. Schultes regards Scripture as a written form of active tradition (cf. pp. 577, 588, 589) although he grants it a value of its own by reason of inspiration and calls it a source of Revelation in its own right (p. 581).

[2] op. cit., p. 590.   [3] Schell, op. cit., pp. 161, 162, 167–9.

[4] B. Bartmann, *Lehrbuch der Dogmatik*, vol. I. ed. 5, Freiburg i. B., 1920, p. 36.   [5] ibid.   [6] Bartmann, op. cit., p. 31.

Finally, does this factual approach to the definition of Tradition have anything specific to offer on the subject of development of dogma? Franzelin looked for charismatic infallibility in those who would directly prepare for a new definition.[7] Lercher with a more factual approach, maintains that some— he calls them 'magistri'—do at times propose a truth which slowly wins the unanimous approval of the whole Church, pastors and faithful.[8] The teaching of the few in this case is active tradition even though it is not yet infallible. It is an instance of non-infallible Tradition,[9] before it attains universal acceptance and becomes infallible. Again a factual account of events without predispositions.

The realism of this approach, its freedom from preconceptions is readily admitted, but it is necessary also to question the adequacy of these results of it that have just been described.

A difference of activities—rather than a numerical distinction of persons—differentiates between a number of bodies or organs active in the Church. That difference of activities indicates a difference of qualifications which in turn distinguish these organs one from another. Since the qualifications belong to the organs or bodies it is not sufficient simply to describe a series of activities in an attempt to give a realistic account of Tradition. It is necessary to describe these same activities precisely as belonging to a body or organ or to a number of organs in the Church so that the activity may be evaluated by the qualifications and positions of the organ. Oral teaching is an activity in Tradition. It was exercised by Fathers of the Church and by Theologians, as we have noted Schultes to say. But precisely as oral teaching it is better connected with the Magisterium of which they were members; if they were members. Schultes, when he wrote of the Fathers and Theologians as oral teachers, was not describing the activities that admittedly go to make up Tradition in such a way that their value and guarantee could easily be seen. It is realistic to describe these activities in their variety; it is necessary to describe them in their connection with an organ. It is better to connect the preaching of the ordinary priests with

[7] op. cit., pp. 273 ff.   [8] op. cit., p. 312.
[9] Diekamp, op. cit., p. 49.

the episcopate which authorises it, than to leave it a factor in itself (as Schell would) where it has no guarantee proper to it.

The searcher for Tradition must have no 'a priori' ideas of the guarantee required but he must describe what he finds so that at once a relatively autonomous value (at least) and a guarantee follow. Without these two inseparable things an activity cannot be regarded as tradition in its own right.

A similar criticism applies to a factual description of development of dogma, such as Lercher's. It is too easy to say: a truth is first proposed by a few teachers and then slowly grows into a unanimity of teachers and believers. That is too much a 'post factum' view of the matter. It is easily said once this truth in question has become sufficiently distinguished from the truths of the deposit in which it was implicit to be called—in an orthodox sense—a new dogma. Then perhaps documents may show that some few announced it in explicit form before others. To isolate this few and this first explicit expression of the truth, to regard that precisely in its isolation as Tradition and to be asked consequently to consider non-infallible as well as infallible Tradition is to be asked to approach the problem of Tradition and its guarantees from the wrong angle.

The more explicit expression of truth by some individuals cannot be isolated from the less explicit expression which will grow to be explicit and common in this class if it is in fact orthodox. For Tradition is a living thing and so it grows. (Tradition certainly loses vitality, too, in periods of decadence; but here we confine our attention to growth.) No section of it can be isolated and described as if it were self-contained. Hence Tradition is best discussed in reference either to complete organs or to the organic whole, the Church.[10]

2. TRADITION IS THE LIFE OF THE CHURCH

In order to indicate at once the variety of activity involved in Tradition and the subject of this activity which guarantees

[10] Hence the teaching or belief of an organ of Tradition can be called a criterion of Tradition, too: the word 'criterion' merely indicates that as well as handing on tradition the teaching or belief also guarantees it.

it, some theologians simply define Tradition as 'the life of the Church'. This is the approach of Dubarle, for instance. To his way of thinking Tradition is continuous religious life in the Church.[11] This life carries, at least virtually, an intellectual content. Liturgical rites and Church institutions can transmit, as integral parts of a life that is essentially divine, truths that words or writing cannot fully express.[12] Dubarle does not say explicitly that teaching or writing are activities that are part of this life of the Church which expresses its beliefs, but that is not ruled out in any way. He is satisfied to say that Tradition is the continuity of life in the Church.

That would presumably be a description of active tradition and objective tradition would be the doctrine so handed on. But then an editorial in *Istina* is a sharp reminder that this line of thought can go much farther.[13] The editor asks if, before being and in order to become a handing on of truths, it is necessary for Tradition to be first a handing on of things or realities.[14] He proceeds to claim that what Christ entrusted to his Apostles to be handed on to us was the Church itself with an essential structure and a life of its own:[15] that, since the Church is lately becoming more conscious of her life, the newest tendency is to identify Tradition with the life of the Church, i.e. to regard the Church, its life and its structure as not only the organ but also the object of Tradition.[16]

It is true that supernatural life is handed on by acts of the Church, that hierarchical powers in the Church are passed on from generation to generation and that, in these ways, the Church itself can be said to be handed on. The conferring of life or of a power can obviously be called tradition. But it is as misleading, when discussing the theological concept of Tradition, to call the objective element in Tradition a thing rather than a doctrine as it is to equate Tradition with the Magisterium and thereby to throw the active element out of

[11] A-M. Dubarle, art. 'Introduction a L'Écriture Sainte', in *Initiation Théologique*, vol. I, Paris, 1952, p. 83.   [12] ibid.

[13] Editorial: 'Pour une notion "réaliste" de la Tradition', in *Istina*, n. 2 (1958). The editor was C. J. Dumont, O.P.

[14] loc. cit., p. 130.   [15] loc. cit., p. 131.   [16] ibid.

perspective. Tradition in theology is the handing on of Revelation. As such it has always been discussed.

Admittedly doctrine can be handed on by activity outside
of those formal acts of preaching and writing. That we have
seen to be a commonplace of the theology of Tradition, and
Ortigues, who also describes Tradition as the general life of
the Church, gives the key to the explanation of this fact. The
Church, he explains, is essentially sacramental. It is a sign of
the divine reality which it contains within itself.[17] By the very
same activity by which it perpetuates its own existence the
Church perpetuates its doctrine. Whatever the Church does
is an affirmation of the presence of the divine reality within
it, and so of the belief of the Church by which alone this
divine reality is grasped. The life of the Church is an intelligible sign of what the Church believes herself to possess and
to be. By seeing to the propagation of her life and of herself,
the Church automatically provides for the handing on of her
beliefs—and that even apart from the formal activity of teaching which is also an essential part of her life.

To say that Tradition is the whole life of the Church as that
propagates itself down the centuries is one way of defining
the concept of Tradition and perhaps the best way in short
accounts of the matter such as those we have been examining.
With this definition it is more legitimate, too, to account for
the integrity and indestructibility of Tradition by simply indicating the divine character of the Church—its institution
and endowments. But now one has gone to the opposite extreme to those who list a series of activities. The Church is
not a simple organ with a uniform activity. Individuals act
as members of the Church, certainly, and to that extent the
Church acts and lives, but individuals can and do act first as
members of organs in the Church. A full account of Tradition
cannot discuss all activity together and en masse any more
than it can discuss a series of activities independently of their
organs.

[17] art. cit., p. 290.

3. TRADITION IS THE 'SENSUS FIDEI'

A third approach, rather than attach different activities to different organs of the one Church, prefers to connect active tradition with a supernatural factor that is in fact common to all members of the Church, the 'sensus fidei'. We have already examined the nature and value of the 'sensus fidei', as one criterion, one expression of tradition. Let us see now how it fares when asked to account for the whole of Church Tradition.

Perhaps it is unfair to take Dillenschneider's essay as an attempt to describe Church Tradition in this way. From the title of the work it seems to be concerned with the 'sensus fidei' only as a factor in the development of Marian dogma.[18] But as the book proceeds it becomes clear that the author thinks of Tradition as the handing on of doctrine by development; of the development of doctrine precisely as the work of the 'sensus fidei'; and of the importance of some recent Marian definitions as pointers to these facts. Consequently the work contains many definitions or descriptions of Tradition in terms of this understanding of the faith and qualifies for examination here.[19]

Tradition is defined as "the living understanding of the faith which manifests itself, in the ensemble of the teaching and hearing Church".[20] Tradition is the 'sensus fidei' in the universal Church, but manifested, expressed—"qui se manifeste". An intuition of the revealed truth, a grasp of revelation, an internal faith or belief, no matter how vital or developing cannot be called Tradition. By such internal faith doctrine may be conserved by an individual or group for one generation but it cannot be handed on—and such handing

---

[18] Dillenschneider, *Le Sens de la Foi et le Progrès Dogmatique du Mystère Marial.*

[19] op. cit., p. 106. For a practical illustration of his concept of Tradition, cf. Dillenschneider, art. 'L'Assomption Corporelle de Marie in *Assomption de Marie; Études Mariales, 6e année* (1948), pp. 43, 46 ff.

[20] Dillenschneider, op. cit., p. 113.

on of truth is Tradition—unless it be expressed in some way.[21] The faith of the individual member and that of the whole Church is always an essential factor in Tradition for the truths of Revelation are possessed by being believed, but they cannot be handed on without an activity that is external. Much of the value of the external expression depends on the depth and perspicacity of the internal faith. Yet it is this external activity that forms the active element in Tradition properly speaking.

What part does the Magisterium play in Dillenschneider's view of Tradition? In the section of the work in which he specifically deals with the relationship of the Magisterium with the 'sensus fidei', he describes that relationship as threefold. First, the Magisterium exercises a watching brief over the 'sensus fidei' in its expressions.[22] Secondly, since definitions of the Magisterium are not arbitrary and it receives no direct inspiration but only a divine assistance to decide what is in fact the faith of the Church, the 'sensus fidei' is for the Magisterium, not indeed a regulator to be obeyed—but a datum to be known.[23] Lastly, the Magisterium and it alone discerns infallibly what is in fact the universal belief of the Church.[24]

From this account of the doctrinal activity of the Magisterium it is obvious that it should be incorporated into a full concept of Tradition: unless Dillenschneider is thinking of the activity of the Magisterium as the mechanical handing on of truths—which are explicit or already fully developed by the 'sensus fidei'—which he has shown himself loth to term Tradition earlier on.[25] All the more will the term Tradition need to cover a wider sphere of activity than the 'sensus fidei' once Dillenschneider himself restricts the efficacy of the 'sensus fidei', as do most theologians, to truths of the faith which

---

[21] Strictly, then, the active tradition described should be an external activity. So that the description of active tradition given by Berthier: "mens Ecclesiae sub speciali Dei providentia est medium necessarium, quo transmittendae sunt traditiones divinae"—J. J. Berthier, *Tractatus de Locis Theologicis*, Taurini, 1900 (reprint), p. 42—is unsatisfactory.

[22] Dillenschneider, op. cit., p. 343.   [23] op. cit., p. 349.
[24] op. cit., p. 357.   [25] op. cit., pp. 108, 109.

directly affect the general body of the faithful in the Church.[26] Yet he always defines Tradition simply as the 'sensus fidei'. And that neither does justice to the role of the Magisterium in Tradition nor does it even fully describe the role of Tradition in the development of Marian dogma. Dillenschneider has certainly formulated a definition of Tradition but the principal object of his work—the description of the role of the 'sensus fidei' in doctrinal development—hindered him from completing it. Let us consider Koster's contribution, then, for he also defines Tradition with reference to the 'sensus fidei' or 'Glaubensinn' in the universal Church but he expressly attempts to connect it with a variety of activities according as it belongs to the different organs that are active in Tradition.

Koster will have the activity of the Magisterium in presenting the deposit to the faithful and in defining the result of authentic development to be counted part of active tradition, but then Koster links the activity of the Magisterium as such in a particular way with 'Glaubensinn'. Where Dillenschneider regarded that development of dogma which was in fact Tradition as proceeding apace in the whole Church and according to a universal developing 'sensus fidei', Koster envisages different parts or organs of the Church developing dogma as their own particular 'Glaubensinn' develops.[27] We have already described how he distinguished and treated separately the 'Glaubensinn' of the ordinary faithful, the 'Glaubensinn' of the Fathers and that of the Theologians. The 'Glaubensinn' of the Magisterium is also for Koster a thing apart.[28] A particular truth may develop from the deposit of Revelation in any of these four ways: it may be drawn from its implicit state in the deposit and be brought to the notice of the Magisterium by any of these four agencies, or by a

[26] op. cit., pp. 329 ff.
[27] cf. J. Beumer, art. 'Glaubensinn der Kirche', in T.T.Z., 61 Jahrg. (1952), pp. 137, 138, for a criticism of Koster's claiming official support for his teaching on the nature and function of the Glaubensinn from statements of Trent, the Vatican and 'Mystici Corporis'. The claim is unjustified. Cf. Koster, op. cit., p. 68.
[28] op. cit., p. 73.

combination of them.[29] Hence Koster's account of the complexity of active tradition in the Church involves a numerical division of members of the Church into four groups, all mutually exclusive.

Active tradition in the Church is thought to take place in three stages. In the first stage—"general elementary tradition"[30]—the deposit is made available to the faithful by presenting to them the simple Creeds or the Scriptures or by teaching them the practice of the Christian Religion. This is apparently the work of the Magisterium, and it seems to be an expression of 'Glaubensinn'.[31] This 'Glaubensinn' of theirs is endowed with the charism of infallibility.[32]

The second stage in Tradition—"incomplete active tradition"—is seen in a constant teaching of the Magisterium that has not reached yet the universality or certainty that would show it to be infallible, a constant and universal practice of the faithful, a universal teaching of the Fathers or Theologians.[33] At this stage there is no infallibility.

The third and final stage of Tradition—"complete Tradition"—is reached with an infallible and express teaching by the Magisterium of the truth developed in any of the ways mentioned in the second stage.[34] As in the first stage of Tradition this, too, is the expression of the 'Glaubensinn' of the Magisterium which is infallible. Here, then, is a complete attempt to explain the whole of Church Tradition in all its complexity in terms of 'Glaubensinn' or 'sensus fidei'.

In criticism it must be said that the distinction between the witnessing of Fathers and Theologians and the witnessing of the faithful is not sufficiently expressed, as Koster thinks, solely in terms of 'Glaubensinn'. The activity proper to Fathers and to the great Theologians, i.e. the writing

---

[29] Koster, op. cit., p. 135.   [30] op. cit., p. 95.

[31] Beumer's criticism of Koster for some confusion in discussing subjective and objective Glaubensinn is not altogether just. Cf. Beumer, art. cit., p. 130.

[32] op. cit., p. 73.

[33] op. cit., pp. 95, 96. In view of this stage it is very hard to understand why Müller (art. cit., p. 180) and Schmaus (op. cit., p. 773) link Koster with Deneffe and Dieckmann in a purely Tradition-magisterium concept.   [34] cf. op. cit., pp. 96, 135.

proper to ecclesiastical writers, indicates more than a higher degree of gifts and graces from the Holy Spirit—although it indicates that, too. It indicates great natural gifts of intellect and powers of expression. The distinction between the organs in the Church is a distinction of activities indicating a distinction of qualifications. Perhaps it is better to say: a distinction of levels of activity indicating a distinct level of qualifications, for the same persons can be active on different levels and so can belong to different organs. Hence Koster is wrong in maintaining that these organs are mutually exclusive. A Theologian can act on the level of the ordinary faithful and have his activity judged as part of the activity of the universal Church, as an expression of 'Glaubensinn'. He does so whenever his acts are the acts of everyday life that express his beliefs. When he engages in activities proper to a Theologian— the theoretical research, in writing, into revealed truth—his activity is judged as part of the activity of another group. It is no longer evaluated in terms of 'Glaubensinn' and certainly not in terms of a 'Glaubensinn' described as simply as Koster describes it, simply the result of graces and gifts.

But more serious is Koster's connection of the infallibility of the Magisterium with the 'Glaubensinn' of the pastors. If the nature and value of the active tradition of the Fathers cannot be explained solely in terms of 'Glaubensinn', 'a priori' that of the teaching of the Magisterium cannot. As Müller very rightly points out, the infallibility of the Magisterium is regarded by theologians as a charism that belongs to an office independently of the personal graces and gifts of the incumbents.[35] The teaching of the Magisterium is not formally 'Glaubensinn'; it is not formally just an expression of the personal grasp of the truth by men equipped with the graces and gifts of ordinary dispensation. It is an expression of faith personally possessed, of course, but it is more than that. It is an official and authoritative public activity of teaching in the Church, commissioned by God and guaranteed by a special charism that is independent of any personal supernatural equipment.

Koster's account of the three stages of Tradition is too

[35] art. cit., pp. 184, 185.

mechanical. It is true, as Dillenschneider wrote and as Koster clearly implies, that the first and last word lies with the Magisterium, but the three-staged account of Tradition with which we are here presented gives no true picture of the constant communion between the Magisterium and those other bodies that are active in Tradition. It is not as if—and this is the impression we are given by Koster—the Magisterium presented simple truth to the universal Church and then withdrew its infallible teaching, at least in respect of the item of truth being developed, while one of the four activities mentioned in the second stage were developing that item of truth; only to become active again, to lend its decisive infallibility when the developing activity is over. If Scheeben writes that the belief of the faithful works back in influence upon the teaching of the Magisterium he does not mean that the Magisterium at a certain stage has suddenly to take notice of a development in which it had no integral part.[36] It is much more a question of continual dialogue of ever-developing infallible teaching and ever-developing belief that constantly influences infallible teaching. It is because of this uninterrupted dialogue over periods of time and development that the 'sensus fidei', the unanimous teaching of Fathers and Theologians can as we saw be called infallible, too. Koster does not wish these various witnesses to be called infallible and it is easy to see now why he does not.

4. TRADITION IS A DIALOGUE BETWEEN MAGISTERIUM AND FAITHFUL

Some contemporary theologians have sought to express a comprehensive concept of Tradition in these terms. In this way they hope to do justice to the complexity of Tradition while at the same time describing the activity in the setting of a supernatural organism.

[36] Such is the impression given by Koster when he writes that when the Holy Spirit chooses to bring a newly developed truth to the notice of the Magisterium by means of the Glaubensinn of the faithful, the Magisterium must follow his indication: cf. op. cit., p. 129, and Beumer, art. cit., p. 185.

The Magisterium and the general body of the faithful, to Geiselmann's way of thinking, are the parts which build the organism of which Tradition is a function.[37] The Magisterium has a particular teaching function to perform for the benefit of the whole Church while the activity that is proper to the faithful is simply the profession of personal belief.[38] But these two activities do not exist in isolation from one another. They affect each other and benefit each other. The dependence of the belief of the faithful on the teaching of the Magisterium is by far the more marked and the more beneficial to the faithful "for faith comes by hearing".[39] But the influence and benefit is not all one way. The faith of the Church professed in the lives of all the faithful can act too as an assistance and a support for the teaching of the Magisterium. Geiselmann says most of what Scheeben says about the belief of the faithful and in much the same language; but he does not call it, as Scheeben does, a "guiding factor", a guide for the teaching of the Magisterium, although he equivalently regards it as such in the context.[40]

Some contemporary theologians are so intent on assuring that Tradition belongs to the whole Church and is not confined to the Magisterium that they do not emphasise enough the part which the Magisterium plays in Tradition. Ternus[41] and Semmelroth[42] are examples of this eagerness, but any lack of due emphasis found in their treatment is corrected by others like Bacht and Schmaus who also use the 'dialogue' approach.[43] None of them do justice to the further complexity of active tradition that derives from the fact that other bodies can also be distinguished within the universal Church whose activities must be described if a complete picture of active tradition is to be attained.

Tradition is a function of the Church, the Mystical Body of Christ, in which organs act and re-act on each other. And there are more organs than the term 'dialogue' suggests. Because

---

[37] art. cit. *Die Tradition*, p. 105.   [38] ibid.   [39] art. cit., p. 106.
[40] cf. Geiselmann, art. cit., p. 106 and Scheeben, op. cit., p. 99.
[41] art. cit. Beiträge, pp. 38–40, 49–51.   [42] art. cit., pp. 7, 8.
[43] H. Bacht, art. 'Tradition als menschliches und theologisches Problem', in S.Z., 159 (1957), p. 297; Schmaus, op. cit., p. 774.

the Church is a living thing its activity involves development and, at times, decline. So it is in doctrinal activity,
too. In discussing the activities of the Magisterium, of the
Fathers of the Church, of Theologians and of the faithful,
we have already seen theologians describe something of the
interactivity between these organs in the Church and of the
development of dogma that is involved in this interactivity.
The doctrine assumes a different form in its passage from the
preaching of the Magisterium into the minds and works of
the Fathers and Theologians, into the faith and lives of the
faithful. It is somewhere along these lines that the activity
which is at once tradition and development of dogma is likely
to be found fully described.

Before examining what we think to be the best description
of a comprehensive concept of Church Tradition found in
this period, it is useful to devote a short section to Catholic
thought on Apostolic Tradition.

5. Apostolic Tradition

The Tradition of the Apostles has begun to loom large in
the inter-confessional discussions on Tradition in recent times.
It is normal nowadays to find Neo-Protestants emphasise the
existence of oral Tradition in apostolic times, a factor in the
apostolic Church that is described by the Scriptures themselves. "Of the existence in the primitive Church of a large
body of oral tradition which antedated the New Testament
there can no longer be any doubt"—so wrote J. R. Nelson.[44]
This oral Tradition of the Apostles transmitted the Christian
truth in its earliest stages. It does not follow, however, that Neo-
Protestants now admit that a later oral Tradition transmits
Christianity with an equal or an equivalent right. Cullmann
particularly, as we shall see, placed Apostolic Tradition in a
place apart. To him it had no successor in any way comparable
to itself. Hence Catholic theology must say what it thinks of
Apostolic Tradition, what was special about it and if that speci-
ality prevented a later transmission from carrying on its task.

[44] J. R. Nelson, art. 'Tradition and Traditions as an Ecumenical Problem', in *Theology Today*, 13 (1956), p. 155.

In recent Catholic theology much of the reference to Apostolic Tradition has been used to offset the Tradition-magisterium trend of thought. So when Dejaifve has to reply to the objection that the Magisterium defines what it likes, what it finds in its own heart,[45] he emphasises the fact that the Magisterium is at all times subject to the apostolic teaching—i.e. a body of truth constituted by the activity of the Apostles in the Church.[46] We have seen something similar in Proulx; and Baumgartner puts this in a slightly different way when he maintains that the active tradition of the Magisterium is essentially subordinate to the active tradition of the Apostles.[47] And lest it be thought that Catholic theologians write such things merely under pressure of a strong objection, it can be pointed out that the same type of thought is found in more disinterested contexts. Bartmann[48] and Schultes[49] are both concerned primarily with Apostolic Tradition. Bartmann is more interested in the objective element in working out his definition and they both insist that Apostolic Tradition is a rule of faith for the Church of all ages.

Catholics and non-Catholics find themselves in agreement on this one point, then, viz. that the Apostolic Tradition is normative for the whole future of the Church. But Cullmann deduces from this that the Apostolic Tradition is found now in Scripture and that nothing else can strictly be called a norm in the post-apostolic Church. Catholic theology, on the other hand, holds that the Apostolic Tradition has been transmitted integrally also by the life and preaching and faith of the Church and that, furthermore, there exists in this Church a divinely commissioned and guaranteed body of teachers to express for the benefit of individual believers the content of this Apostolic Tradition as it is held in the life and faith of the whole Church. The teaching of this body is normative in its own way. The precise point with which we are here concerned, however, is this: how does Catholic theology describe the special position allowed to Apostolic Tradition? Later on it will be useful to see if Cullmann in particular allows any

---

[45] cf. Chapter I, sec. 5.   [46] Dejaifve, art. cit. Bible, pp. 146, 147.
[47] Above, pp. 47 ff.   [48] op. cit., pp. 28–30, 36.
[49] op. cit., pp. 575, 576, 581 ff.

more to Apostolic Tradition than Catholic theology does, for, if not, he has little solid justification on that score for denying it any comparable successor.

The question of the precise nature of Apostolic Tradition is, naturally, a question of Biblical exegesis to a great extent. And Lengsfeld complains that the Biblical theology of Tradition has so far been largely neglected by Catholic theology. Ranft and Geiselmann have provided much of the material for such a theology[50] and Lengsfeld himself makes a contribution to it.

It has been noted already in dealing with the Tradition-magisterium concept that Deneffe distinguished what he termed the constitutive Tradition of the Apostles from the continuative Tradition of the Church but that he was mainly interested in the similar authority which characterised both Traditions; that Journet, on the other hand, spoke of an illumination, equivalent to revelation which was proper to the Apostles in their activity and which marked off their Tradition from that of the later Church.[51] Now Geiselmann also lays much stress on the fact that the Apostles were taught by the Holy Spirit.[52] He knows that they were eye-witnesses but if that means only that they actually witnessed with the senses a certain number of physical events it does not go far to explain their place in the Christian economy. It was the revealed word, the teaching which specified the nature and the significance of the salvation events, the supernatural faith which enabled them to receive this teaching and, above all, the revelatory influence of the Holy Spirit which showed them the truth in it; that is what made the Apostles' teaching so important.[53] The Apostle Paul was not an eye-witness of the earthly life of Christ (he did, of course, come in contact with the risen Lord on the road to Damascus) and yet he could say that he did not receive his gospel from men but "by the revelation of Jesus Christ" (Gal. i. 12).[54] What marks off the high importance of the Apostles therefore is not so much the

---

[50] Peter Lengsfeld, *Überlieferung*, Paderborn, 1960, p. 17.
[51] Above, pp. 34 ff.   [52] art. cit. *Die Tradition,* p. 99.
[53] Geiselmann, art. cit. *Die Tradition,* pp. 83–4, 99.
[54] cf. Lengsfeld, op. cit., p. 41.

fact that they witnessed physical events or heard words, for so did many others, nor the fact that they had the faith to receive the teaching of Christ concerning the events, for so have we, but the fact that Christ sent his Spirit with a special mission to them. "I have yet many things to say to you: but you cannot bear them now. But when he, the Spirit of truth, is come, he will teach you all truth" (John xvi. 12–13).

It is this special mission of the Holy Spirit to the Apostles that Geiselmann and Schell have mainly in mind when they say that the Apostles were "the ones who received the Revelation".[55] It is this, too, they have in mind when they say that the teaching of the Apostles was more divine where the preaching of the Church is more human, that the teaching of the Apostles could be called God's Word in a sense in which the teaching of the Church could not be called God's Word.[56] Of course, they do not mean to say that the teaching of the post-apostolic Church is a purely human affair, for the activity of the Holy Spirit did not cease completely with the death of the Apostles. But, as Congar puts it, "now there is only *assistance* to transmit, whereas then there was *inspiration* or the gift of revelation. Certainly, the same Holy Spirit is at work now as he was then: that is the reason for the fundamental homogeneity of the two times. But he does not intervene in the same way now." [57] Before describing more fully this fundamental homogeneity, can anything further be said about this special influence of the Holy Spirit on the Apostles? Geiselmann is inclined to limit it somewhat in extent because, he writes, there were instances of Tradition within the Apostolic Body itself and that would make revelation or illumination unnecessary. Paul received some of his teachings when he went to Jerusalem and he had the benefit therefore of other Apostles' inspired knowledge of Revelation. Geiselmann suggests that there may have been more instances of this type of Tradition within the Apostolic Body itself.[58]

Because of this prophetic illumination which the Apostles

[55] cf. Schell, op. cit., p. 160.
[56] cf. Geiselmann, art. cit. *Die Tradition*, p. 81 and Schell, op. cit., pp. 159, 160.   [57] op. cit., *Die Tradition*, p. 259.
[58] Geiselmann, art. cit. *Die Tradition*, pp. 85, 86.

received the faithful of apostolic times exercised at most a negative influence on the development of doctrine that took place in the apostolic Church.[59] They did not have a positive contribution to make as they did in the post-apostolic Church,[60] but in so far as particular difficulties arose in the lives of the new communities or particular questions came from the faithful of those years, one development of apostolic teaching rather than another was demanded. "Suppose", writes Journet, "that the Corinthians, instead of provoking Paul to speak of marriage, idolatry and the Lord's Supper, had asked him if original sin in its universal application had reached even the Mother of the Son of God." [61] The Apostles did not need to examine the faith of the Church as the later Magisterium needs to do.

In view of the special qualifications of the Apostles, then, what is to be said on the subject of the special authority of Apostolic Tradition? The truth taught can be authoritative because the teacher was divinely commissioned to teach it. In this sense Apostolic Tradition has no authority that is proper to it alone. The Apostles were the first teachers commissioned by Christ but, in the Catholic view, they were not the last. The truth can be authoritative in a looser sense because of the qualifications of those who taught it. And in this sense the Apostolic Tradition had an authority that was not transmissible. The Apostles taught under an influence of active revelation which did not outlive them. Hence they constituted the deposit of Revelation and closed it when they ceased to preach. This apostolic deposit was made over into the faith of the Church and the preaching of the Church has been bound to its limits ever since.

So the preeminent position of the Apostles must be maintained but a fundamental homogeneity of Tradition in apostolic and post-apostolic times must also be admitted. There was teaching of the faith commissioned by Christ and with help from his Spirit in each of these times. But the homogeneity is wider than that. The Apostles were not the only ones who were active in Traditions in apostolic times. Tavard

[59] cf. Geiselmann, art. cit. *Die Tradition*, p. 90; Proulx, op. cit., p. 283.
[60] cf. Scheeben, op. cit., pp. 109, 110.   [61] op. cit., *Esquisse*, p. 27.

has written: "As 'God's own people' (1 Pet. ii. 9), the Christians of apostolic times would declare the wonderful deeds of God: they had heard from the apostles the message of apostolic faith and they were able, with the help of the Paraclete, to transmit it. 'God's own people', as a fellowship of prayer which is also bound by a consensus in faith, could not be wrong in their declaration of the wonderful deeds of God." [62] And Schell has added further to the description of homogeneity: the Apostles handed on truth not only by oral preaching but by action and institution. Their preaching obviously had a content of truth but the handing on of truth was implied in their building up the Church institutions and in their ordering of Church worship, too. [63]

6. Tradition according to Scheeben [64]

If Tradition is regarded as something extraordinarily difficult to define, it is more because so many elements go to make up the concept of Tradition that a full definition would be unwieldy and a short definition insufficient than because these elements cannot be fairly accurately isolated and described in themselves. In Heinrich's work most of the elements that belong to the definition of Tradition can be found but his definition of Tradition—although it is unwieldy enough— does not contain many of them. [65] Scheeben nowhere presumes to define Tradition. He describes it at length and with many cross-references to other contexts. He did not say everything that is to be said about Tradition, nor even everything that we have seen the other theologians in the period say. But he did account for all the essential elements that go to make up the concept and described their relationships to each other so well that the last word may safely be left to him.

Scheeben is as much conscious as any theologian in the

[62] Tavard, art. cit., p. 239.   [63] Schell, op. cit., p. 158.
[64] For an introduction to Scheeben's ecclesiology and for a slightly different view of some of the matter presented here, see W. Bartz, *Die Lehrende Kirche; Ein Betrag zur Ekklesiologie M. J. Scheeben*, Trier, 1959. Also idem, art. 'Le Magistère de l'Église d'après Scheeben', in *R.S.R.*, 124–6 (1960), pp. 309 ff.   [65] Heinrich, op. cit., vol. II, p. 11.

period of the Protestant position on Tradition and of the necessity of an answer for it.[66] He begins to answer the Protestant position and to describe the fate of Christian doctrine after its revelation by insisting, as much as Franzelin insists, on the divinely appointed teaching body as not only an organ willed by God but an organ without which the task of bringing revealed truth integrally to all those people for whom it is intended could not be accomplished.[67] But he does not end by describing Tradition only in terms of the authentic teaching of this body. His concept of Tradition is much wider.

He describes the constitutive Tradition of the Apostles—without using that term. The Apostles handed over to the communities which they had founded the whole content of the Revelation they had received.[68] They handed on also the hierarchical powers to those who should follow them and lead their communities after them. Hence the apostolic deposit or the apostolic tradition was placed in the Church as in a living treasury, for all time. This handing over of the content of Revelation on the part of the Apostles was twofold—by writings and by word of mouth. Yet, since the written deposit had a worth and an existence of its own beyond that which belonged to the spoken word, the truth passed on orally is generally called Apostolic Tradition in the narrower sense; the spoken word exists only in the living act of tradition. Hence Apostolic Tradition is distinguished from the Scriptures at this stage. Both make up the apostolic deposit which is a source of faith for all future time.[69]

The whole apostolic deposit—the Apostolic Tradition properly so-called, i.e. the truth that came to the Church by word of mouth, together with the Scriptures—is handed on in the Church and by the Church as a living body, but particularly by the perennial Magisterium which succeeds to the functions of the apostolate. Nor is this further handing on a mechanical business of mere continual reference to truths once received. It involves insight. Clarification and development of the truth

---

[66] Scheeben, op. cit., pp. 41 ff.   [67] op. cit., pp. 46 ff., and esp. p. 63.
[68] op. cit., pp. 110, 111.
[69] This is a résumé of Scheeben, op. cit., p. 111.

such as the Apostles themselves would have provided had they lived on are now demanded of the Church.

This activity of the post-apostolic Church is called active Church tradition while the whole deposit as it is now the object of this activity and as, through this activity, it reaches future generations, is objective Church Tradition.[70] Yet here again, since the written deposit has an existence and a worth of its own apart from this activity of the Church, while the oral deposit exists only in and through this activity, Church Tradition in the narrower and traditional sense refers only to the handing on of the oral deposit.[71]

In this second and more proper sense of the word, then, Church Tradition formally and materially, in act and object, represents the oral Tradition of the Apostles and is an adequate stream or canal through which the truths of the source, the oral deposit of the Apostles, reach down the ages. Since from this stream the men of all times can derive the truth which the Apostles taught in constituting the deposit of faith, it is also called a source of Revelation for them but in a secondary sense: the title belongs primarily to the deposit as it was constituted by Apostolic Tradition.[72] The word 'stream' expresses better than the word 'source', Scheeben seems to think, the transmission down the ages. It remains now to describe Church Tradition in detail.

It is immediately after he has described the setting up of the authentic Magisterium in the Church and in connection with its preaching activity that Scheeben begins to discuss Tradition.[73] And his first distinction is important. Authoritative preaching, he writes, is distinguished from Tradition but not separable from it. By one and the same activity the characteristics of Tradition and the characteristics that are proper to authoritative preaching are placed. For authoritative preaching does in fact bring truth forward from the past and passes it on to the future generations.[74] And that is the characteristic of Tradition. Yet authoritative preaching has characteristics proper to itself by which it is formally distinguished from Tradition. It places its own official stamp

---

[70] op. cit., p. 112.   [71] ibid.   [72] ibid. Cf. Schell, op. cit., p. 158.
[73] op. cit., p. 108.   [74] op. cit., p. 109.

on truth. It vindicates, authenticates, officially recognises the truth. Scheeben uses the word 'Geltendmachung' for this effect.[75] When Tradition is seen precisely as truth that is handed down the ages, truth in transit, it seems destined for this final vindication. So the act that is characterised by its handing on of truth involves or demands an act that will authenticate the truth handed on. In authoritative preaching both elements or characteristics are present. Under the aspect of the former it is Tradition; under the aspect of the latter it is formally authenticating and authoritative.[76]

Although Billot did show some tendency to distinguish two formalities in magisterium, two aspects of official teaching, and to regard it as Tradition under one aspect only, he almost nullified the impression later on.[77] Semmelroth, on the contrary, insisted so much on the formality of authoritative preaching by which it authenticated truths handed on by Tradition that one was left wondering whether this preaching were itself Tradition at all or not.[78] To Scheeben's way of thinking authoritative preaching has the characteristics that make it Tradition but it also has characteristics which make it something more than Tradition and, to that extent, distinct.

The distinction is of importance for this reason. It prevents one who seeks to know what Tradition is and where it is from looking first for that final authoritative and authenticating element which belongs only to the one organ possessing the charism of infallibility in view of its mission. That precise type of authority and that official authentication is not demanded of Tradition as such. It was precisely for including this characteristic, this authority of divinely instituted teaching in the concept of Tradition that Scheeben criticised Franzelin. "The word (Tradition) is too weak in itself to express the authoritative aspect of preaching and . . . normally it is understood to specify only the transmission of doctrine." [79]

We have already noticed that Scheeben pointed to a distinction between the Tradition of the Apostles and the Tradition of their followers in office. In the apostolic body the whole of Revelation was grasped as a personal possession with un-

[75] ibid.   [76] ibid.   [77] cf. above, p. 26.
[78] art. cit., pp. 8 ff.   [79] op. cit., p. 110.

equalled depth of insight. The Magisterium is not expected to be in the same immediate and full possession of the truth of Revelation at any particular time. Most likely here, when there is question of the Magisterium not being in as full a possession of revealed truth as the Apostles, it is a matter of depth of insight or powers of insight rather than a matter of extent of knowledge. Scheeben presumably does not mean that some part of Revelation is not in the possession of the Magisterium at times and is supplied by other bearers of Tradition, but only that other bearers of Tradition can help supply a new insight now as they could not to the Apostles. For the deposit of Revelation is channelled down from the source, from apostolic preaching, by the activity of the whole Church.[80]

As a result of the difference between apostolic and Church Tradition, then, a further distinction can be seen, within Church Tradition itself, between Tradition and authoritative preaching. In Church Tradition these are no longer merely distinct aspects of one and the same act, for Tradition is now a wider thing than authoritative preaching: it belongs to the whole Church.[81] Authoritative preaching belongs to one organ in the Church that carries Tradition. Yet even after this further distinction it must be noted that authoritative teaching and the whole Church Tradition are intimately bound together: "by reason of the organic and vital unity of the Church".[82] This close relationship we shall consider later on.

This is the type of thought on Tradition that should satisfy Baumgartner and all the exigencies which he places for the concept of Tradition in view of the 'modus loquendi' of official Church proclamations. Here is a Tradition which is a source of Revelation distinct from magisterium in that it is broader than it and even formally distinct from it in its material coincidence with it: a real source of doctrine for the Magisterium of each age.

[80] op. cit., pp. 109, 110.
[81] Michel unceremoniously—and wrongly—numbers Scheeben with those who identify Tradition with magisterium, on the strength of a single quotation. Cf. Michel, art. cit., col. 1339.
[82] Scheeben, op. cit., p. 110.

As Scheeben has described Church Tradition in general as an activity of all those who have part in the life and riches of the Church, so he now describes in general the value and guarantees of Church Tradition. It involves a human contribution, he writes, but not merely that. Not every one can take part in Tradition; only those who are members of the Church and as long as they remain members of the Church. Tradition belongs to that organic community which is vivified and guided by the Holy Spirit.[83] Hence the witness which Tradition bears and is, is witness of the Holy Spirit; the value of that witness is not derived from a natural community of men whether simple or learned but from a community's relationship to the Holy Spirit. The witness, then, is always guaranteed, infallible.[84] Because it is men who are active, however, the witness will never reach ideal and absolute perfection. Because the Holy Spirit does not influence the Church today to the same extent as he influenced the Apostles, the witness of the truth of Revelation will not reach the perfection which the Apostles' witness reached.[85] Yet that Tradition which belongs to an infallible and indefectible Church will always be present integrally in the Church.[86]

Scheeben has said that all who take part in the life and riches of the Church play their part also in handing on the truth "each in his own way".[87] He has thereby indicated a variety of activity in Tradition. It is now necessary to describe these various activities and yet in such a way that the guarantees which belong to Church Tradition can all the time be clearly seen.

Tradition belongs to the category of expression. Truth is only handed on by being expressed. Hence Scheeben describes the variety of activity which belongs to Tradition in the Church by writing of the various forms of expression, the various manifestations of Tradition in the Church.[88]

Because the Church is a living organism the expressions of the truth it possesses can be varied. Because development of

---

[83] Scheeben, op. cit., p. 152.   [84] op. cit., pp. 152, 153.
[85] op. cit., pp. 153, 154.   [86] op. cit., pp. 154 ff.   [87] op. cit., p. 110.
[88] op. cit., p. 152: "Äusserungen". op. cit., p. 169: "Erscheinungsformen der aktuellen Tradition".

truth is involved and it is not to be expected that truth will develop 'pari passu' in all parts or organs of the Church, the expressions of that truth must be varied.[89] But, keeping always in mind that guarantee which must belong to Tradition, Scheeben discusses the forms of expression which appear as guaranteed forms and, in fact, as infallible testimonies of the Holy Spirit.[90] He could distinguish and discuss the different forms of expression in terms of the different types of acts of expression—practical, oral, written, etc.—but he discusses them, in fact, in terms of the different organs in the Church from which they proceed. For then he can indicate the guarantee that goes with them because of the places of these organs in the Church. And the different types of activity involved are mentioned in passing anyway.[91] Two themes have already helped him to explain the nature of Church Tradition, namely, the organic nature of the Church and the perennial magisterium that is in it. These same two themes now help to explain the nature and value of the different forms of expression, the activities which can be distinguished in Church Tradition as well as that development of doctrine which is inseparable from it.[92]

We have already—in Chapters I to III—examined the organs in the Church which express and so hand on truth and we have seen the guarantees which their various expressions possessed. It suffices to enumerate them from Scheeben here. He first mentions the belief of the faithful as a secondary expression of revealed doctrine.[93] It is the profession of the faith which every member of the Church receives from the Magisterium by the grace of the Holy Spirit and makes part of everyday life: a relatively autonomous and immediate testimony of the Holy Spirit who is active in the whole Church. It is a profession of personal faith undistinguished by any great gifts, natural or supernatural.[94]

---

[89] op. cit., p. 159.   [90] ibid.   [91] ibid.
[92] op. cit., pp. 151, 152.   [93] op. cit., pp. 160 ff., 97 ff.
[94] Mainly for lack of this necessary and continuous connection with the true and infallible Magisterium of the Roman Catholic Church, the profession of such orthodox faith as they possess (by e.g. Protestants) is not counted in Tradition although they, too, have the graces and gifts

The primary form of expression of revealed truth is that which belongs to the Church Magisterium. It has its own charism of infallibility. It is the authentic witness to tradition.[95] As well as pointing out this organ of Tradition Scheeben also indicates where in practice its teachings are most readily seen. They are seen in the teaching of the ordinary clergy (who are instruments of the Magisterium by ordination and mission in a way that Fathers and Theologians as such are not)[96] and of the theological schools. Scheeben writes of 'a certain autonomy' in this teaching of the clergy as a middle factor between bishops and faithful.[97] But it is not "a relatively autonomous and immediate witness of the Holy Spirit" as the belief of the faithful, for instance, is.[98] No direct influence of the Holy Spirit to the clergy as such and sufficient to allow their teaching to be called Tradition in its own right is envisaged. The part of the ordinary clergy in Tradition here described is that of an instrument of the episcopacy.

The central bearer of Tradition within the Magisterium itself Scheeben names the 'Sedes Apostolica'. The expression of truth from this organ is seen in the infallible teaching of the Pope himself. In an analogous way to that in which the teaching of the universal Magisterium can be known from the teaching of the clergy, so the teaching of the Popes is preserved and expressed in the Roman Church.[99]

Finally there is the teaching of Fathers and Theologians par excellence; a written expression of their insights into doctrine taught them by the Magisterium, from men of outstanding natural and supernatural gifts.[100]

In the light of this description of the complexity of active

---

of the Holy Spirit and are therefore attached to the Church in a way. They are not fully guaranteed agents in Tradition according to this Catholic view.

[95] Scheeben, op. cit., pp. 161, 162.   [96] op. cit., p. 95.   [97] op. cit., p. 162.

[98] op. cit., p. 160. Cf. op. cit., p. 96, for a similar appraisal of the teaching of Fathers and Theologians.

[99] op. cit., pp. 163 ff. There is more to Scheeben's thought about the local Roman Church as the centre of orthodoxy but it is not easy to say to what exactly it amounts. In any case it does not essentially affect the main sequence of his thought on Tradition which is presented here.

[100] op. cit., pp. 166 ff.

tradition or expression of revealed truth in the Church and
of what we have already learned from Scheeben about the
Magisterium, the faithful, the Fathers and Theologians, it becomes clear that Scheeben's concept of Tradition is as follows:
the revealed truth is expressed or handed on by these various
organs in the Church, by the faithful mostly in the practice
of their daily life, by Fathers and Theologians in writing, by
the Magisterium in teaching that is infallible ex officio. The
organs act and re-act on one another in the organic unity of
the Church. The Magisterium infallibly teaches all members
and so all organs, but the Magisterium can be helped and
guided by them, too, since it does not possess the same equipment and the same depth of insight as the Apostles possessed.
Individual members of the Church can belong to more than
one of these organs in so far as they possess the characteristics
and perform the activities proper to more than one organ. The
value and guarantee which the activity or expression of truth
by any organ possesses comes from its connection with magisterium and its direct connection with the Holy Spirit. Because
of the inter-activity between the organs, development of doctrine is inseparable from Tradition.[101] For none of the organs
receives the truth mechanically from the Magisterium and
none of them mechanically hands it back. The Fathers of the
Church were men of great endowments. So were and are the
Great Theologians. The truth reveals depths to them that
other members of the Church could never see without them.
But every member of the Church who weds the truth to daily
life is open to his own peculiar insights for the revealed truth
has its own dynamism. It is no lifeless formula that comes
from the Magisterium and returns to it again. Here is expressed at once the vitality of Tradition, the complexity of
Tradition and the unity of Tradition—in terms, as Scheeben said, of two themes: an organic Church and a perennial
Magisterium.

[101] B. Fraigneau-Julien, *L'Église et le Caractère Sacrementel selon
M. J. Scheeben,* Desclee de Brouwer, 1958, p. 264.

F

Chapter Five

THE TWO SOURCES

"Tradition is not simply a reflection of the light which shines from Scripture, it is itself a source of light."
PROULX, *Tradition et Protestantisme*, p. 188

ACCORDING to Catholic theology there are two sources of Revelation; Scripture and Tradition. These two sources do not exist in isolation from each other. Their relationships can be usefully discussed here in order to throw a little further light on the theology of Tradition in this period.

1. PARTIM-PARTIM

The first effect which a consideration of the relationships of Scripture to Tradition can have on the thought of theologians is to induce them to limit Tradition in its objective element to truths which, they claim, are not contained in Scripture. The tendency to such limitation derived some of its force, no doubt, from its apparent usefulness in polemics against the early Protestants.[1] But the concept of Tradition that results from such limitation has found little enough support in the period under review.

It is sometimes found enumerated in a series of concepts or definitions which are graded according to strictness or accuracy. So we get it from Muncunill, for example.

> Generally speaking, Tradition can be defined as the speculative or practical doctrine received from Christ or the Apostles and transmitted to us; but more properly it is this speculative or practical doctrine received *orally* from Christ or the Apostles and transmitted to us; and in its most strict sense it is that doctrine received orally from Christ and the Apostles and trans-

---

[1] cf. Pohle, art. cit., col. 1940.

mitted to us, which is not contained either explicitly or implicitly in the Holy Scripture.[2]

But we are not told if this last and strictest sense of the term is to be regarded as the proper concept of Tradition in Catholic theology.

Some theologians begin plainly with a definition of Tradition in which the objective element is limited to truths allegedly not contained in Scripture.[3] This is the case with Tanquerey who defines Tradition as: "doctrine, not found in the Scriptures, but transmitted infallible from age to age by the authentic pastors of the Church".[4] but as his discussion proceeds he nullifies the effect of this definition by writing of objective tradition in terms of 'inherent tradition, declarative tradition and purely oral tradition', i.e. tradition which is also contained explicitly or implicitly or not contained at all in Scripture.[5] He does at one stage refer to this wider objective tradition as belonging to a concept of Tradition in a wider sense,[6] but this wider concept is the one that underlies the subsequent treatment of Tradition in his work. The same inconsistency between definition and further discussion is found even more clearly in Hervé's treatment of the subject.[7]

There are very few theologians in the period, but there are some, who define Tradition with this limited objective element and maintain that definition in their further treatment of the subject. Zubizarreta is perhaps the best example of such an approach.[8] And yet, almost as if this position on Tradition just cannot be consistently maintained, he writes

[2] Muncunill, op. cit., pp. 109, 110.
[3] If the word 'allegedly' is used in this context it is not with any intention of prejudging an issue yet to be raised but only to indicate that another view does hold that there are no truths of Revelation not contained somehow in Scripture.
[4] Tanquerey, op. cit., p. 619.   [5] ibid.   [6] op. cit., p. 618.
[7] Hervé, op. cit., pp. 537, 538. Cf. also Perennes, art. cit., cols. 1784, 1785; he gives a list of concepts similar to that noted above from Muncunill, declares that the last and strictest one is the normal concept of Tradition in theological use and yet distinguishes inherent, declarative and constitutive tradition.
[8] V. Zubizarreta, *Theologia Dogmatico-Scholastica*, vol. I, ed. 4, Bilbao, 1948, p. 506.

later that Tradition preceded Scripture in time and that the material extent of Tradition is wider than that of Scripture doctrine,[9] both of which statements would seem to involve a wider concept of Tradition than that allowed in his definition.[10]

There is no need to prove at any length at this stage that this notion of Tradition, the objective element of which is so limited, is not an adequate notion. It is legitimate, provided that it can be shown that there are truths of Revelation not contained in Scripture either explicitly or implicitly—for the notion depends entirely on this fact—and provided, too, that it be admitted that the objective element in this notion of Tradition changed constantly in extent until such time as the Canon of Scripture was materially complete. This limited notion of Tradition is one which has found adherents not only in the period under review but in most centuries of Christian thought. This Proulx very fairly admits and illustrates.[11] But he insists too that the notion of Tradition which regards it as containing all of Revelation as its objective element is the adequate notion.[12] He points out in this connection that the Apostles were ordered to preach and did in fact preach all the truth committed to their care by Christ.[13] The whole deposit was transmitted to the Church independently of the writing of Scripture and it has been transmitted by the preaching and teaching and practice of the whole Church since that. An oral deposit was thus constituted and transmitted in ways other than scriptural. Tradition, then, is the complete deposit of Revelation—the oral deposit—transmitted in this way.

2. THE SUFFICIENCY OF SCRIPTURE

It is obvious that the limited notion of Tradition discussed above could not be upheld if it were found that the whole

---

[9] op. cit., p. 511. He also mentions inherent and declarative tradition but adds in a footnote to these: "Inhaesiva et declarativa non sunt proprie traditiones," p. 507.

[10] cf. also J. V. De Groot, *Summa Apologetica de Ecclesia*, Ratisbonne, 1892, pp. 666, 667; Simar, op. cit., p. 19.

[11] Proulx, op. cit., pp. 172 ff.   [12] op. cit., p. 185.   [13] ibid.

deposit of Revelation were contained also in the Scriptures. That the whole deposit is in fact in Scripture is a contention found in some modern Catholic theology. It is not part of our business to discuss in detail the controversy that still continues on this point. We can show the inadequacy of the limited notion—as shown above—without appealing to this controversial sufficiency of Scripture. Yet a brief discussion of the controversy has its relevance here. It presents an opportunity of pointing out that such a sufficiency of Scripture as is here in question, if it were granted, does not affect the existence or the nature of Tradition as that has been described; of showing, too, the unfairness of a criticism of a modern theologian's theory of Tradition, a criticism that is based on his holding for this sufficiency of Scripture; an opportunity, lastly, of recognising how some points made legitimately in connection with the relationship of Scripture and Tradition would be enhanced if in fact Scripture contained the whole of Revelation. Let it be stated immediately that the sufficiency of Scripture discussed here and in the thought of theologians who favour it involves no taint of unorthodoxy. It is one thing to say that there is only one source of Revelation. It is another thing altogether to say that both sources of Revelation are materially complete—while admitting that one of them, Scripture, is sufficient in no other sense.

It seems that we can only regard the material sufficiency of Scripture as, at most, a hypothesis here since the outcome of the present debate appears to be still uncertain. Lennerz does maintain that the question of the material insufficiency of Scripture has been decided by Trent and is not any longer open to discussion amongst Catholics. This is the net result of an article of his.[14] The fact of the matter is, however, that the discussion has gone on and that at least one theologian involved in it has used the same Council of Trent to reach an almost diametrically opposite conclusion to that of Lennerz. He would not claim that Trent decided in favour of the material sufficiency of Scripture but he would claim that it

[14] H. Lennerz, art. 'Sine Scripto Traditiones', *Greg.*, vol. 50 (1959), pp. 624 ff. Cf. Lengsfeld, op. cit., p. 118 ff., on this question.

deliberately left the way open for that view since the view was expressed by some of those present at the Council.[15]

The majority of theologians in the period do hold that there are truths in Tradition that are not contained in Scripture and many attempt a list of these truths—principally such truths as the inspiration of all the books of Scripture, the validity of baptism by heretics and the justification of infant baptism.[16] Yet these theologians are not always sure as to what they mean when they say that some truths are not contained in Scripture. Lercher is only sure that the inspiration of all the books of the Canon is certainly not contained in Scripture in any way; of other truths mentioned he will only say that they cannot certainly be known from Scripture—which equivalently admits the possibility of their being implicit in Scripture.[17] And when Heinrich wants to show that Tradition complements the doctrinal content of Scripture he will only write: "there are many revealed truths transmitted to us by Tradition which the Holy Scripture does not contain explicitly or with sufficient clarity".[18]

In favour of the argument that the whole corpus of Revelation is contained in Scripture, there is Geiselmann's research into traditional Christian thought on the subject.[19] But perhaps the best basis is given to the argument by Dubarle. He says that if Revelation is regarded as a series of propositions, in so far as we can enumerate such propositions, then undoubtedly all Revelation is not contained explicitly in Scripture. But he points out that Revelation was bound up with a gift of God, it was a teaching concerning the salvation

[15] J. R. Geiselmann, art. 'Un Malentendu eclairci: la relation "Écriture-Tradition" dans la théologie catholique', *Istina*, 1958, no. 2. esp. pp. 198 ff. Few would go so far as Charlier when he writes: "The Fathers from the beginning maintained, and the Council of Trent repeated it, that the Bible enshrines the whole of the Revelation which is the object of Christian belief"—C. Charlier, *The Christian Approach to the Bible*, Glasgow, 1958, p. 234.

[16] cf. Mazella, op. cit., p. 491, for example.

[17] Lercher, op. cit., p. 315. Cf. also W. Wilmers, *Lehrbuch der Religion*, vol. I, ed. 2, Pustet (Regensburg), 1875, pp. 142, 143.

[18] Heinrich, op. cit., vol. I, p. 829.

[19] Geiselmann, art. cit., 'Un Malentendu'.

event,[20] and since Scripture described the salvation event very thoroughly it can be seen to contain all Revelation at least implicitly.[21] Journet makes an impressive attempt to show how many of the truths often claimed by theologians to be outside of Scripture's contents are in fact contained in Scripture. His generalisation on the point maintains that Scripture contains: "at least the essential truths, the principles, the articles of faith from which the whole deposit of Revelation can, with the assistance of the Holy Spirit, become ever more explicit".[22]

Just as the opposition were not always sure how strongly to express the exclusion of some truths from Scripture so the theologians who opt for the material sufficiency of Scripture are not always sure how to describe the inclusion of the whole deposit of Revelation in Scripture. There is here an echo of a difficulty from another discussion—the discussion concerning the nature of development of dogma and the difficulty of deciding what is meant when one says that truth is contained implicitly in truth. So that it is probably De Voogt who best expressed the present status of our knowledge of the contents of Scripture when he writes in an article that presents the relative merits of Geiselmann's contribution and of one by Ortigues:[23] "we content ourselves with the statement that all the Christian truths find some point of contact in the Scriptures".[24] For if it has been always the practice of the Church to give her references to Scripture for each truth she teaches[25] it is also true that, at least to the logical reason, the line connecting some truths with the scriptural basis seems a slender one.[26]

[20] cf. Semmelroth, art. cit., p. 4.
[21] Dubarle, art. cit., pp. 80, 81.
[22] op. cit., p. 36 and ff.
[23] Ortigues, art. cit.   .
[24] P. De Voogt, art. 'Écriture et Tradition d'après des Études Catholiques Récentes', Istina, 1958, no. 2, p. 191.
[25] idem, art. cit., p. 196.
[26] idem, art. cit., p. 192. "S'il est admis qu'il y a toujours un lien, il faut se rendre a l'évidence qu'il est parfois tenu, au moins devant la raison raissonnante".

3. TRADITION IS A COMMENTARY ON SCRIPTURE

It is Remberger who has suggested that Geiselmann's thesis on the material sufficiency of Scripture leads to a concept of Tradition as a continual interpretation of Scripture down the ages.[27] There are two senses in which that sentence: Tradition is an interpretation of or a commentary on Scripture could be true. Tradition could be a commentary on Scripture by the very fact of transmitting the same truth as that contained in Scripture but which it had received and still retained in a manner other than Scripture. Tradition could also be a commentary on Scripture in the sense of an exegesis of Scripture; as if the bearers of the oral deposit had retained no memory of it except for what Scripture now reminded them was contained in it, so that their doctrinal activity would now confine itself to exegesis of the Scriptures. It seems that Remberger attributes the latter view to Geiselmann's theory of Scripture for he opposes to it "some criticisms urged by the traditional view of the matter". One criticism he draws from a teaching of the Vatican Council when it declared that we must believe on divine faith all that is contained in the Word of God which is written or ('vel') handed down. Remberger argues that the dichotomy expressed by the 'vel' here implies that the truths of faith can be derived from Scripture alone or from Tradition alone, that Tradition is materially complete in its own right, that it is not merely a presentation of truth as contained in Scripture.[28] It seems then that Geiselmann is accused—and apparently as a result of his theory of

[27] X. Remberger, art. 'S. Scrittura e Tradizione', *Dig. Rel.*, 1958, n. 2, pp. 15, 16. He ends an account of Geiselmann's article referred to above with: "La formula definitiva dovrebbe piutosto essere questa: Tutta la parola di Dio e contenuta tanto nella Scrittura che nella Tradizione, varia soltanto il modo di trasmissione: la Scrittura ci trasmette il messagio di salvezza come verita rivelata; la Tradizione ci trasmette la verita rivelata in forma di interpretazione e di comprensione autoritativa".

[28] art. cit., p. 16. "Ma alloro la Tradizione non e forse una grandezza a se stante ed una fonte di fede egualmente valida, accanto e con la S. Scrittura? Non e detto, con questo, che la sua funzione non e solo quella di spiegare la Scrittura?" This objection should trouble R. Kehoe who writes in his art. 'The Scriptures as Word of God', in *E.C.Q.*, 7 (1947),

the material sufficiency of Scripture—of holding that Tradition is in effect the continual exegesis of Scripture in the Church.

Such a view of Tradition is neither involved in a theory of the material sufficiency of Scripture nor is it held by Geiselmann. It is obvious that the mere existence of the whole deposit of Revelation in Scripture does not preclude another existence of the same deposit with the bearers of Tradition.[29] And although Geiselmann makes his own the theory of Kuhn with the words: "Tradition is the living interpreter of Scripture",[30] it cannot be inferred from this that he regards Tradition as an exegesis of Scripture while it can be shown from elsewhere in his writings that he thinks of Tradition as a commentary on Scripture in the acceptable sense of that phrase. In his article in 'Fragen der Theologie Heute' Geiselmann reviews his own work on this question of the material sufficiency of Scripture and he carefully points out there that Tradition is not Scriptural exegesis but by being an interpretation or understanding of the oral apostolic deposit, it is automatically an interpretation of or commentary on Scripture, since the deposit of Revelation is wholly contained in Scripture, too.[31]

Schmaus takes over Geiselmann's findings on the question of the material completeness of Scripture[32] and he makes a statement on Tradition in connection with it from which one could infer, although unfairly and on insufficient evidence, that he held Tradition to be no more than Scriptural exegesis: "The living Tradition is, in the Church, the way in which the Word of God, which is contained in Holy Writ, is developed and made accessible." [33] But he, too, is careful to preclude just such a false interpretation of his remarks and he points

p. 76: "The Scriptures give us the very word of God. What Tradition gives us is the true sense of the Scriptures . . . It is not in the same sense a source of revelation."

[29] This handing over and handing on of an oral deposit Dejaifve has for his theme in art. cit., p. 147.

[30] Geiselmann, art. cit., *Un Malentendu*, p. 214.

[31] idem, art. cit., *Die Tradition*, p. 98. Tradition "ist ausschliesslich Interpretation, aber nicht der Schrift, sondern der apostolischen Tradition".   [32] op. cit., pp. 775 ff.   [33] op. cit., p. 776.

out that with Geiselmann Tradition was another source, "echte Quelle".[34] As Heinrich writes, it is because Tradition contains the fulness of divine truth in its own right that it is an interpretation of Scripture.[35] Tradition then is a commentary on Scripture but not by way of exegesis.[36] The whole deposit was committed by Christ to the care of the apostolic preaching and it has been handed down by an unbroken succession in the Church and guarded infallibly by the Magisterium. All this is true before the influence of the Scriptures on the process is taken into account at all.

In practice, to what does this statement amount: that Tradition is a commentary on Scripture but not by way of exegesis? It means that Tradition is not formally 'teaching the Bible', its activity is not primarily directed towards interpreting the books of the Bible. But by the very fact that it teaches and develops a body of truth which is also contained—at least in part—in the Bible, it automatically becomes an unintentional commentator on the Bible. In practice this amounts to the saying that the Bible must be read in the light of Church teaching and belief. It is the man who already possesses the faith of the Church who can see so much of what the Bible has to teach and see it clearly. And as the doctrine in the Church develops, more can be seen in Scripture. Tavard instances such a possibility: "The Roman primacy is one of those elements that have passed from a stage when it was understood by the faith of 'God's own people' to a subsequent stage when it has become so inseparably agglutinated to the understanding of the apostolic Scripture that the Church of one age receives from the Church of the preceding age" and he adds: "Christology and Mariology offer many instances of the process." [37] It is in this sense that Ortigues is to be understood when he writes of the Church possessing a certain spontaneity in handing on the message.[38]

---

[34] op. cit., p. 777. Bévenot also bears out Geiselmann on this point: M. Bévenot, art. *Tradition, Church and Dogma*, H.J., vol. 1 (1960), p. 37.
[35] Heinrich, op. cit., vol. I, p. 830.   [36] Proulx, op. cit., p. 173.
[37] art. cit., p. 242.
[38] Ortigues, art. cit., p. 293: "elle posséde une certaine spontanéité dans l'économie du message".

De Voogt takes the argument a step further when he is writing of the possibility of deducing truth from the Bible. He makes it clear that there is practically no truth which can be certainly deduced from the Bible by the generality of men once these are cut off from the teaching of the Church. He instances the misunderstandings concerning the Real Presence, the sacrifice of the Mass, the Holy Trinity, that are so common outside the Church.[39] It was to be expected, then, and it did in fact happen that the truth of Revelation was committed also to the care of a living and perennial body which would always be in possession of it.[40] At this stage it certainly does not matter to the existence and to the nature of Tradition whether it is held that Scripture is or is not materially complete. There will always be demanded what in fact most theologians of the period expressly admit to exist, a complete corpus of revealed truth borne by the bearers of Tradition and in itself something other than their possession of or understanding of the Scriptures.

4. SCRIPTURE IS NOT A DOCUMENT OF TRADITION

Draguet has objected to Deneffe because the latter did not include Scripture amongst the records of Tradition. He suggests that the Scriptures represent a means of knowing the ecclesiastical preaching of the time of their composition and that the further fact of their inspiration should not prevent them from being counted, with other documents which witness to Church preaching, amongst the records of Tradition.[41] And to Van den Eynde Scripture is a document of Tradition for the reason suggested by Draguet—that it represents the teaching of the Church at the time of its composition.[42]

It is true to say that the New Testament was written by the

[39] De Voogt, art. cit., p. 192. It is essential here, of course, to leave intact the value of Scripture texts for apologetic use—to prove historically the setting up of an authentic Magisterium. Nor is it claimed that this truth and others mentioned above are not clearly in Scripture, but only that Scripture is liable to misinterpretation. The truth is defenceless in written form.   [40] idem, art. cit., p. 193.
[41] Draguet, loc. cit., Review of Deneffe's book, p. 95.
[42] Van Den Eynde, art. cit., p. 235.

Apostles or 'apostolic men' and that it contained the truth which they were preaching in the Church at the time. But it is better to say, too, that its inspired character does prevent it from being numbered amongst the documents of Tradition just as that character makes it a source of Revelation in its own right. In order to be directly and formally a document of Tradition a writing must not only contain objective tradition but be produced by a bearer of Tradition.[43] It must be a result of that type of active tradition which is writing. For, as any other act performed by just anybody at all which happens to have a truth of Revelation for object is not automatically counted in Tradition, so not every document which happens to contain some revealed truth is counted as a formal record of Tradition. Only those documents produced by the agents in Tradition (already described) in carrying out the activity that is proper to them, are records of Tradition in the strict sense.

The Scriptures resulted from the activity of men who were agents in Tradition but not from their activity precisely as agents in Tradition.[44] For, as Scheeben remarks, the writers of Scripture were instruments in the hands of the inspiring Holy Spirit so that the Holy Spirit is the principal author of the works produced.[45] The writers of Scripture are instruments of the Holy Spirit in a way that bearers of Tradition as such are not. The Scriptures, therefore, are documents produced by God.[46] They have a particularly close claim on the authorship of the Holy Spirit. Because of that special characteristic of theirs, the Scriptures had an independent worth that placed them outside Tradition in the strict sense —although they were handed over to the Church by an activity of the teaching office of the Apostles.[47] So the Scriptures are part of the apostolic deposit, they were handed over to the Church and in this handing over their special

---

[43] cf. Scheeben, op. cit., pp. 172 ff. On p. 173 he lists monuments indirectly or 'materially' pertaining to monumental Tradition such as writings of the later and heterodox Tertullian.

[44] This point is well made by Deneffe, op. cit., p. 151.

[45] Scheeben, op. cit., pp. 115, 116.

[46] idem, op. cit., p. 111.   [47] idem, ibid.

character was infallibly guaranteed. They would always, therefore, belong to the Church to be handed on and to have their character guaranteed by the successors of the Apostles in all ages.[48] The continuous teaching of the Church regarding their authoritative or inspired character is, no doubt, Tradition. But Scripture itself in its composition was not strictly part of the active tradition of the Apostles and in its continued documentary existence it is a record of Inspiration rather than a record of Tradition. Consequently the Scriptures are not counted as part of the documentary Tradition by Scheeben where he treats that aspect of the subject; in fact Scripture and documentary Tradition are implicitly distinguished.[49] Scripture is not a document of Tradition but —and this is particularly true if it somehow contains the whole deposit of Revelation—it exercises a more important influence in the living Tradition than any of the actual documents of Tradition do.

The influence which the continued presence of Scripture in the Church does exercise on Tradition is described by theologians under many aspects. It is probably overstated in the thought of Söhngen: "over and above oral tradition, we possess in Scripture another self-existent source for our knowledge of Revelation. Without the written word, the objectivity of apostolic teaching would vanish into pure data of consciousness."[50] Certainly the apostolic preaching was received in understanding in the consciousness of the Church, particularly of the teaching Church. But it was neither received (even apart from Scripture) nor handed on in this subjective understanding alone. It could only have been received and preserved by being expressed, formulated in words or implied in activity or 'institutions'. Just as it never remained subjective so it never remained, even apart from its Scriptural form, completely oral, the affair of transient words. As Tavard points out, there is nothing exclusively oral about Tradition and that is even more true as time goes on.[51]

Therefore from the very nature of the activity essentially

[48] idem, op. cit., p. 134.   [49] idem, op. cit., pp. 170 ff.
[50] G. Söhngen, *Einheit in der Theologie*, Munich, 1952, p. 322.
[51] Tavard, op. cit., p. 56. Ortigues, art. cit., p. 293.

involved in Tradition there is no danger of the apostolic doctrine vanishing into pure data of magisterial consciousness.
If apostolic traditions needed 'objectification' they had that
independently of the writing of Scripture and that 'objectification' has been handed down as Scripture has. In this
thought of Söhngen the roles normally assigned to Scripture
and Tradition are practically reversed. The element of truth
contained in the position is expressed more moderately by
other theologians.

First a point is made by Schmaus which contrasts with the
insistence laid by so many theologians on the 'occasional' character of Scripture.[52] These usually lay great stress on the fact
that individual books of Scripture were written with particular purposes in view in order to show that Scripture could
not be expected to contain and in fact does not contain the
whole deposit of Revelation. Schmaus maintains that Scripture had a more definite place in the dispensation envisaged
and set up by Christ than this insistence on its 'occasional'
character would indicate. He does not maintain this with any
immediate intention of showing the material sufficiency of
Scripture by depriving the opponents of that theory of one
of their usual arguments.[53] His concern is more to show the
important help which Scripture continually offers Tradition,
and that in Christ's plan of things. And so, granting that
Christ, to the best of our knowledge, left no command that
the Apostles should write, Schmaus stresses the fact that it
was the Holy Spirit, "der Geist Christi", who inspired the
Apostles to write, that it was therefore according to the mind
of Christ that Scriptures come into existence at this particular
time.[54]

The importance of Scriptures for the Tradition of all times
can be summed up briefly in the statement of Tavard's that
it is "the embodiment of the unique original source of faith,
the 'kerygma' or preaching of the Apostles".[55] In order to explain, in turn, why this makes the Scriptures so important,

[52] Pesch, op. cit., p. 383; Schultes, op. cit., p. 580; Salaverri, op. cit.,
p. 751; Pinard de la Boullaye, art. cit., p. 845 footnote; etc.
[53] This is sufficiently well done by Journet, op. cit., pp. 38 ff.
[54] Schmaus, op. cit., p. 763.   [55] Tavard, op. cit., p. 246.

Schmaus is inclined to insist mainly on the fact that the Apostles were 'eye-witnesses' of the salvation event, a fact that is stressed in the writings of the Apostles themselves.[56] The situation in which the Apostles found themselves was unique when compared to that of later preachers.[57] Their direct experience of the Saviour in His life and actions on earth was not granted to the preachers of later generations.[58] It seems that Schmaus relates a special value of apostolic preaching to this characteristic of theirs: that they were eye-witnesses. And he hazards the guess that the Scriptures were part of the new dispensation in order that this apostolic teaching with this special value should be preserved for us in an original form.[59] His thought here can, without distortion, be linked up with what we have seen written already about revelation not being a series of teachings given in the abstract. In Tavard's words: "The core of Revelation was not the teaching of a doctrine. It was the coming of a Presence among men: 'We saw his glory, the glory, as it were, of the only-begotten of the Father' (John i. 14)." [60]

We must maintain that revelation is formally in teaching, in a 'locutio Dei', whether that be by speech or some equivalently direct communication between God and the human mind, such as for example infusion of knowledge. We must admit too, of course, that revelation did not come about in statements isolated from an event or a Presence. But, whatever may be said about the core of revelation, the formal element in it has always been regarded as the direct teaching which gave the events or the Presence their significance in the minds of those who experienced them. It is true to say that the eye-witness of the events or of the Presence was in a special position, but that would appear to bear more directly on the apologetic value of his witnessing than on its dogmatic value. Hence, without lessening the force of this point of view in the least, an aspect of the matter noted by Heinrich is even more important. He traces the fact that the Apostles had a deeper grasp of revealed truth than any of their successors more immediately to a greater influence of the Holy Spirit upon

---

[56] Schmaus, op. cit., p. 764.   [57] op. cit., p. 763.   [58] idem, ibid.
[59] idem, op. cit., p. 764.   [60] Tavard, op. cit., p. 4.

them.[61] And he traces the fact that the Scriptures present the truth of Revelation with unexampled depth and insight, more immediately to this aspect of the matter.[62]

In any case it is obvious that the Scriptures do contain in written form the first and deepest grasp of the deposit of Revelation from those who first received it whole. Scripture is a source of Revelation for the Church of all succeeding generations. In practice how does that affect Church Tradition?

Although the Scriptures must be read in the light of the faith of the Church—for otherwise neither the whole of inspired Scripture can be recognised as such nor can much of its content be understood clearly—they provide, when they are so read, a constant reminder of the truths of Revelation and they are to that extent a guarantee of stability and of integrity to Tradition. So Ortigues regards the influence of Scripture on Tradition, according to his own notion of Tradition, as the Church's interpretation of a reality which she bears sacramentally within herself.[63]

The Bible, however, is not reduced to the status of a handy reference book; no matter how valuable a reference book it may be in view of its inspiration. The Church can and does always read its own beliefs in the Scriptures, always gives its scriptural references for its dogma. But the Scriptures mean more than that to the faith of the Church and so to its Tradition.

Precisely because it is the depositary of the deeper insight of the Apostles, Scripture can give the Church deeper insights into her own faith. It is the same faith which the Apostles preached and which the Church now possesses, and the Apostles' expression of it can obviously help the Church's understanding of it. De San even says that Scripture is necessary if the Church is to strive for perfect understanding of the truth.[64] So Ortigues remarks that, although we could never simply deduce the dogma of the Immaculate conception from Scripture, once it has begun to be explicit in the faith of the

[61] Heinrich, op. cit., vol. II, p. 30.   [62] op. cit., vol. II, p. 31.
[63] art. cit., p. 296. "Mais ce que l'Église interprète, ce n'est pas seulement un text: c'est la realité divine qu'elle porte en elle 'sacramentellement' et que l'Ecriture *lui indique*."   [64] De San, op. cit., pp. 120, 121.

Church Scripture can help us to see deeper into the meaning
of it, can help define its true sense.[65] The two sources of Revelation, then, act and re-act on each other almost as the different
organs of Tradition itself can do. As Schell remarks, the two
sources of Revelation should be thought to perfect each other
organically rather than mechanically or materially.[66] And it
is probably only to such mutual relationships that Tavard
refers when he writes: "we ought not to speak of 'two sources'
of faith: as though tradition and Scripture had nothing to do
with one another".[67]

5. EXEGESIS IS NOT TRADITION

We have already noted in section 3 of this chapter that
theologians refuse to reduce Tradition to an exegesis of Scripture, on the grounds that it is itself in autonomous possession
of the deposit of Revelation. We have noted in section 4 that
Scripture, although it is not a document of Tradition, is a
source of truth in its own right and can help the bearers of
Tradition to a deeper understanding of the truth which they
possess already. One further question needs to be discussed
before the two sources are properly seen as at once distinct
from each other and yet essentially related to each other.
Apart from that commentary on Scripture which is automatic
from the Church's teaching and believing the same truth as
Scripture contains, there is an activity known properly as
scriptural exegesis. This is in effect the derivation of truth
precisely from Scripture and precisely as scriptural, i.e. with
the guarantees that scriptural inspiration and inerrancy give
it rather than the guarantees it derives, for example, from
being also taught in the Church. We have seen that Tradition
cannot be reduced to exegesis. It is a further question as to
whether exegesis—whether it be by an infallible decision of
the Church or by an interpretation of Fathers or theologians
—is Tradition. The question has given rise to a small controversy in the period.

It is Burghardt who holds the most extreme view here. "An
argument from Scripture", he writes, "is theologically an

[65] art. cit., p. 295.   [66] op. cit., p. 176.   [67] art. cit., p. 243.

argument from the Church's understanding of her own book; and that is an argument from tradition." [68] This postulates, in effect, that the sense of every text used to prove a truth from Scripture be interpreted by the Church.[69] And it must be official exegesis, for only that would be Tradition—always an affair of the Magisterium—for Burghardt. This rules out the possibility, always admitted at least in theory, that an exegete could know the inspiration of some books of Scripture and the meaning of some texts and thereby arrive at the certainty of faith on Scripture alone.[70] On the more practical level it rules out the possibility of deriving an argument from Scripture where the Church has not published official exegesis of a text. Even when one knows the inspired character of Scripture and only understands its doctrine because one already has the faith of the Church, the argument one derives from Scripture where there is no official exegesis, the certainty of the truth one gains in this way, is now conditioned by its being truth presented in inspired Scripture and not by its being a truth taught from Scripture by the Church.

Let the discussion come down then, to where there does exist an exegesis of Scripture and that by the Magisterium, for here Burghardt will have some support in regarding this as Tradition. He will be supported by Deneffe, for example, because to Deneffe's way of thinking the exegesis of Scripture, the teaching of truths out of Scripture and as scriptural truths, is an instance of 'active tradition'. To bear this out Deneffe claims that theologians regard the 'mode of transmission and of preservation' as that which constitutes Tradition as distinct from Scripture. In official exegesis one has the mode of transmission proper to Tradition; hence one has Tradition.[71] Semmelroth, too, appears to be in agreement with Deneffe on this point, if we can judge his position from a rather brief statement. He is objecting in this context that if the notion of Tradition is based on the 'partim-partim' theory, anything said subsequently about the transmission of truth involving

[68] Burghardt, op. cit., p. 27.
[69] "It is the Church's task to tell us what, e.g., Mt. XVI, 16 means"— Burghardt, ibid.   [70] cf. Zapelena, art. cit., p. 60; op. cit., p. 274.
[71] Deneffe, op. cit., pp. 134, 135.

development will have no significance for the deposit of truth in Scripture. Hence, he declares that active tradition has a twofold object: the written deposit in the Bible and the deposit existing apart from that in the Church.[72] Finally, Franzelin has been accused of holding this position by De San and Proulx.

De San's arguments from Franzelin's text are not at all cogent.[73] And yet is not the very fact that Franzelin regards the active element in Tradition as the formal element an indication that he falls under the objection now urged against him? For if it is the activity of handing on in a particular way that makes Tradition in distinction from anything else, is not the handing on in this way of Scriptural truth precisely as such (i.e. exegesis) Tradition? On this point—we have already seen Deneffe make it—Proulx mainly upholds De San's objection to Franzelin.[74]

Proulx is correct when he insists that the transmission of the oral deposit and that alone is Tradition in the proper sense of the word. Yet to say that the active element in Tradition is the formal element does not involve one in any different concept, as Proulx thinks it does. When Franzelin called the active element in Tradition the formal element he was mainly concerned with distinguishing Tradition as a means of transmission and of preservation of doctrine, from another means of dissemination, i.e. inspired Scripture.[75] Proulx realised as much.[76] Now that which distinguishes the sources cannot later identify them. The solution to the problem here depends upon realising what first or immediately specifies the objective doctrine. As Scheeben points out, the Apostles when writing and giving the Scriptures to the Churches were exercising their teaching function in the Church also. But that did not make the writing of Scriptures Tradition since the Scriptures as inspired documents had a worth and a standing

[72] art. cit., p. 5.
[73] De San, op. cit., pp. 99–101. Franzelin, op. cit., pp. 214, 242.
[74] Proulx, op. cit., pp. 92 ff. De la Barre holds this view of Tradition and claims Franzelin's support for it. Cf. R. P. De la Barre, *La Vie du Dogme Catholique*, Paris, 1898, pp. 137 ff.
[75] cf. Franzelin, op. cit., theses I–III.   [76] Proulx, op. cit., p. 91.

of their own prior to that.[77] When it comes to post-apostolic times and the Scripture truths are also the object of official Church teaching, because the Scriptures are documents and they survive with their original inspired character and particular worth, such official teaching is 'Scripture' still rather than Tradition in the proper sense of the word.[78]

The active element is the formal element in Tradition when it is allowed immediately to specify the doctrine as traditional. If the element of inspiration enters in, if a doctrine is taught as inspired, as it is in exegesis, then that doctrine is already specified as 'Scripture': its further proposal as scriptural truth does not deprive it of its characteristics or specification. When Proulx himself is faced with the task of distinguishing the sources of Revelation he must say that what formally constitutes truth as tradition is its consignment to the belief of the spirits of the faithful; especially of the pastors of the Church.[79] But this in effect is no different from saying that what formally makes a truth tradition, what formally specifies Tradition, is the consignment of the truth to the expression of the faith of the faithful and especially to the teaching of the pastors of the Church. It is no different from saying that the formal element in Tradition is the active element.

It is not maintained that Franzelin clearly decided that exegesis was not Tradition. It appears that he did not specifically address himself to that question. Still, the case made against him by De San and Proulx will not hold.

At this point the distinction of two sources of Revelation can be clearly seen and yet without any injury to their essention relationships. Scripture presents revealed truth by means of inspired writings. It stamps its own deposit of truth with the character of inspiration. Whoever teaches Scripture after that and adds his own authority in his teaching does not disturb that stamp or change the source of that truth. Tradition is the transmission of truth by the preaching of the Apostles and of the Apostles' successors and by the life of the whole Church. In this way the whole deposit of Revelation is trans-

[77] Scheeben, op. cit., p. 111.   [78] idem, op. cit., p. 112.
[79] Proulx, op. cit., p. 172.

mitted. It is still disputed whether Scripture does or does not contain the whole deposit in its particular way. If it does it is all the more valuable as a reminder to the Church of the deposit committed also to its care, and as a record of a deeper insight into this deposit which was proper to the first bearers of Tradition and which will help the Church towards its own deeper understanding. But the Scriptures are not fully intelligible except when read in the light of the faith of the Church. To that extent Tradition is of its very nature a commentary on Scripture and essential to it.[80] More than that, inspired Scripture cannot even be fully recognised as such apart from the teaching that all the books of the Canon of Scripture are inspired, a teaching which has come down to us in Tradition.

[80] cf. Scheeben, op. cit., p. 148.

Chapter Six

TRADITION IN NON-CATHOLIC THEOLOGY

"The Reformers are the real traditionalists."
EMIL BRUNNER,
The Misunderstanding of the Church, p. 45

IT would obviously be impossible to do any justice to the variety of non-Catholic thought on Tradition, and to the depth and richness of much of it, in one short chapter (the term 'non-Catholic' is here, for convenience, taken to mean non-Roman-Catholic). That would need at least one other book. So if the present writer relegates non-Catholic thought to one and the last chapter of this book, he does not mean to show any disregard for it. He is not sufficiently well informed to write a book on it and yet he feels that to omit all reference to it might seem neglectful. Furthermore it does not require too detailed a knowledge of all non-Catholic thought on Tradition, it requires only a knowledge of some general trends of that thought to make the main point which this chapter attempts to make.

The Modernist movement attacked the immutability and authority of defined dogma. Then Billot saw that Catholic writing on Tradition must emphasise the infallibility and authority of its bearers. But we did not have to wait for Billot or for Modernism to have this pointed out to us. Franzelin, examining the implications of the 'Scripture Alone' principle, saw it first. He realised that the 'Scripture Alone' principle of the Reformers did not raise only a question of 'de facto' existing sources, or 'loci' from which revealed truth in fact reached individuals. He saw that it was primarily a question of the authority or guarantee or equipment which any alleged sources must be shown to possess. His emphasis on one non-Scriptural 'locus'—the one for which he thought guarantees could be irrefutably established—led him to an over-simplified definition of Tradition. That is the obvious criticism of Franzelin's treatment of Tradition. Yet there is something to be said for that treatment, too. It may have over-simplified the concept of Tradition but it did at least set in relief the principal point of controversy between Catholics and Reformers. When that principal point of controversy is forgotten polemics become futile. Sometimes non-Catholics accuse Catholics of placing Church teaching or Tradition above the Word of God or Scripture and Catholics reply that Church teaching is not above the Word of God but subordinate to it or beneath it. If the charge is put in these terms, perhaps it must be answered in these terms but so often when words like 'above' and 'below', words with a spacial reference primarily, are thought to be magical deciders of a man's orthodoxy, the debate about Scripture and Tradition reminds one of an unseemly scramble of schoolgirls for a better place, and the more essential issues are forgotten. Tradition cannot be defined adequately as the official teaching of the Catholic Magisterium, yet the debate between Catholics and non-Catholics concerning Tradition can never be resolved until they agree on the nature and function of the teaching authority in the Church. That is the key point of their difference and this chapter hopes to illustrate it.

The slogan 'Scriptura Sola', Scripture alone, has undoubtedly led some Catholic controversialist writers to attack the Scriptures when they should have been attacking the Reformers' theology of the Church. But if it has misled the Catholics, it has misled the non-Catholics sometimes, too. Amongst the latter the plea is often heard nowadays for a realistic discussion of Tradition as a real agent in the propagation of the Christian truths of each sect. With Krüger, for example, the plea finds its way into the world of encyclopedias.[1] Yet it is not true to say that Neo-Protestants are discovering a Tradition in their midst of which the Reformers, the first exponents of the 'Scripture Alone' principle, knew nothing. In fact 'Scripture Alone' is one of the most misleading slogans extant.

[1] G. Krüger, art. 'Tradition' in 'Die Religion in Geschichte und Gegenwart', vol. 5, *Tübingen*, 1931, cols. 1249–50.

Lengsfeld has quite recently published an accurate and sympathetic account of the inter-confessional debate on Tradition. In this work he describes the attitude of the Reformers and of their modern disciples. He finds that Luther ultimately did not betray as much practical interest as Melanchthon in a restoration of the primitive purity of the Church. His contribution to the theology of the Reformers was more negative.[2] When Luther rejects Papacy, Councils and Church authority in general he does so finally because they lessen or threaten the absolute authority of Scripture. Of course, Melanchthon also places the absolute authority in Scripture. But he is not quite as extreme in rejecting other authority. He is more concerned with ridding the contemporary Church of what he regards as corrupt beliefs and practices than with any final rejection of Church authority. He did hope that union with Rome could once more be realised through renewed understanding. And so he sought a common ground for discussion. He appealed to the early Creeds and to the writings of the early Fathers. Not that he thought these to have an authority equivalent in any way to Scripture. He thought, rather, that the early Fathers were such saintly and learned men, and also so near to the time of the original apostolic preaching, that in practice their teaching could be taken as an exact expression of the revealed truth found in the Scriptures. Under circumstances such as these in which the early Fathers lived and taught and wrote, the danger of mistaking the original and Scriptural faith was negligible. Further, Melanchthon did not wish to confine this service which the Fathers rendered the Church to any one age in the history of the Church. He would wish that a Synod of truly learned and pious men should always exist to protect the purity of the faith; to see that it always remained in harmony with its earliest and most faithful expressions. Obviously Melanchthon did not see in the early Fathers, nor did he recommend in this Synod of learned and holy men, anything like the authoritative and infallible hierarchy of the Church of Rome. Any teaching by any organ other than Scripture, he thought, was liable to error. Yet in ideal circumstances—such were present in Patristic teaching

[2] P. Lengsfeld, op. cit., pp. 150–5.

and would again be present in the Synod he wanted—the fear of error would be negligible. But there is never any question of more than human authority for an organ of teaching other than Scripture.

In the theological thought of Lutherans from the beginning, therefore, there was a place for Tradition—understood on their own terms. Pelikan's commentary on the Augsburg Confession reveals an attitude to Tradition similar to that which Lengsfeld finds in Melanchthon's writing.[3] The Confession did not appeal explicitly to a principle called Tradition. Like Melanchthon, it appealed to the teachings of the early Church. It was mainly Chemnitz, Pelikan says, who reinstated this explicit concept in Lutheran thought. But the principle was there before the concept was formally reinstated.

If the Reformers had never appealed to a principle that can be called Tradition, Tradition possesses the incontrovertible status of a fact. A Christian child receives its faith first from its parents. This parental teaching is its first source of Revelation, its first rule of faith. Tradition is a fact in a society and no abstract theorising can altogether dismiss it or arbitrarily confine it to select groups. Each Church, each Christian sect or society has its own Tradition. If they all lived and taught in exact accordance with the Scriptural doctrines, there could be no differences between them. A confession of any kind inaugurates a Tradition and a sect hands it on. "All men are heirs of traditions, even the most apparently spontaneous of sectarian Protestants, and when they imagine that they are effectively emancipated from one set of traditions it is the most natural thing in the world for them to fall under the sway of another", so wrote Jenkins.[4] And Kinder also writes of the factual influence of some form of Tradition as a constant factor in the Reformed Churches.[5]

In short the 'Scriptura Sola' principle must not be taken

---

[3] J. Pelikan, art. 'Die Tradition im konfessionellen Luthertum', in *Lutherische Rundschau*, 6 (1956, 1957), pp. 228 ff.

[4] D. Jenkins, *Tradition and the Spirit*, London, 1951, cf. pp. 10 ff.

[5] E. Kinder, 'Schrift und Tradition', in *Asmussen–Stählin, Die Katholizität der Kirche*, Stuttgart, 1957, p. 19.

to mean that the early Reformers did not or that the Neo-Protestants do not admit another agency in bringing the Scriptural faith to individual men. The appeal to Tradition was already clear in Melanchthon's writings and the concept was firmly reinstated in the Lutheran thought of Chemnitz. And in our own times Neo-Protestants are constantly writing about Tradition as an essential factor in their own concept of Christianity. The point at issue between Catholics and Neo-Protestants, therefore, is not whether there be a Tradition-principle in the make-up of Christianity or not but rather the way in which this principle is to be described and evaluated. In fact, it is on its attempt to defend its own description and evaluation of the Tradition within it that a sect's claim to represent true Christianity must stand or fall. We all possess substantially the same Scriptures. It is our Traditions that differ.

Of course, there is much talk and writing nowadays concerning ecumenism and some theologians prefer to say that the fulness of the authentic Tradition is not possessed by any one of the existing sects. It will be found by a critical collaboration of the authentic elements in the doctrine and structure of all the sects. So Schlink has written: "Our main concern must be to discover the spiritual wealth concealed in the different traditions, and to seek the unity of the Church not in uniformity but in a fellowship of different traditions." [6] Such a statement at first sight holds some promise of unity. But of course it conceals an attitude to the nature of Tradition and to the nature of the Church which must cause the most radical disagreement. For that apparently reasonable plea for a return to unity through sympathetic and understanding acceptance of our differences betrays a theory of Tradition and a theory of the Church—these are inseparable —which could not be acceptable to those sects that claim to point out one true and visible Church existing today and one true and authentic Tradition transmitting the whole of Christian Revelation. You cannot invite people to work towards a true Church and a true Tradition before you prove

[6] E. Schlink, 'The Significance of Eastern and Western Traditions for the Christian Church', in *E.R.*, 12 (1960), p. 142.

first that they do not already possess it and second, that the Church and Tradition you envisage are the true Church and Tradition founded by Christ.

Let us return, then, to the main point here. The Christian sects are agreed that Scripture has an absolute and supreme authority. But they differ in their interpretations of Scripture. That is actually another way of saying that they embody different Traditions, for Scripture is read in the light of Tradition. Each sect reads its own faith in Scripture. Therefore each sect must give its authority for its own reading of Scripture. Each must give its authority for the faith it holds and which it claims to find in Scripture. Each Church, in other words, must explain the authority it claims to possess. It cannot refuse to claim authority; at least in the secondary sense of the word—authority from the possession of special endowment or guidance. For in the very teaching of a recognisable brand of Christianity as the authentic and Scriptural Christianity lies an implicit claim to authority. Each sect must describe its guarantees, otherwise it can be ignored. If my 'yea' is as good as any man's 'nay', if neither of us can claim any special authority, then Christianity is in a hopeless plight and pays no compliment to its founder. In the Catholic concept of Tradition we found guarantees belonging to that part of Tradition called magisterium by reason of the office of those who exercised magisterium, and guarantees belonging to other parts of Tradition which derived to a great extent from magisterium. These were infallibility and derived infallibility. When we now ask non-Catholics for their guarantees, we question them about Church authority; in fact, about Church Tradition.

1. THE NEO-PROTESTANTS AND AUTHORITY

By Neo-Protestants is meant the modern exponents of the Reform theology. Here we confine attention to Cullmann and Skydsgaard. We are forced to make a selection and we hope to make it representative. For an introduction to a wider selection of modern Protestant thought, the reader might consult Lengsfeld, who deals with Peter Brunner, Ebeling,

Campenhausen, Gloege, Barth and Bultmann.[7] For some of them—Barth particularly—would take at least a chapter to themselves. Cullmann is playing a very large part in current inter-confessional debate and Skydsgaard's theology of Tradition is amongst the most advanced.[8] Cullmann's particular insight centres on Apostolic Tradition. "The work of the form-critics on the Gospel has directed our attention more than ever before to the development of the oral tradition which preceded the fixing of the Gospels in writing." [9] Emphasis on this Tradition in the apostolic age is common now amongst non-Catholics who seek a more realistic attitude to Tradition in the texture of Christianity.[10] Cullmann allows this Apostolic Tradition a value which he grants to no later Tradition: "whatever the respect owed by the Church to the ecclesiastical tradition . . . it can never assume the same value as the apostolic norm, and it can never itself become a norm. . . . The uniqueness of the apostolate is annulled by this (Catholic) teaching norm." [11]

What makes Apostolic Tradition unique and why is it alone normative? It is in answering this question that we meet Cullmann's particular thesis on the identification of 'Kyrios' (Lord) and 'paradosis' (Tradition). He derives this thesis first from 1 Cor. ii. 23. In this verse St Paul, referring to the doctrine of the Eucharist which he is about to record, says "I received from the Lord". It is Cullmann's contention that St Paul means neither that he received direct revelation of this doctrine nor that he received it from a chain of witnesses

[7] Lengsfeld, op. cit., *Überlieferung.*
[8] For Oscar Cullmann's concept of Tradition the following works of his have been used: (i) art. ' "Kyrios" as Designation for the Oral Tradition concerning Jesus', trans. in *S.J.T.*, 3 (1950), 180 ff. (ii) art. 'Scripture and Tradition', trans. of art. in *D.V.*, 23 (1953), 47 ff., as in *S.J.T.* (1953), 113 ff. (iii) *Die Tradition als exegetisches, historisches und theologisches Problem,* Zürich, 1954. This is a translation of the French *La Tradition,* 1953, and it takes account of objections raised by Danielou and Bavaud to the French edition. (iv) *The Early Church,* ed. Higgins, London, 1956. A collection of translations from Cullmann's works. The chapter on 'The Tradition' is a translation of *Die Tradition* in (iii) above and takes account of Catholic objections to his Petrusbuch.
[9] *The Early Church,* pp. 59, 60.   [10] cf. Nelson, art. cit., pp. 151 ff.
[11] Cullmann, op. cit., *Die Tradition,* p. 38.

the first of whom, in the chronological order, was the Lord; but that St Paul here reveals the nature of all Apostolic Tradition as something in which the 'exalted' Lord is immediately at work.[12] Because the Lord has an essential part to play in apostolic 'paradosis', an Apostle could say with equal accuracy: 'I received from the Lord' or 'I received from Tradition'.

Now how is this part of the exalted Lord described which makes Apostolic Tradition so unique? At first it might seem that the Lord is active in Apostolic Tradition through his Spirit, who came to the Apostles at Pentecost. "Henceforth the Holy Spirit, who is identified with the 'Kyrios', takes the place of the 'paradosis' of the law." The Lord imparts his Spirit and so is active in Apostolic Tradition. But Cullmann is conscious of the fact that the Holy Spirit is given to the whole Church and he shows no tendency to distinguish the effect of the Spirit on the Apostles from his effect on the later Church.[13] Furthermore, there is no attempt to analyse the effect which the gift of the Spirit might have towards infallibility or inerrancy. Wherever the human element enters in there is the possibility of error. "This human element (present even where there is inspiration by the Holy Spirit) is present also in the apostolic writings themselves. . . . But behind them there are the apostles as eye-witnesses. The human element is here reduced to an inevitable minimum inherent in the very notion of a divine revelation to man." [14]

It is not so much the help of the Holy Spirit, then, it is the fact of being eye-witnesses that lends a special security to the Apostles' teaching: "in the transmission of tradition proper, an exceptional place belongs to them as eye-witnesses commissioned directly by Christ".[15] Paul was an eye-witness to the risen Lord and received his commission on the road to Damascus. The other Apostles were eye-witnesses of the earthly life of Jesus. Hence the Apostle is essentially one who passes on what he has received by revelation. "But since everything has not been revealed to each individual apostle, each

[12] Cullmann, op. cit., *The Early Church*, p. 62.
[13] *The Early Church*, pp. 71, 72.
[14] Ibid., p. 85.   [15] Ibid., p. 72.

one must first pass on his testimony to another . . . and only the entire 'paradosis' to which all the apostles contribute, constitutes the 'paradosis' of Christ".[16]

Cullmann is really concerned with two distinct propositions: (1) that apostleship and its witness is unique, (2) that only Apostolic Tradition is normative. Since he will have the first of these propositions imply the second (for he says that Catholics destroy the uniqueness of the apostolate by claiming a later normative Tradition) he must hold that the factor which makes apostolate and its witness unique is also the factor which makes Tradition normative. What is this factor? In so far as it can be gleaned from the account of his thought just given, it comprises these elements: (1) the Apostles were eye-witnesses or the first recipients of revelation; (2) the Apostles were directly commissioned by Christ.

Two criticisms might be offered. First, Cullmann has not now explained as clearly or as emphatically as many Catholic theologians the grounds of apostolic uniqueness. Secondly, if a Catholic with a more emphatic insistence on the uniqueness of the Apostles and of their witness sees in this no objection to a normative Church Tradition, there is little hope of seeing such an objection in Cullmann's account of the uniqueness. To expand these points:

It almost seems as if Cullmann finally places the uniqueness of the Apostles' position and of the value of their witness in the historical fact that they were nearest to the events they report: so when he writes of the Apostles: "The human element is here reduced to an inevitable minimum inherent in the very notion of a divine revelation to man." But, of course, when it is a question of receiving and transmitting revealed doctrine it is not mere spacial or temporal nearness to the source that is decisive. The human element is not reduced to a minimum by that alone. Many people were as near to Christ as the Apostles were, and did not understand him. Cullmann does not emphasise the role of the Holy Spirit to point the unique value of apostolic witness and yet none of the other elements in his picture of the apostolate will explain that unique value. Catholic readers at least will be dis-

[16] *The Early Church,* p. 73.

appointed in Cullmann. The first statement of his theme—
the identification of 'Kyrios' and 'paradosis'—sounds original
and promises a new insight. When its content is analysed,
however, it seems to say no more than Catholic theologians
have always said about the Apostles, and some of them have
explained the uniqueness of the apostolate and of its witness
more clearly than Cullman (cf. Chapter IV, sec. 5).

The question of the normative character of Church Tradition is not affected one way or another. Catholic theology
insists that the apostolate was unique and that the value of
its teaching was also unique. It is inclined to see the reason for
this more in the special influence of the Holy Spirit on the
Apostles than in the fact that they were eye-witnesses, a fact
that has reference primarily to their historical nearness to
Christ. "It seemed good to the Holy Spirit and to us", wrote
the Council of Jerusalem (Acts xv, 28): "and I think that I
also have the Spirit of God", said St Paul (1 Cor. vii., 40).
Catholic theology also insists, and Cullmann admits, that the
later Church has a similar if not exactly comparable help of
the Holy Spirit. Danielou, in fact, accused Cullmann of a certain inconsistency where the latter recognises a real and effica-
cious activity of God in the sacramental life of the Church
while denying it any comparable value in the Church's doctrinal life.[17] Cullmann answered this objection in a way by
saying that infallibility and error are not categories that are
applicable to the sacraments.[18] But that is not the point; they
are applicable to the doctrine and infallibility is the quality
which God's activity might be supposed to lend the doctrine.[19]
Unfortunately Danielou did not press the point in a later
article.[20]

Cullmann's conclusion, whatever his evidence is worth, is
as follows: "The Apostle cannot, therefore, have any successor
who can replace him as bearer of the revelation for future

[17] J. Danielou, art. 'Réponse a Oscar Cullmann', in *D.V.*, 24 (1953),
114 ff.   [18] *The Early Church*, p. 83.
[19] H. Bacht, art. 'Tradition und Sakrament', in *Schol.*, 30 (1955), pp.
27 ff.
[20] J. Danielou, art. 'Qu'est ce que la tradition apostolique?' in *D.V.*,
26 (1954), 73 ff.

generations, but he must continue himself to fulfill his function in the Church of today: *in* the Church, not *by* the
Church, but *by his word* . . . by his *writings.*" [21] Again the
two propositions are found in this conclusion. Certainly the
Apostles cannot be replaced and certainly they still bear
unique witness in their writings, but the evidence for this
point will not also prove his second proposition: that no other
bearers of Tradition can succeed them with similar although
not exactly comparable equipment.

Finally Cullmann's interpretation of the significance of a
historical fixing of a Canon of Scripture is already well
known. We need only remark that when Cullmann claims
the only possible meaning of the fixing of a canon of Scripture
to be the acknowledgment of apostolic Scripture as the sole
norm of Christian belief thenceforward, he has once more
gone a long way beyond his evidence.[22] There are, in fact,
other possible explanations of the event. In the end Cullmann's contribution to our knowledge of the nature of Tradition is much less than his terminology would lead us to expect.
On the point that interests us most here—the authority of
Church Tradition—he is almost entirely negative. Let us turn
to Skydsgaard, then, in search of a more positive account.

By far the most accurate and understanding account of the
doctrine of Tradition held in modern Catholicism that has
been presented by an outsider is found in Skydsgaard's article
on Scripture and Tradition.[23] And yet Catholics would take
exception to many of his judgments. He thinks that Trent
expressed a concept of Tradition rather than a statement concerning traditions and that it embraced the view that Revelation is only partly contained in Scripture.[24] He is aware and
approves of Geiselmann's interpretation of the Tridentine
decree—according to which Trent did not decree the material
incompleteness of Scripture. He regards that interpretation
as something "that will cause considerable controversy and
upheaval in present-day Roman Catholic theology".[25] In that

[21] *The Early Church*, p. 80.   [22] Ibid., pp. 88, 90.
[23] K. E. Skydsgaard, art. 'Scripture and Tradition: Remarks on the
Problem of Tradition in Theology To-day', trans. in *S.J.T.*, 9 (1956),
337 ff.   [24] art. cit., pp. 338, 339.   [25] ibid.

prediction he was mistaken. Geiselmann's presentation of evidence for his interpretation may have been justly criticised but the interpretation itself has been easily accepted in modern Catholic theology (cf. Chapter V, sec. 2).

Skydsgaard's question is: "whether the Roman Catholic concept of tradition is not too uncritical in its attitude to the 'status quo' in the Church. Does not the whole of living tradition . . . show that the ultimate court of appeal and critical authority—which decides what is true and what is false— has wielded too little genuine authority and has been too uncritical? And 'critical' here means 'true to the Bible'." [26] He has recognised the fact of development of dogma but he wants the Bible to be the rule of authentic development.

Quoting Cullmann on the connection between 'Kyrios' and 'paradosis', Skydsgaard describes a concept of Revelation which he too easily assumes to be alien to Catholic thought. The content of divine Revelation—and, therefore, of authentic Tradition—is not only a set of abstract doctrines but a message concerning a salvation event and concerning a Person who continues to act on men in Word and Sacrament for their salvation.[27] And active tradition? "Tradition is fulfilled when the Church—on the basis of the Apostles' message which rests on the person and work of Jesus Christ—lives in accordance with the message by celebrating Baptism and Holy Communion. When the Church preaches the message, teaches, bears witness, baptises, celebrates Holy Communion, and praises God . . . then tradition is being carried on." This is a living Tradition because the Spirit of Christ is in the Church, quickening it.[28]

To all this, if we understand it correctly, a Catholic could subscribe. Apart from the five other Sacraments, where lies the difference between us? According to Skydsgaard, "we cannot accept the Roman Catholic concept of Scripture within tradition as an organ (although a fundamental one) of the living stream of tradition through the ages. This view amounts to saying 'Scripture extended in tradition'." The first of these sentences is hardly an accurate appraisal of the Catholic theology of Scripture and (therefore) it is hard to

[26] art. cit., p. 345.   [27] art. cit., pp. 352 ff.   [28] art. cit., pp. 353, 354.

G

see that the second sentence means anything different for Catholics than the sentences in which Skydsgaard himself describes development: "A Protestant concept of tradition is concerned primarily with an event, i.e. handing down the sacred Word of God that people may hear and believe and with penetrating deeper and deeper into the biblical insights connected with this act of salvation." [29]

Is the precise point of difference between us found in his contention that "it is solely through Scripture that true authority can maintain itself in the Church"? It depends on what he means by that. Cullmann was afraid that the admittance of a later Magisterium would destroy the uniqueness of the apostolate and Skydsgaard is afraid that a Magisterium would replace the authoritative Scriptures.[30] But the uniqueness of the apostolate cannot be destroyed and neither can the Scriptures be replaced for we have nothing exactly comparable to them with which to replace them. Where then is the point of Skydsgaard's case against the Catholics? When he admitted that the Holy Spirit quickened the tradition of the Church, he equivalently admitted that the Church has an authority at least in the secondary sense of the term. If the Church is helped by the Holy Spirit in bearing witness, then she is 'an authority' on Revelation. But Skydsgaard claims that all Church teaching and all development is subject to the test of Scripture. All its teaching must answer the question: is this biblical? A Catholic, once he admitted the material completeness of Scripture, could admit that, too. But he would have to add two paragraphs.

First, he would have to point out that the biblical test is not the only test of authenticity. The Catholic Church when it teaches, gives its references to Scripture. But it appeals to its own authority, too, for the Holy Spirit is with it. These two authorities, these two tests of authenticity do not replace each other. They are both unique in kind. Neither is there much point in deciding which is the superior norm, which the 'ultimate' court of appeal. They are too different to be easily compared and words like 'superior' and 'ultimate' tell us precious little about either of them.

[29] art. cit., p. 356.   [30] art. cit., p. 355.

Secondly, he would have to point out in order to be realistic that to say 'the Bible judges the authenticity of Church teaching' is not to say anything very practical. In practice the Bible has not judged. Men have judged and have appealed to the Bible. Each sect has decided what the Bible teaches. Now they can debate their different interpretations on the principles of exegesis if they wish but ultimately *the very fact that they have differed* must prove to them that if Christianity is to succeed at all one of them must be right not only 'de facto' but 'de jure'. Some of them must be guided to the truth. It cannot be left to chance discussion amongst men of good will. Ultimately a sect's claim to teach true and whole Christianity will stand or fall by its success in describing and vindicating its authority as a teaching Church. Skydsgaard has said too little on the subject of Church authority to allow us to judge his Church's claim. And few of his fellow Protestants say more.

The first of these paragraphs above points out that to recognise the authority of Scripture—even to call it superior or ultimate—is not to imply the absence of other authority. Protestant theologians are inclined to think (as are Catholics) that when they say that Church teaching must be submitted to the test of Scripture they have also said that Church teaching has no full guarantee or final authority in its own right. In fact, the first of these statements does not imply the second and the evidence offered for the first will not prove the second. Few Neo-Protestants will deny that the Church has doctrinal authority over the individual. The majority speak of it at some stage, however reluctantly and guardedly. But their descriptions of it differ from the Catholic theory at least verbally.

Some of the non-Catholic theologians we shall now examine claim that Church teaching can be revised or reversed at a later stage. They maintain that a teaching of the Church has no final authority. When they say, therefore, that Church teaching must pass the test of Scripture they mean much more than that. They mean to say that Church teaching could be revised in the light of later reading in Scripture. If that is what Skydsgaard meant by saying: "it is solely through Scripture that true authority can maintain itself in the Church",

then he does disagree with Catholics. But the second paragraph above maintains that in actual history the Bible does
not revise Church teaching. Men do and they appeal to
the Bible. Hence, the paragraph maintains, the question of
authority must be faced again. Of course, a sect may have
to appeal to the Bible for one proof at least if it claims that
it possesses the authority in question. But if the possession
of irrefragable authority is admitted to be an integral part
of true Christianity that latter will be an easier problem of
exegesis to solve.

To ask whether there is in the true Christian Church a
doctrinal authority the decisions of which are not reversible,
is to ask about infallibility.

2. THE ANGLICANS AND INFALLIBILITY

Around 1950 three reports were submitted to the then
Archbishop of Canterbury. They were reports on doctrine
from the Free Churches, the 'evangelical' group within the
Anglican communion and the 'catholic' group within that
communion. The report of the Free Churches had this to say:
"We suggest that the underlying cause of our differences lies
in the doctrine of the Nature of Authority, and in the attitude
of the separated communions to tradition, especially as this
question affects the structure of the Church." [31]
Since most non-Catholic sects admit that the Church has
some authority in teaching—the authority which comes from
special equipment if not the authority which comes from
office—we wish to ascertain what some of these think of the
nature and limits of this authority. There, as the Report just
quoted points out, is the point of disagreement. For very few
would nowadays agree with the sentiments of N. P. Williams:
"The Thirty-Nine Articles characteristically take up a position which may be interpreted as consistent either with the
Catholic view of tradition and Scripture as joint authorities
for the truth of the deposit or with the Protestant conception
of the Scriptures as the sole authority, independent of any

[31] *The Catholicity of Protestantism* (eds. Flew and Davies), 1953, p.
132.

living exponent." [32] Most admit a second authority, and commentators on the Thirty-Nine Articles, too. But they differ in describing it. According to the Report of the Free Churchmen there are three witnesses to divine Revelation: "The apostolic Church and its Scriptures, the Church of the ages, and enlightened individuals." [33] For the Church has received from God the task of preserving the Christian truth, and not only that but also the task of drawing out its further implications, of interpreting the Scriptures, of applying the truth to the needs of each generation. What equipment does the Church have in carrying out this task? The Church is the fellowship of the Holy Spirit, who has guided and inspired it throughout its history. Yet we cannot in any real sense say that the Church is infallible. Why not? Because "it is composed of human beings, and consequently fails from time to time to conform in life and doctrine to the Word, to the Church of the apostolic age, and to the Scriptures".[34] Can the Church fail in its doctrinal mission then? Can it, because it is composed of fallible human beings, slip farther and farther from the original Scriptural truth? It cannot. The Holy Spirit has other means of preventing such a final lapse. "From time to time also, during periods of decadence within the institutional Churches, He has illuminated the conscience and understanding of individuals who are earnestly seeking to find the truth which is in Christ, and he has used such people to recall the Church as a whole to a knowledge of the Gospel . . . Here is a third witness to the Word of God." [35]

Much the same sequence of thought on Tradition and Church authority comes from within the Anglican communion. In Bicknell's commentary on the Thirty-Nine Articles development of doctrine is seen to be an essential part of its transmission by the Church down the ages. The Church is granted judicial authority in matters of faith.[36] And if we

---

[32] N. P. Williams, art. 'Tradition' in *The Encyclopedia of Religion and Ethics,* vol. 12, Edinburgh, 1921, p. 414.
[33] op. cit., *The Catholicity,* p. 118. [34] op. cit., *The Catholicity,* p. 117.
[35] op. cit., *The Catholicity,* p. 118.
[36] E. J. Bicknell, *The Thirty-Nine Articles,* 3rd ed. (rev. Carpenter), Longmans, 1955, pp. 233, 234.

wish to find the views of the commentary on the nature and limits of this authority we can look to where "one of the burning questions of the day" is discussed: "How are we to distinguish between legitimate developments and illegitimate?" [37] The question is asked. We are told that we must consider the Roman Catholic and Modernist answers to it. Both are rejected. And the section ends. This type of writing is too common in the inter-confessional debate to avoid an expression of annoyance. It is too easy to have and to give the impression that because one has attacked something definite, one has also defended something definite. And the reader often has to roam far from the scene of the attack to find something to put in the place of the thing attacked. In this case, luckily, he does not have to roam farther than the next section, on the authority of Church councils.

"If even a general council, fully representative of the whole Church, may err, what guarantee do we possess that the whole Church may not fall into error on some point?" [38] If this question is answered then we will have an answer to the question posed above: how can one know with certainty that a certain development of dogma is authentic? If the Church were infallible we would have certain criteria of legitimate development. But the whole Church is not infallible any more than a general council is infallible, according to the commentary. The Church is composed of individuals who can sin and fall into error. Again we ask, can it not happen, then, that a false development of doctrine gradually achieve universality and ultimately obscure the original truth? And again there is an appeal to the inspired individual: "we do believe in the perpetual guidance of the Holy Spirit and that he will not suffer the Church to go far astray without revealing the truth to faithful servants of God within the Church. An Athanasius is raised up to stand against the world. Thus the way is prepared for a return from error." [39]

It would not be fair, of course, to suggest that all Anglican writers face the difficulty raised by a non-infallible Church in this precise way. But it is sometimes disconcerting to find that they do not face it at all. The Report of the 'evangelical'

[37] E. J. Bicknell, op. cit., p. 256.   [38] op. cit., p. 273.   [39] ibid.

group within the Anglican communion affords an example. "Tradition", it says, "represents the Church's apprehension of the revelation attested authoritatively in the Bible; an apprehension truly made possible by the Holy Spirit's guidance and inspiration, yet an apprehension which is incomplete and fallible because the Church's membership is not yet complete and because the Church is still made up of sinful and ignorant men." [40] Here the Church is thought to be fallible for the reasons already noted above, i.e. that it is made up of sinful and fallible members. But no attempt is made to face the difficulty that a fallible Church may more and more obscure the truth of Christ. No attempt is made to indicate a remedy for errors into which the Church may fall in its apprehension of the faith and in its interpretation of Scripture.

Prestige, to take another example of Anglican thought, does face the difficulty of a fallible Church, but tries to solve it by a further appeal to Scripture. He opens the Prologue to his book *Fathers and Heretics* with a sentence which he himself describes as 'provocative': "tradition is the true ground, both historically and rationally, of such authority as can properly be claimed for the Christian religion".[41] There were no angry shouts of 'Papist' from his audience at St Mary's in Oxford (this was one of the Bampton Lectures for 1940) and if there had been they would soon have been proved premature by some precisions which quickly followed. He derives his concept of Tradition from the Fathers and he now anticipates his findings by claiming that in patristic theology whatever authority Tradition possessed was directly connected with (1) the fact of revelation, (2) the primacy of Scripture as a guide to faith.

In one sense of the word, he writes, Tradition refers to the 'philosophical' elaboration of the primitive Revelation when it was dealt with by human reason as human reason had come to deal with all the fundamental facets of human existence. In this case the primitive Revelation is "out at interest with the intellectual banks" and he writes: "modern auditors have every right to inquire how far the interest paid was properly

---

[40] Report: *The Fulness of Christ*, London, 1950, pp. 62, 63.
[41] G. L. Prestige, *Fathers and Heretics*, London, 1940, p. 3.

credited".[42] But that is not the precise concept of Tradition found in the Fathers. "The word 'paradosis' they reserved in its strict sense for something yet more fundamental . . . so far were they from distinguishing tradition from the deposit of faith or from the contents of the Bible, that, broadly speaking, it signified to them the actual divine revelation, the substance of which was to be found in the Scriptures and, with certain simple qualifications, nowhere else."[43] The authority of Tradition derived from its first deliverers, the prophets and Apostles who were raised up by Christ to speak his truth; "authority is claimed for Christian truths on the ground that they are an 'apostolic tradition' or a 'tradition of the apostles' ".[44] Prestige also writes of authority in later Church transmission, of "subsequent teachers, who with an authority no less assured delivered it once more to people of a later age"[45] and of the inspiration by which the Church is enabled to give a true interpretation of the records.[46] So this Tradition of the Apostles is found now in the Bible and in the safe keeping of the Church.

To the question that always lies just beneath the surface: what is this authority of the teaching Church? his answer is a scattered one. He has said that the Church possesses sufficient inspiration for its task of discerning the faith in its records, that its continual preaching, its creeds and its sacramental practices aid its interpretation of Scripture, but he also maintains that the final vindication of the true faith can come only from the Bible.[47] So he seems to make Church Tradition the interpreter of Scripture and Scripture the only absolutely certain criterion of the true Tradition, for the underlying assumption is that Church Tradition by itself can err. He knows he is open to a charge of circularity and he tries to avoid it as follows:

Appealing again to patristic thought—although now without apposite quotation—he claims that the tradition was contained in a comparatively small part of the Bible, in those parts of the Bible which represent the Gospel, the historicity

[42] Prestige, op. cit., pp. 10, 11.   [43] op. cit., pp. 12–13.
[44] op. cit., pp. 21, 24.   [45] op. cit., p. 25.
[46] op. cit., p. 44.   [47] op. cit., pp. 30–4.

of which and of the events which they recount can be critically established beyond doubt.[48] The original facts and convictions related in the four Gospels are the last court of appeal. Here is the criterion by which Church preaching and Church interpretation of Scripture is judged true or false.

Is it unfair to Prestige to conclude that the last court of appeal in the attempt to ascertain the authentic deposit of faith is the literary and historical criticism of the Bible? And how far shall this criticism be allowed to go? If the deposit of faith is already 'out at interest in the intellectual banks' with the evangelist Mark, "the oldest and least sophisticated of them", then how much of Mark's Gospel is the original "evidence", the fundamental Revelation, and how much is Mark's own "inference"?[49] We have already admitted that an appeal to Biblical exegesis will help decide the structure of Church authority and that this exegesis will be more likely to result in agreement once the sects agree that Church authority of a certain quality is indicated for Christianity. But it takes a brave man to maintain, in face of the historical and contemporary divergence on almost every point of Christian doctrine, that the Bible will furnish clear and critical evidence of the essentials of the Christian faith by reference to which all further Church preaching and interpretation of Scripture can be verified.

So we are thrown back on the other explanations of Church authority and indefectibility. It is probable that the 'evangelical' Anglicans do not call the Church infallible ultimately because the Church to them has many denominations belonging to it.[50] These differ, and they cannot all be correct. It is certain that the Bicknell commentary and the Free Churchmen do not admit the Church to be infallible because it has a human element and that human element is sinful and fallible. The 'evangelical' Anglicans also use this factor to rule out the possibility of an infallible Church for to claim Church infallibility "would be to posit an over-ruling of the fact of human ignorance and fallibility which would do

---

[48] op. cit., pp. 44, 45.   [49] op. cit., pp. 7, 8.
[50] cf. Report: *The Fulness of Christ*, p. 63; also Report: *The Catholicity*, pp. 138, 139.

G*

violence to men's personality and freedom".[51] Hence Bicknell's commentary declares: "What our Lord promised to His Church was not infallibility, but an infallible guide, the Holy Spirit." [52] And, like the Free Churchmen, he ultimately appeals to the presence of individuals to whom the Holy Spirit "reveals" the truth and who will save the Church from protracted error.

Now all this seems to the present writer to be an unnecessarily elaborate means of avoiding a doctrine of Church infallibility. In the first place it sounds rather weak to say that the Church has an infallible guide but is not itself infallible. For what good is an infallible guide who does not guide infallibly? A fallible guide would do just as well or, rather, just as badly. We are told that the Holy Ghost will not allow the Church to continue in error. He will raise up individuals and equip them to correct it (notice that the Holy Spirit can equip individuals without over-ruling the fact of their human ignorance, their liability to sin and their fallibility, but he cannot equip the Church or its teaching organ without doing this). But this appears to be simply a kind of long-term infallibility. The Church can err, but not for long. The Catholic says that there can be error in parts of the Church but that the whole Church can never be in error, nor can the whole teaching episcopate be simultaneously in error, nor can the Pope be in error when he commands the faith of the whole Church. The Anglican says that the whole Church can be in error but that its error will be redeemed by extraordinary means. This is not the place to discuss the pros and cons of these positions. It is enough to say that it would be more reasonable to expect—and it would be easier to prove from Scripture—that the Holy Spirit, the infallible guide of the Church, keeps the Church from error through its ordinary and appointed ministry than through extraordinary agents who could hardly be as easily recognised.

It is not easy to find a clear and definitive statement of a theory of Tradition and Church authority to which 'catholic' Anglicans would subscribe. The section on the doctrine of the Church and Authority in their Report to the Archbishop

[51] Report: *The Fulness*, p. 62.   [52] Bicknell, op. cit., p. 273.

of Canterbury is concerned with that doctrine as it is taught by orthodox Protestantism. Hints of the 'catholic' view are only found in its criticisms of others. The Report states: "It is necessary, in appealing to the Bible, to appeal also to the Tradition of the primitive Church as the context in which the Bible had its origin and meaning," [53] but there is little or no elaboration of such statements. Perhaps Mascall will help us.

It is most unusual to see a non-Catholic write: "From an 'a priori' standpoint there might seem to be no need for a divinely inspired Bible at all." [54] But the statement is only a measure of Mascall's belief in the existence of an ordinary and continuing teaching body and of the presence of Christ and of his Spirit in the Church. He writes: "however different her interpretation of it may be from that of Roman curialism the Anglican Church does presumably believe that the Church has an authority to teach, a magisterium, and it appears that, in common with the Church of the early centuries, she locates it primarily in the bishops, who corporately form the earthly manifestation of the apostolic body".[55] This Magisterium has an organic place in the Church, the Mystical Body of Christ.[56] For the episcopate is not a human institution. It is a continuation by divine right of the Apostolate instituted by Christ.[57] To Mascall's mind it is this ordinary teaching authority, and not any extraordinary charismatics, that accounts for the success of the Church's doctrinal mission.

If he does not appeal to charismatics, however, neither does Mascall formally decide the question of infallibility or indefectibility of the Church in her teaching mission. It appears that he would allow the Church such prerogatives only in its undivided state; for it is the undivided Church that possesses the true Tradition: "the Anglican maintains his appeal to Scripture and the Fathers and the undivided Church and persists in prayer for the unity of all Christendom".[58] Mascall believes in the validity of Anglican orders and hence he

[53] Report: *The Catholicity*, p. 28.
[54] E. L. Mascall: *Christ, the Christian and the Church*, London, 1946, p. 231.   [55] op. cit., p. 243.
[56] op. cit., p. 244.   [57] op. cit., pp. 123, 124.
[58] E. L. Mascall, *The Recovery of Unity*, London, 1958, p. 232.

believes that the Magisterium is divided. So he quotes a concept of Tradition, too, in terms of an undivided Church—the quotation is taken from an agreed statement in the Report of the Anglican and Rumanian Conference at Bucarest, June 1935—"We agree that by Holy Tradition we mean the truths which have come down from our Lord and the Apostles and have been defined by the Holy Councils or taught by the Fathers, which are confessed unanimously and continuously in the Undivided Church and are taught by the Church under the guidance of the Holy Spirit." [59]

3. THE EASTERN ORTHODOX AND THE PAPACY

Up to this point in the discussion of non-Catholic thought and from the evidence which non-Catholic thought has itself provided, two things appear to be verified:

First, any claim to possess or to point out true Christianity can only be judged according to the authority which that claim vindicates for the teachers or possessors of Christianity. Finding the true and integral faith is a matter of finding those who have authority in expressing the true faith. The interconfessional debate, therefore, must concern itself primarily with finding agreement on an adequate authority in Church teaching or belief, an adequate authority for Tradition. So much appears from the first section of this chapter.

In the second section, in discussing Anglican theology, one ground of authority was considered: infallible guidance by the Holy Spirit. Since it is reasonable to envisage—as so many non-Catholics nowadays do—that this guidance is given the Church through a teaching organ, a 'teaching Church', rather than in a diffused fashion and directly to individuals, we can now confine the question to the infallibility of the Magisterium. If the true Magisterium possesses this infallible guidance —which does not rule out the existence of error *in* the Church or over-rule any human aspect of it—it is 'an authority' on Revelation. Of course some Anglicans would maintain that the teaching Church has authority in a primary sense also; that its bishops succeed to the commission given the Apostles

[59] E. L. Mascall, *Christ*, p. 241, note 4.

to teach all nations and that they are, therefore, by reason of their office in authority over those who freely submit to the faith. But it is authority in the secondary sense, the authority that comes from infallibility or guidance by the Holy Spirit, that is important in the discussion of Tradition. It was because Franzelin failed to distinguish types of authority that he limited Tradition to an organ which possessed both types.

We now come to the third aspect of this essential centre of the inter-confessional debate. Even if we agreed that the true Tradition and therefore the true Magisterium must be infallible, it would not necessarily follow that we would agree in pointing out the true Magisterium. It may be agreed that those who have authority in the primary sense will have first claim to authority in the secondary sense: those who have the perennial mission to teach will be found to have charismatic and not merely derived infallibility. But there may be disagreement as to who these are. This disagreement has been already hinted when 'catholic' Anglicans appeal to an undivided Church. It is stated more clearly when the Eastern Orthodox theologians talk about Tradition.

Arseniev is very insistent upon the part played by the Holy Spirit in the witness of the Church but he is less enthusiastic about distinguishing Tradition from Scripture. In the primary sense of the word, the Apostolic Tradition has for its content "the concrete historic fact—the fact of his having come, of his measureless condescension, of his death and resurrection". This is at once "the contents of the Gospel and the essence of Scripture, the foundation stone of the whole faith". Now this presence which once came amongst us is still dwelling amongst us, in the Blessed Eucharist, and the Spirit of God still works in the Church.[60] And the witness of the Church both to the historical salvation-event and to the continuing presence of its Saviour is possible only through the presence of the Spirit in the Church. "What the Spirit of God (penetrating in the hidden depths of the Divine Life present in the Son of God who was made flesh) bore witness of, only the

[60] N. Arseniev, art. 'The Teaching of the Orthodox Church on the Relation between Scripture and Tradition', in E.C.Q., 7 (1947), pp. 21, 22.

Spirit of God living in the Church can really apprehend." [61]
In this witness of the Church or, rather, in this witness of the
Holy Spirit in the Church, Scripture and Tradition inter-
mingle and are not easily distinguished. He illustrates this
intermingling from that witness which the Church bears in
her liturgical life. Here, where the Church prays and expresses her beliefs, she constantly uses the texts of Scripture to
do so. Arseniev really does not want to distinguish Scripture
and Tradition. He only wants to insist that: "It is the Spirit
of God inhabiting the Church which is decisive." [62]

Konstantinidis, on the other hand, does discuss Tradition
in itself and states the strongest claim of the Eastern Orthodox
Church. He spoke at a meeting of the World Council of
Churches in Rhodes, 1959, and when there had already been
much well-meaning if rather vague talk about a fellowship of
divine traditions, he indicated kindly but firmly that Divine
Tradition exists today, one and undivided, in the Eastern
Orthodox Church and that other 'traditions', other differ-
entiated Churches are in error, heretical. [63]

He refers to the fact—commonly admitted in Neo-Protes-
tantism—that the New Testament times witnessed an oral
tradition of the revealed truth. But, he insists, Scripture never
replaced Tradition. The oral Tradition of the Apostles,
formed under the influence of the Holy Spirit, has been preserved in the Church, first orally and then in the form of
literary records as the Divine Tradition of the Church. "This
Tradition—static in its divine origin, like Scripture, but
dynamic in its external forms—remained integral and undivided in the Church, as a living and continuous expression
of the revelation." [64] Today it still exists integral and undivided. It is the teaching and belief of the Eastern Orthodox
Church. That is the claim of Konstantinidis, but by no means
peculiar to him amongst Eastern Orthodox theologians.

Obviously some claim for the authority of the teaching
and belief of the Eastern Orthodox Church must under-

---

[61] art. cit., p. 18.   [62] art. cit., p. 25.
[63] C. Konstantinidis, art. 'The Significance of the Eastern and Western
Traditions within Christendom', in E.R., 12 (1960), pp. 148, 149.
[64] art. cit., p. 147.

lie this position. What is this claim? What is the effect of the Holy Spirit in that Church of which Arseniev spoke? Bratsiotis gives the answer. In short it reads: infallibility. But the Orthodox theologians do not convey the impression of unanimity in describing the conditions of this infallibility. Bratsiotis claims that the integral Divine Tradition, as it existed in the undivided Church of the Fathers, exists today in the Eastern Orthodox Church. This is a claim to immutability of doctrine through admitted doctrinal development.[65] The doctrine of infallibility is the basis of this claim.

According to Bratsiotis the Orthodox people as a whole, the body of the Church, are regarded as the guardians of Orthodoxy: "the highest authority in Orthodoxy is the Church as a whole . . . the whole body of the Church is considered in Orthodoxy to be infallible".[66] And he refers to the hierarchy as the 'voice and instrument' of the body of the Church[67] (the exact contrary of the teaching of some Catholic theologians that the faithful are the voice and instrument of the hierarchy). At one stage he writes that the supreme authority in the Orthodox Church lies in the Ecumenical Councils but then he qualifies that by writing that it is 'administrative authority' which is in question and he further insists that the ecumenicity of such a council must be recognised and witnessed by the conscience of the whole Church: "In other words, the decisive criterion of an Ecumenical Council is the recognition of its decrees by the whole Church, which is therefore in fact the sole authority in Orthodoxy."[68] It does seem, then, as if he is saying that the Holy Spirit makes the hierarchy infallible by making the whole Church infallible; that it is the hierarchy who have derived infallibility while the faithful possess the charism.

Whether that is Bratsiotis' view of the matter or not, it is probably not the view of Florovski. Florovski, too, is concerned with the question: "Is the contemporary Orthodox

[65] P. P. Bratsiotis, art. 'The Fundamental Principles and Main Characteristics of the Orthodox Church', in E.R., 12 (1960), pp. 155, 156.   [66] art. cit., p. 161.
[67] art. cit., p. 160.   [68] art. cit., p. 161.

Church the same Church, as in the age of the Fathers?"[69] The answer is affirmative. For the Orthodox Church "is not *a* Church, but *the* Church. It is a formidable but fair and just claim. There is here more than just an unbroken historic continuity, which is indeed quite obvious, there is above all an ultimate spiritual and ontological identity."[70]

The appeal to the Fathers was always an appeal to authority rather than just to antiquity. The witness of the early Church does not hold its value simply from its temporal proximity to the original Revelation. What, then, is the value of the Fathers' witness, the criterion of the truth of their teaching? "this true tradition, according to St Irenaeus, is grounded in, and guaranteed by, that 'charisma veritatis certum', which was *deposited* from the very beginning in the Church and preserved in the uninterrupted succession of Apostolic ministry: 'qui cum episcopatus successione charisma veritatis certum acceperunt' (Adv. haereses, IV. 40. 2)".[71] Did the authoritative Tradition cease with the Patristic Age? Neither the 'consensus quinquesaecularis' which restricted the authoritative period of the Church to the period ending in Chalcedon —a Protestant formulae, he says—nor the Eastern formula of 'Seven Ecumenical Councils', which restricts the authoritative period to eight centuries, satisfies Florovski. He is not happy to affix limits to a Patristic period—indeed the limits that are fixed are varied and there is little agreement on them —for great theologians lived after all the affixed limits. But more fundamental still is his objection to those who think that the Byzantine Church or the contemporary Church is confined in its kerygmatic activity to simple repetition of Patristic doctrine, borrowing Patristic authority and never developing another insight with equal right.[72]

Ultimately the modern Orthodox Church is identical with the Patristic Church, not because it traces historic continuity of doctrine—although it is important that it do that, too— nor because it still contains great theologians, but because it is the 'locus' of the same authority from the same source, be-

[69] G. Florovski, art. 'The Ethos of the Orthodox Church', in *E.R.*, 12 (1960), p. 185.   [70] art. cit., p. 186.
[71] art. cit., pp. 186, 187.   [72] art. cit., pp. 190, 191.

cause it contains the true, dogmatic Tradition. "The same Spirit, the Spirit of Truth, which 'spake through the Prophets', which guided the Apostles, which illumined the Evangelists, is itself abiding in the Church, and guides her into the fuller understanding of the divine truth, from glory to glory."[73] And it does seem from the sequence of his thought —even if he does mention a Father like Damascene, who was not a member of the Episcopacy, and later Theologians—that the primary recipient of the guidance of the Holy Spirit, the primary possessor of authority, is the apostolic succession, the hierarchy.

The Eastern Orthodox Church laid official claim to infallibility in the Council of Constantinople, 1672. Since the Great Schism, the Eastern Orthodox Church has developed its dogma. Many fundamental doctrines of Eastern Orthodoxy, such as the doctrine of the Sacraments and of Justification, were not fully elaborated until after the Schism. According to Androutsos, the organ which formulates developed doctrine is the Episcopate and when it represents the whole Orthodox Church, it functions 'ipso iure' infallibly.[74] Hence the decrees on an Ecumenical Council are infallible and irreformable. The consent and acceptance of the whole Church is nothing more than an external criterion of ecumenicity. To the question: can the Eastern Orthodox Church as it now exists convene a truly ecumenical council from its bishops? Androutsos answers in the affirmative. The fact that it has not done so must not be taken as an indication that it cannot.

It is a tenet of modern Eastern Orthodox theology, then, that the Eastern Orthodox hierarchy is infallible and that the true, integral and authoritative Tradition is the teaching and belief of the Eastern Orthodox Church. Of course, there is not complete unanimity on the point. Some older writers especially—Mesolora is an example—imply that true ecumenicity and final authority in teaching belongs only to the undivided Church before and, if it ends, after the Schism.[75]

[73] art. cit., p. 187.
[74] cf. F. Gavin, *Some Aspects of Contemporary Greek Orthodox Thought*, Milwaukee, 1953, pp. 255 ff.
[75] cf. Gavin, op. cit., p. 29.

But the strongest claim of Eastern Orthodoxy is that described above and it has substantial theological backing in modern times.

The question now at stake is really the question of identifying the authentic Magisterium. The Catholic Church maintains that in order to act within the moral body known as the Magisterium or teaching organ of the Church, a bishop needs to be not only validly consecrated—and it admits the bishops of the Eastern Orthodox Church to be such—but in communion with the primatial See of Rome, the centre of magisterial unity. The Eastern Orthodox theologians who make the strongest claim for the Tradition of their Church claim that the sole authentic Magisterium which has infallibility and authority is the episcopal body of the Eastern Orthodox Church. The Catholic Church does not recognise the validity of Anglican orders and, hence, the question of Anglican bishops acting within the Magisterium does not arise for it. Some 'catholic' Anglicans hold that the apostolic succession comprises all the bishops of the undivided Church, including their own, and that the Magisterium cannot act as such, e.g. in Council, until the Church is no longer divided.

The question of identifying the Magisterium, of deciding between these rival claims, is beyond the scope of this book; only this much can be said. If a concept of Tradition which will fit the historical nature of Christianity is worked out, it will be seen to involve a Magisterium, i.e. an ordinary teaching office that is an organic part of Christ's Church. Christianity simply reveals itself to be a religion based on Tradition. It is thought to be indefectible and that ultimately involves a claim to infallibility in its doctrinal mission. It is more reasonable and more (Scripturally) defensible to seek that infallibility primarily in an ordinary teaching organ than to seek it primarily in any extraordinary charismatics (although the existence of such is not denied) or in some diffused state in the whole Church (although the whole Church must derive infallibility from the teaching organ). But if the study of the nature of Tradition within Christianity should lead one to see the need for an infallible or guaranteed teaching organ it does not serve to identify that organ amongst rival claimants. That is because the tract on Tradition cannot be placed before the tract on the Church. The Catholic concept of Tradition which has taken up the major part of this book presupposed the whole Catholic doctrine of the Church.

CONCLUSION

ONE short chapter on non-Roman Catholic thought does not merit the drawing of any definitive conclusions. The chapter sought to point out the fact—recognised by non-Catholics generally—that Tradition transmits the beliefs of their sects also; therefore, that they would need to say something more definite about the guarantees of their Traditions. The chapter suggests that some non-Catholics need to concentrate on this point: where *in fact* did their present beliefs come from, directly from the Bible, or from some historical interpreter of the Bible? And if they came more immediately from historical interpreters, what authority does this interpretation possess? The chapter suggests that non-Catholics who admit Church authority and infallibility have to settle their differences on one point: on the identification of the legitimate teaching hierarchy which possesses the charism of infallibility. The longer discussion of the Catholic teaching merits more extensive conclusions.

We were introduced to the discussion of Tradition in this essay by the Catholic theologians who believe that it should be defined as magisterium. No other single definition or description of Tradition in the period reviewed can count on the same theological support. The theologians who seek to develop the description of Tradition beyond that of the Tradition-magisterium school do not betray any great unity of outlook amongst themselves. If a more adequate notion of Tradition does emerge, it is found by synthesis and based essentially on Scheeben.

The definition of Tradition in terms of magisterium is bound up with three concepts: the concept of a divine teaching mission, of a charism of infallibility and of authority. These three concepts are essentially inter-related. The authority of magisterium comes from the official divine mission which the Magisterium received and because of which the charism of infallibility was conferred on it. It was this official authority that alone belongs to men with a mission to teach, that the theologians who followed Franzelin demanded wherever Tradition was to be found. Hence they defined Tradition as magisterium.

But the word 'Tradition' is too weak to express the authoritative aspect of preaching. It is such words, from Scheeben, that indicate the Achilles' heel of the Tradition-magisterium position, and open the way to a fuller concept. The qualities that are proper to the teaching of the Magisterium come from its mission and from its charism. It can not only guarantee a truth with absolute certainty, it can also provide the official authentication of truth in the Church and simultaneously command its acceptance. There are other organs in the Church and the truths they profess have certain guarantees from derived infallibility; therefore a certain authority. This is an authority of qualification merely—we speak of 'an authority' on a subject—not the authority of office. Behind all this, of course, there is the primary authority of God who revealed the truth.

It was Franzelin's opinion that the authority of Tradition could not be discussed at all unless the authority of the Magisterium was first placed beyond doubt. In a sense he was right and in a sense wrong. He was wrong in thinking that the authority of Tradition is authority in the strict sense, the authority that belongs only to the teaching of those divinely appointed to teach. But he was right in a sense, too. For authority in the wider meaning of the word, the authority of qualification, cannot belong to Tradition in any part of the Church unless the infallibility of the Magisterium is defended, unless a Magisterium is 'an authority' on Revelation. For each body in the Church is 'an authority' only as long as it receives its truth from the Magisterium. So much has appeared from the discussions of the infallibility in the belief or teaching of these bodies. It follows that the non-Catholics who do not recognise an infallible Magisterium cannot satisfactorily account for the authority of Tradition.

The other organs have no mission such as the Magisterium has and hence no charism of infallibility. But the word 'Tradition' and the concept covered by it, does not of itself express or demand the precise authority of the Magisterium or the charismatic aspect of infallibility. The teaching of the Magisterium is Tradition, a guaranteed handing on of revealed truth, before ever we take into consideration the fact that its infallibility is of the charismatic type which belongs only to men with a divine mission and that its teaching is authoritative as no other teaching in the Church is. Once so much is admitted, it is seen that other organs in the Church teach or profess doctrine that is guaranteed or infallible without being authoritative: and the infallibility in belief has its part to play now in Tradition.

The first magisterium was that of the Apostles. It had its differences from any teaching that has been in the Church ever since, but these differences did not prevent it from being Tradition, too. As the divine truth came from Christ and the Holy Spirit it was Revelation. As it was handed on by the Apostles it was tradition. Yet the Apostles were the immediate recipients of the final and complete Revelation and that gave their Tradition special characteristics. One of these is pointed by the name given it: constitutive Tradition. By it a completed body of truth was deposited in the Church which would have to be transmitted without addition or loss from that time onwards. The Apostles and 'apostolici viri' wrote Scripture, too, under the inspiration of the Holy Spirit and committed the Scripture to the Church. But this was not Tradition. The New Testament, like the Old, was written by men who were instruments of the Holy Spirit in a way in which they never were in any other activity. The Scriptures, therefore, are attributed to the Holy Spirit in a way in which no other human effect is. They have a dignity and a value that marks them off. So theologians say: it is the 'oral' deposit and not the written deposit that belongs to Tradition.

A second characteristic of the Apostolic Tradition concerns the depth of the Apostles' insight. Revelation is formally made by teaching. But the persons and events described in the teaching were amongst the actual experiences of the Apostles. Because the teaching of Christ did not itself meet with much understanding on the part of the Apostles its meaning was revealed to them by the Holy Spirit. The Scriptures are our record of their penetrating knowledge. They are not themselves documents of Tradition but their value for the progress of Tradition down the centuries is immense.

There is more to be said of Tradition in the apostolic age. For the Church existed in apostolic times, too, and the apostolic body was but a part of it, however important a part. The apostolic preaching was received obediently by the Christian community. The members of the community believed the preaching and professed it, at least virtually in the living of their lives. They handed on their faith. Yet even here there is something different about the apostolic age. There was not here the same interplay of community faith and magisterium that the later Church was to know. The community faith was never a norm for the Magisterium but in the apostolic age it was not even a datum to be examined, to be known. It was at most a negative influence, in so far as its questioning and difficulties prompted then that development of doctrine which is inseparable from Tradition in all ages. The Apostles stood above the Christian community in a way that no succeeding Magisterium could do. Ultimately again that is because they were the immediate recipients of revelation, their Tradition was constitutive, and its profundity has never been equalled.

When the apostolic age had passed Divine Tradition could be simply referred to as Church Tradition although that term must not be confused with 'traditio ecclesiastica', which indicates some truth or institution originating in the post-apostolic Magisterium. The nature of Church Tradition can be explained with the aid of two ideas: the idea of a perennial magisterium and the idea of an organic Church. The truth of Revelation came into the Church first through the ministry of chosen Apostles. It comes into the Church always through the ministry of those who have succeeded them in their mission. But it is not received in passive receptacles, and the reaction it provokes is not uniform in the whole Church.

The teaching of the Magisterium is received actively by different organs in the Church. In treatises on Tradition it is usual to enumerate these as the Fathers of the Church, the Theologians and the 'corpus fidelium'. As far as membership is concerned, these organs are not mutually exclusive. One belongs to one or more of them because of the type of activity contributed by him rather than because of his person. Every member of the Church belongs to the third group, the 'corpus fidelium', so that it is only improperly called an organ of the Church.

The teaching of the Magisterium is received by the Fathers of the Church, by a group of men of outstanding natural qualifications who were equipped by the Holy Spirit to be the eyes by which the Church could see deeper into her doctrine. Their activity was primarily writing. It was through their writings that they bridged the gaps of time and space separating them and formed a unified body of teaching. The infallible teaching of the Magisterium took new form in the writings of the Fathers, in so far as it was now expressed by the intelligentsia of the Church. Thus the belief of the Church came to be handed on by the Fathers as patristic doctrine: infallible doctrine when unanimous, because it was received from the Magisterium and assimilated with the help of the Holy Spirit. Much the same can be said for the Great Theologians, since there is no reason to suspect that the Church was less well equipped after the eighth century than she was before it.

The teaching of the Magisterium is received by every faithful member of the Church. It is professed by every member, sometimes in the clarity and conviction of martyrdom, usually in more mundane ways such as the teaching of children and the practice and piety of daily living. The beliefs of the Church are expressed and handed on in this way, too. As the possession of the faithful they come in contact with the problems that everyday life poses and with the spirit of every age. The faith of the whole Church is infallible.

The flow of doctrine, however, is not all one-way. The Magisterium of later days does not stand in the same independence as the Apostles with their immediate source of doctrine in revelation and their unequalled grasp of it. While the charism and the authority 'ex officio' are proper to itself, the Magisterium continually consults the Fathers and Theologians and enquires about the faith of the universal Church.

Its own teaching is carried forward by these organs, and understood and expressed by each in its own way. There is a continual interplay, therefore, between the Magisterium and the other organs of Tradition. It is that interplay which explains at once the development that is essential to Tradition, and, together with the direct influence of the Holy Spirit upon them, guarantees its integrity in the organs that are without a special charism.

As remarked at the beginning, Tradition is a complex thing. It has all the vitality and variety of an essential function of a living organism. Its full description, such as modern theology can present it to us, is not easily stated or understood. There are shorter definitions of Tradition that are more convenient both in polemics and in current theology: and their use—once their limitations are known—is always legitimate. But Tradition is a reality in the Church before it is a notion for theology, and its richness can never be sacrificed to convenience. It belongs to the daily life of the Church and that life has its roots in mystery.

ABBREVIATIONS

A.A.S.	*Acta Apostolicae Sedis*
A.Cl.	*L'Ami du Clergé*
Cl.R.	*Clergy Review (The)*
D.A.F.C.	*Dictionnaire Apologétique de la Foi Catholique*
D.T.C.	*Dictionnaire de Théologie Catholique*
D.V.	*Dieu Vivant*
D.R.	*Downside Review (The)*
D.T. (Fr.)	*Divus Thomas (Freiburg)*
Dig. Rel.	*Digest Religioso*
E.C.Q.	*Eastern Churches Quarterly*
E.R.	*Ecumenical Review (The)*
E.T.L.	*Ephemerides Theologicae Lovanienses*
Est. Ecl.	*Estudios Eclesiasticos*
Greg.	*Gregorianum*
H. J.	*Heythrop Journal (The)*
I.T.Q.	*Irish Theological Quarterly (The)*
Kl.	*Kirchenlexikon*
L.T.K.	*Lexikon für Theologie und Kirche*
M.T.Z.	*Münchener Theologische Zeitschrift*
N.R.T.	*Nouvelle Revue Théologique*
N.V.	*Nova et Vetera*
R.D'H.E.	*Revue D'Histoire Ecclesiastique*
R.S.R.	*Recherches de Science Religieuse*
S.C.	*Scuola Cattolica (La)*
S.J.T.	*Scottish Journal of Theology*
S.Z.	*Stimmen der Zeit*
Schol.	*Scholastik*
T.D.	*Theology Digest*
T.R.	*Theologisches Revue*
T.T.	*Theology Today*
T.T.Z.	*Trierer Theologische Zeitschrift*

BIBLIOGRAPHY

MONOGRAPHS

Adam, K. *The Spirit of Catholicism* (trans. McCann), London, 1952.

Bainvel, J. V. *De Magisterio Vivo et Traditione*, Paris, 1905.

Bartmann, B. *Lehrbuch der Dogmatik*, I, (5.a.) Freiburg, 1920.

Bartolo, S. Di. *I Criteri Teologici*, Torino, 1888.

Bartz, W. *Die Lehrende Kirche. Ein Beitrag zur Ekklesiologie M. J. Scheeben*, Trier, 1959.

Bellamy, J. *La Theologie Catholique au XIXe Siècle*, Paris, 1904.

Berdyaev, N. *Freedom and the Spirit*, London, 1935.

Bernard, R. *La Foi, I, in Somme Théologique* (ed. de la Revue des Jeunes), Paris, 1939.

Berthier, J. *A Compendium of Catholic Theology*, I, ed. 5 (trans. Raemers), London, 1931.

De Ecclesia Christi, ed. 2, Rome, 1903.

Berthier, J. J. *Tractus de Locis Theologicis*, Taurini, 1900.

Bicknell, E. J. *The Thirty-Nine Articles*, 3rd. ed. (rev. Carpenter), Longmans, 1955.

Billot, L. *De Sacra Traditione contra Novam Haeresim Evolutionismi*, Rome, 1904.

De Immutabilitate Traditionis contra Modernam Haeresim Evolutionismi, ed. 3, Rome, 1922.

Brunner, E. *The Misunderstanding of the Church* (trans. Knight), London, 1952.

Das Missverständnis der Kirche, Stuttgart, 1951.

Burghardt, W. J. *The Catholic Concept of Tradition in the Light of Modern Theological Thought, Proceedings of the Sixth Annual Convention of the C.Th.S.A.* (Reprint), 1951.

Charlier, C. *The Christian Approach to the Bible* (trans. Richards and Peters), Glasgow, 1958.

Congar, Y. M-J. *Jalons Pour Une Théologie du Laicat*, Paris, 1954.

Lay People in the Church (trans. Attwater), London, 1957.

La Tradition et Les Traditions, Paris, 1960.

Cullmann, O. *Die Tradition*, Zürich, 1954.

Dabin, P. *Le Sacerdoce Royal des Fidèles*, Paris, 1950.

De Groot, J. V. *Summa Apologetica de Ecclesia*, Ratisbonne, 1892.

De la Barre, R. P. *La Vie du Dogme Catholique*, Paris, 1898.
De Lubac, H. *Meditation sur L'Église*, Paris, 1953.
Deneffe, A. *Der Traditionsbegriff*, Münster i. W., 1931.
Denzinger. *Enchiridion Symbolorum*, ed. 31 (Rahner), Rome, 1957.
De San, L. *De Divina Traditione et Scriptura*, Bruges, 1903.
Dieckmann. H. *De Ecclesia*, Freiburg i. Br., 1925.
Diekamp, F. *Katholische Dogmatik*, ed. 8, 9; Münster i. W., 1938 (tr. *Theologicae Dogmaticae Manuale, Paris*, 1949).
Dillenschneider, P. C. *Le Sens de la Foi et le Progrès Dogmatique du Mystère Marial*, Rome, 1954.
Dorsch, A. *Institutiones Theologicae Fundamentalis*, II, ed. 2, Oeniponte, 1928.
Dunin-Borkowski, S. von. *Die Kirche als Stiftung Jesu: aus Religion, Christentum und Kirche*, Munich, no date.
Filograssi, I. *De Sanctissima Eucharistia: Quaestiones Dogmaticae Selectae*, ed. 6, Rome, 1957.
Fraigneau-Julien, B. *L'Église et le Caractère Sacramentel selon M. J. Scheeben*, Desclee de Brouwer, 1958.
Franzelin, J. B. *Tractatus de Divina Traditione et Scriptura*, ed. 4, Rome, 1896.
   Tractatus de Deo Uno, ed. 3, Rome, 1883.
Gavin, F. *Some Aspects of Contemporary Greek Orthodox Thought*, Milwaukee, 1923.
Geiselmann, J. R. *Die Lebendige Überlieferung als Norm des christlichen Glaubens*, Freiburg, 1959.
Heinrich, J. B. *Dogmatische Theologie*, I–II, Mainz, 1873.
Hervé, J. M. *Manuale Theologicae Dogmaticae*, I, Paris, 1947.
Hocedez, E. *Histoire de la Theologie du XIXe Siècle*, III, Paris, 1947.
Hurter, H. *Theologiae Dogmaticae Compendium*, I, Oeniponte, 1896.
Iraqui, P. S. and Aberzuza, P. F. *Manuale Theologiae Dogmaticae*, I, Madrid, 1959.
Jenkins, D. *Tradition and the Spirit*, London, 1951.
Journet, C. *Esquisse du Developpement du Dogme Marial*, Paris, 1954.
   L'Église du Verbe Incarné, I, Paris, 1941.
   The Church of the Word Incarnate, I (trans. Downes), London, 1955.
Koster, M. D. *Volk Gottes im Wachstum des Glaubens*, Heidelberg, 1950.

Lengsfeld, P. *Überlieferung: Tradition und Shrift in der evangelischen und katholischen Theologie der Gegenwart*, Paderborn, 1960.
Lercher, L. *Institutiones Theologiae Dogmaticae*, I, ed. 4 (Schlagenhaufen), Barcelona, 1945.
Loisy, A. *Autour d'un Petit Livre*, Paris, 1903.
Mascall, E. L. *Christ, the Christian and the Church*, London, 1946. *The Recovery of Unity*, London, 1958.
Mazzella, C. *Praelectiones Scholastico-Dogmaticae*, ed. 4, Rome, 1908.
Moffat, J. *The Thrill of Tradition*, London, 1944.
Mouroux, J. *I Believe: The Personal Structure of Faith* (trans. Turner), London, 1959.
Muncunill, P. J. *Tractatus de Locis Theologicis*, Barcelona, 1916.
Murphy, J. L. *The Notion of Tradition in John Driedo*, Milwaukee, 1959.
Pancheri, F. S. *Il Pensiero Teologico di M. J. Scheeben e S. Tomasso*, Padua, 1956.
Parente, P. *Theologia Fundamentalis*, ed. 3, Marietti, Italy, 1950.
Pesch, C. *Compendium Theologiae Dogmaticae*, I, ed. 4, Freiburg i. Br., 1931.
Praelectiones Dogmaticae, I, ed. 4, Freiburg i. Br. 1909.
Pohle, J. and Gierens, M. *Lehrbuch der Dogmatik*, I, ed. 9, Paderborn, 1936.
Prestige, G. L. *Fathers and Heretics*, London, 1940.
Proulx, G. *Tradition et Protestantisme*, Paris, 1924.
Ranft, J. *Der Ursprung des katholischen Traditionsprinzips*, Würzburg, 1931.
Die Traditionsmethode als älteste theologische Methode des Christentums, Würzburg, 1934.
Reid, J. K. S. *The Authority of Scripture*, London, 1957.
Reports. (Presented to the Archbishop of Canterbury.) (i) *Catholicity*, London, 1950; (ii) *The Fulness of Christ*, London, 1950; (iii) *The Catholicity of Protestantism* (ed. Flew and Davies), London, 1953.
Salaverri, P. I. and Nicolau, P. M. *Sacrae Theologiae Summa*, I, ed. 2, Madrid, 1952.
Scheeben, M. J. *Katholische Dogmatik*, ed. 2 (Grabmann), Freiburg i. Br., 1948.
Schell, H. *Katholische Dogmatik*, I, Paderborn, 1889.
Schmaus, M. *Katholische Dogmatik*, III, 1, Munich, 1958.
Schultes, R. *De Ecclesia Catholica*, Paris, 1925.

Simar, T. *Lehrbuch der Dogmatik*, I, Freiburg i. Br., 1879.
Söhngen, G. *Einheit in der Theologie*, Munich, 1952.
Tanquerey, A. *Synopsis Theologiae Dogmaticae*, ed. 16, Paris, 1919.
Tavard, G. H. *Holy Writ or Holy Church*, London, 1959.
Tyrrell, G. *Medievalism, a Reply to Cardinal Mercier*, London, 1908.
Vacant, A. *Études Theologiques sur les Constitutions du Concile du Vatican*, I, Paris, 1895.
Van Noort, G. *De Fontibus Revelationis*, ed. 3, Amsterdam, 1911.
Wilhelm, J. and Scannell, T. B. *A Manual of Catholic Theology*, I, London, 1899.
Wilmers, W. *Lehrbuch der Religion*, I, ed. 2 Regensburg, 1875.
Zapelena, T. *De Ecclesia Christi*, II, ed. 2, Rome, 1954.
Zubzarreta, V. *Theologia Dogmatico-Scholastica*, I, ed. 4, Bilbao, 1948.

ARTICLES

Arseniev, N. 'The Teaching of the Orthodox Church on the Relation between Scripture and Tradition', in *E.C.Q.*, 7 (1947), 16 ff.
Bacht, H. 'Tradition und Lehramt in der Diskussion um das Assumpta Dogma', in *Die Mündliche Überlieferung, Beiträge zum Begriff der Tradition* (hg. Schmaus), Munich, 1957.
'Tradition und Sakrament', in *Schol.*, 30 (1955), 26 ff.
'Tradition als menschliches und theologisches Problem', in *S.Z.*, 159 (1957), 285 ff.
Bainvel, J. 'Tradition and Living Magisterium', in *The Catholic Encyclopædia*, New York, Vol. 15, 1912, pp. 6 ff.
Balic, C. 'Il Senso cristiano e il progresso del dogma', in *Greg.*, 33 (1952), 106 ff.
Bartz, W. 'Le Magistère de l'Église d'après Scheeben' (trans.), in *R.S.R.*, 124–6 (1960), 309 ff.
Bavaud, G. 'Écriture et Tradition selon M. Cullmann', in *N.V.*, 2 (1953), 135 ff.
Baumgartner, Ch. 'Tradition et Magistère', in *R.S.R.*, 41 (1953), 161 ff.
Bévenot, M. 'Tradition, Church and Dogma', in *H.J.*, 1 (1960), 34 ff.
Bennet, V. 'The Assumption: A Postscript', in *Theology*, 54 (1951), 416 ff.

Beumer, J. 'Glaubensinn der Kirche', in *T.T.Z.*, 61 (1952), 129 ff.
'Das Verhältnis von Schrift und Tradition als theologisches Problem bei M. J. Scheeben und H. Schell', in *T.R.*, 55 (1959), 203 ff.
'Heilige Schrift und Kirchliche Lehrautorität', in *Schol.*, 25 (1950), 40 ff.
Bratsiotis, P. P. 'The Fundamental Principles and Main Characteristics of the Orthodox Church', in *E.R.*, 12 (1960), 154 ff.
Bullough, S. 'Scripture and Tradition', in *E.C.Q.*, 7 (1947), 27 ff.
Chamelot, Th. 'Les Pères et les Docteurs de l'Église', in *Initiation Théologique*, I, Paris, 1952.
Colombo, C. 'L'Elemente storico nell' insegnamente teologico', in *S.C.*, 80 (1952), 3 ff.
Congar, Y. M-J. 'Théologie', in *D.T.C.*, vol. 15, part 1, cols. 341 ff., Paris, 1946.
'Sainte Écriture et sainte Église', in *R.S.P.T.*, 44 (1960), 81 ff.
Courtade, G. 'J-B. Franzelin: Les Formules que le Magistère de l'Église Lui a Empruntées', in *R.S.R.*, 40 (1952), 317 ff.
Cullmann, O. ' "Kyrios" as Designation for the Oral Tradition concerning Jesus', in *S.J.T.*, 3 (1950), 180 ff.
'Scripture and Tradition', in *S.J.T.* (1953), 113 ff.
'The Tradition', in *The Early Church*, ed. Higgins, London, 1956.
D'Ales, A. 'La Tradition Chrétienne dans l'Histoire', in *D.A.F.C.*, Paris, 1928, IV, cols. 1740 ff.
Danielou, J. 'Réponse a Oscar Cullmann', in *D.V.*, 24 (1953), 107 ff.
'Qu'est ce que la tradition apostolique?' in *D.V.*, 26 (1954), 73 ff.
Davis, C. 'The Church and Unity: Notes on Recent Work', in *Cl.R.*, 43 (1958), 474 ff.
Davis, H. F. 'Our Lady's Assumption', in *Mother of the Redeemer*, ed. McNamara, Dublin, 1959.
'Immaculate Conception', ibid.
Dejaifve, G. 'Bible, Tradition, Magistère dans la Theologie Catholique', in *N.R.T.*, 78 (1956), 135 ff.
'Bible et Tradition dans le Lutheranisme Contemporain', in *N.R.T.*, 78 (1956), 135 ff.
De Voogt, P. 'Écriture et Tradition d'après des Études Catholiques Recents', in *Istina*, 1958, 183 ff.
Dhanis, E. 'Révélation explicite et implicite', in *Greg.*, 34 (1953), 187 ff.

H

Draguet, R. 'L'Evolution des Dogmes', in *Apologetique*, Paris, 1937.
Review of Deneffe's *Der Traditionsbegriff*, in *E. T. L.*, 9 (1932), 93 ff.
Dubarle, A. M. 'Introduction a L'Écriture Sainte', in *Initiation Theologique*, I, Paris, 1952.
Filograssi, I. 'Traditio Divino-Apostolica et Assumptio B.M.V.', in *Greg.*, 30 (1949), 443 ff.
'Theologia Catholica et Assumptio B.V.M.', in *Greg.*, 31 (1950), 323 ff.
'Constitutio Apostolica "Munificentissimus Deus" de Assumptione B.M.V.', in *Greg.*, 31 (1950), 483 ff.
'Tradizione divino-apostolica e Magistero della Chiesa', in *Greg.*, 33 (1952), 135 ff.
Florovski, G. 'The Ethos of the Orthodox Church', in *E.R.*, 12 (1960), 183 ff.
Geiselmann, J. R. 'Un malentendu eclairci: La Relation "Écriture-Tradition" dans la théologie catholique' (trans.), in *Istina*, 1958, n. 2, 197 ff.
'Die Tradition', in *Fragen der Theologie Heute* (hg. Feiner, etc.), Einsiedeln, 1958.
Holstein, H. 'La Tradition d'après le Concile de Trente', in *R.S.R.*, 47 (1959), 167 ff.
Istina, 'Pour une notion "réaliste" de la Tradition', Editorial, *Istina*, 1958, n. 2, 129 ff.
Kehoe, R. 'The Scriptures as Word of God', in *E.C.Q.*, 7 (1947), 71 ff.
Kinder, E. 'Schrift und Tradition', in Asmussen-Stählin, *Die Katholizität der Kirche*, Stuttgart, 1957.
Konstantinidis, C. 'The Significance of the Eastern and Western Traditions within Christendom', in *E.R.*, 12 (1960), 143 ff.
Krüger, G. 'Tradition', in *Die Religion in Geschichte und Gegenwart*, V. Tübingen, 1931, cols. 1249 ff.
Lennerz, H. 'Sine Scripto Traditiones', in *Greg.*, 40 (1959), 624 ff.
'Scriptura Sola?' in *Greg.*, 40 (1959), 38 ff.
Liege, A-M. 'Parole de Dieu et Tradition', in *Initiation Théologique*, I, Paris, 1952.
Lodrioor, J. 'Écriture et Traditions', in *E.T.L.*, 35 (1959), 423 ff.
Michel, A. 'Tradition', in *D.T.C.*, XV, part 1, Paris, 1946.
'L'Église, l'Écriture et la Tradition', in *A.Cl.*, 8 (1956), 119 ff.

Michel, A. 'Pius XII. Lumiére de la Theologie', in *A.Cl.*, 68 (1958), n. 45, 654 ff.

Mitchell, G. 'Scripture and Tradition: a recent book', in *I.T.Q.*, 23 (1956), 12 ff.

Müller, O. 'Zum Begriff der Tradition in der Theologie der letzten hundert Jahre', in *M.T.Z.*, 4 (1953), 164 ff.

Nelson. 'Tradition and Traditions as an Ecumenical Problem', in *T.T.*, 13 (1956), 151 ff.

Ortigues, E. 'Écritures et Traditions apostoliques au Concile de Trente', in *R.S.R.*, 36 (1949), 271 ff.

Pelikan, J. 'Die Tradition im konfessionellen Luthertum', in *Lutherische Rundschau*, 6 (1956/7), 228 ff.

Perennes, H. 'Tradition et Magistère', in *D.A.F.C.*, t. 4, c. 1783–93, Paris, 1928.

Pieper, J. 'Le Concept de Tradition', in *La Table Ronde*, 150 (1960), 74 ff.

Pinard de la Boullaye, H. 'L'Écriture Sainte Est-Elle La Règle Unique de la Foi?' in *N.R.T.*, 63 (1936), 839 ff.

Pohle, J. 'Tradition,' in *Kl.*, t. 11, c. 1933–71. Freiburg i. B., 1899.

Ranft, J. 'Tradition,' in *L.T.K.*, t. 10, c. 243–8 (2a.), Freiburg i. B., 1938.

Remberger, Fr. X. 'S. Scrittura e Tradizione', in *Dig. Rel.*, 2, Primavera, 1958, pp. 13 ff.

Riudor, I. 'Mision de los laicos en la Iglesia, segun las ensenanzas del Papa Pio XII', in *Est. Ecl.*, 31 (1957), 189 ff.

Schlink, E. 'The Significance of Eastern and Western Traditions for the Christian Church', in *E.R.*, 12 (1960), 133 ff.

Semmelroth, O. 'Überlieferung als Lebensfunktion der Kirche', in *S.Z.*, 148 (1951), 1 ff.

Simmel, O. 'Mariä Himmelfahrt als Frage der Tradition', in *S.Z.*, 148 (1950–1), 381 ff.

Skydsgaard, K. E. 'Scripture and Tradition' (trans. Evans), in *S.J.T.*, 9 (1956), 337 ff.

Söhngen, G. 'Tradition and Apostolic Preaching', as in *T.D.*, 1 (1953), 88 ff.

'Überlieferung und apostolische Verkündigung', in *Einheit in der Theologie*, Munich, 1952, pp. 305 ff.

Tavard, G. H. 'Scripture, Tradition and History', in *D.R.*, 72 (1954), 232 ff.

Ternus, J. 'Zum historisch-theologischen Tradition der Himmelfahrt Mariens', in *Schol.*, 25 (1950), 321 ff.

'Vom Gemeinschaftsglauben der Kirche', in *Schol.*, 10 (1935), 1 ff.

Ternus, J. 'Beiträge zum Problem der Tradition', in *D.T.*, 16 (1938), 33 ff. and 197 ff.

Tisserant, E. Card. 'De Mariologia in ambitu sacrae Theologiae', in *Nuntia Periodica*, Num. 6, Rome, 1959, pp. 12 ff.

Van den Eynde, D. 'Tradizione e Magistero', in *Problemi e Orientamenti di Teologia Dommatica*, I, Milan, 1957.
Review of Deneffe's *Der Traditionsbegriff*, in *R.D'H.E.*, 27 (1931), 852 ff.

Williams, N. P. 'Tradition', in *Encyclopedia of Religion and Ethics*, vol. 12, Edinburgh, 1921, pp. 411 ff.

Zapelena, T. 'Problema Theologicum', in *Greg.*, 24 (1943), 23 ff. and 287 ff., also 25 (1944), 38 ff. and 247 ff.

INDEX OF NAMES